NINO
Lo BELLO'S
GUIDE
TO THE
VATICAN

Also by Nino Lo Bello

The Vatican Empire

Vatican, U.S.A.

The Vatican Papers

English Well Speeched Here

European Detours

Nino Lo Bello's Guide To Offbeat Europe

NINO Lo BELLO'S GUIDE TO THE VATICAN

Nino Lo Bello

CHICAGO REVIEW PRESS

Library of Congress Cataloging-in-Publication Data

Lo Bello, Nino.
[Guide to the Vatican]
Nino Lo Bello's guide to the Vatican/Nino Lo Bello.
Includes index.
ISBN 1-55652-018-2
1. Vatican City—Description and travel—Guide-books.
2. Vatican City—History—Anecdotes, facetiae, satire, etc.
I. Title. II. Title: Guide to the Vatican.
DG792.L6 1987
945'.634—dc19   87-19823
                                                                CIP

On the cover: Vatican Gardens: Garden in the Italian Style, photo by Irene Rooney. Saint Peter's Basilica: Tomb of Saint Peter, Michelangelo's Dome of Saint Peter's; Sistine Chapel: Michelangelo's *Creation of Man*; and Vatican Museums: the *Laocoön*, photos by Carlo Piccolo.

First Edition

Published by Chicago Review Press, Incorporated,
814 North Franklin Street, Chicago, Illinois, 60610

To my three favorite cousins
of Rockford, Illinois—
Sister Mary Immaculate,
Lena Moscarelli,
and Marie Rossi

Contents

splashing their acqueous symphony for any and all cameras. The fountain on the right was put there during the reign of Pope Innocent VIII in 1490, but it was taken down in 1613 by Carlo Maderno on the command of Pope Paul V and rebuilt in such a way that the small upper basin was reversed and the water flowed out of it through seven spouts. As the work of Bernini, the other fountain was put up in 1677 on orders from Pope Innocent XI.

Now here's a tip about something 99 percent of the people who visit Saint Peter's Square overlook completely. There are two black marble discs imbedded in the pavement, both of which are just a few feet from each of the fountains. Position yourself on one disc and cast your eyes on the Bernini colonnades. Except for the first row of columns, all of them disappear from view. Step off the disc, and three other rows of columns suddenly are visible, as if by a magician's wand. This now-you-see-it/now-you-don't optical illusion is an oddity-tribute to Bernini's mathematical genius.

Unknown to most people who head for the basilica, the staircase that leads up to the doors is based on an idea and a design by Michelangelo. Statues of Saint Paul and Saint Peter stand on either side at the staircase foot. Originally, these two statues, made in 1838, were to be placed within the Basilica of Saint Paul Outside The Walls, then in the process of being rebuilt. Pope Pius IX, however, ordered in 1847 that they be placed where they are now found.

Since there are no surviving original plans by Michelangelo for the New Saint Peter's, historians generally give Carlo Maderno full credit for the facade. Maderno gave the basilica a pictorial and decorative character, as well as architectural composition, and saw to it that the facade be subordinate to the dome. The 376-foot wide and 149 high facade is essentially a horizontal affair with eight massive columns, four pilasters, and six half pilasters — all Corinthian. Between each one of them are loggias, nine in all. The central one is used for pontifical benedictions. Actually, the body of the facade goes beyond the span of the basilica itself. On top of the facade there is a horizontal beam that is an additional, undecorated level. At the farther end of this story and the balustrade which crowns it is a tympanum. Decorating this balustrade at the roof are the 18-foot statues which portray the Redeemer who is flanked by John the Baptist and 11 of the Apostles. (The reason Saint Peter is missing is that he is to be found, as mentioned earlier, at the foot of the stairway.) As for the two clocks, both eighteenth century and both made by Joseph Valadier at the behest of Pope Pius VI, they correspond to the first and last of the loggias.

Rising behind Bernini's right colonnade is the Apostolic Palace, in which the pope has his office and bedroom on the top floor. The bedroom is the top right corner chamber through which late at night you can see his light on when he is often reading. The room next to it, on the left, is his office — and it is at this window he often makes a public appearance on Sundays and holidays, usually at noontime. Crowds invariably gather in the Square around midday for a Sunday blessing. When the pope comes out, he usually makes a few comments on some subject that concerns him, like peace, prayer, terrorism, children, etc. Before saying the prayer, he extends a blessing to the throngs down below. The third and fourth windows are part of a library and office, used by the papal secretary, and windows five, six, and seven belong to a large day room; the next two windows lead to reception rooms. The last window you see on the corner over- looks the San Damasus Courtyard and is part of the papal loggia.

While still gazing in this direction, squint a little harder and look for the stovepipe chimney of the Sistine Chapel, which is in front of the gable to the right of the basilica facade. During a papal election, crowds gather to stare at this elongated chimney for *La fumata*, because twice each day everybody waits with suspense for a puff of white smoke or black smoke. The smoke comes from the ballots used by the cardinals to vote on who will be the next pon- tiff. If the smoke is black, then no new pope has been agreed upon — but if the smoke is white, then a new pope has indeed been elected. When that happens, the highest ranking cardinal emerges on the middle loggia and announces the name of the newly elected pope to the crowds assembled below. The new pope puts on a white chasuble, comes out on the loggia and gives his first papal blessing, *Urbi et Orbi* (which means, To the City and

To the World). The coronation ceremony will take place inside Saint Peter's a few week's later, amid grandiose jubilation.

At certain times of the year, mostly during August and part of September, the pope is in residence at the summer palace in Castel Gandolfo in the Alban Hills, some 13 miles away from the Vatican City. On those Sundays when he is in the Castel Gandolfo pontifical palace, he gives greetings at midday when he appears on the residence balcony, below which some 7,000 to 10,000 people are usually waiting to see him. It's about an hour's taxi ride to the summer residence that is nearly 29 acres larger than Vatican City itself (the pontifical complex there includes three main buildings, a model farm, and an elaborate park). There are also special buses that leave at 8 A.M. from the Saint Susanna Church every Wednesday. Around noontime the pope usually holds a general audience in a large assembly hall walled with glass and fully air-conditioned. Admission is free, and tickets can be arranged at the Vatican's Tourist Office in Saint Peter's Square, if you have a letter from your local priest or from a cleric in Rome or elsewhere in Italy.

The Part of the Vatican You Can't Visit

ALTHOUGH THE VATICAN welcomes visitors to its embrace —whether it be the wide expanse of Saint Peter's Square, the multi-museums that comprise the Vatican Museums, the Pontifical Gardens, or the interior of Saint Peter's Basilica (upstairs and downstairs)—there are parts and parcels of the State of Vatican City that are off-limits to the casual tourist. In short, you just can't go there.

Perhaps the most no-no place in all the Vatican City is the elongated piece of land that snuggles between it and Italy. The 1,641 feet of territory neither belongs to Italy nor to the Vatican. Called *"La Terra di Nessuno"* (Nobody's Land), it is one of those geographical curiosities that somehow escapes attention, though it is a parcel of land that belongs to no country.

Just how this bit of no-man's land touching the Vatican came about cannot be fully ascertained. One theory is that it resulted by dint of a measuring error (an unnamed surveyor used the wrong trigonometry formula), and another theory is that the 1929 Lateran Pact between Italy and the Vatican just plain overlooked the stretch. Whatever the reason, it does not appear likely that the strange no man's land will ever be incorporated into Italy proper or become part of the pope's territorial domain. Since the matter would become politically touchy today, officials of both countries prefer to leave it that way. And that's precisely the way it - remains, untouched and neglected. It has been completely deprived of any maintenance; nobody has apparently gone there in years.

From afar this place can be seen in plain view. It is the *Corridoio di Castello,* the corridor built in the thirteenth century by Pope Nicholas III, which stretches from the Castel Sant'Angelo to the Vatican. During the Middle Ages the narrow link was used by the popes whenever they had to flee for their lives from the Vatican to the circular-shaped Castel Sant'Angelo, the former mausoleum of Emperor Hadrian which was converted into a fortress.

The last pontiff to have used the covered corridor, whose walls and windows are so close together that two people can't walk side by side, was Pope Clement VII on the morning of May 6, 1527. As the cutthroat mercenary armies of King Charles V zeroed in on the Vatican and the explosion of cannons was heard on the very steps of Saint Peter's, the pope was persuaded to take flight along the vaulted hallway to Castel Sant'Angelo.

From the top of Castel Sant'Angelo I was able one day to go as far as the locked gate leading to the brick-paved corridor would allow. Helped by unwashed windows perhaps, the thick-walled, narrow-elevated tunnel, which looks like a secret passage, has an air of incredible age hanging over it. At the other end of "Nobody's Land," the part that terminates on Vatican soil, there is a tiny yard surrounded on three sides by an eight-foot wall, an iron picket fence, and the imposing corridor walls. The Vatican post office adjoins one of the walls flanking this triangular courtyard. The wee enclave is the only open part of *"La Terra di Nessuno"* and is often used as a place to park automobiles.

Knowing what Vatican bureaucracy is like (easily the most difficult bureaucracy on the face of the earth, it could give the Communist countries lessons!), I nevertheless made a well-plotted attempt to get whatever special permission was necessary to visit *"La Terra di Nessuno"* (if only to have the distinction of being one of the few human beings to set foot in a real no-man's land). I failed. Though the Vatican has the only set of keys to enter the corridor, it does not have the authority to let anybody go in. Nor was the Italian government eager to make any waves with Vatican officialdom to intercede on my behalf. In one of the most thoroughly astonishing statements ever mouthed by a professional bureaucrat, I was told that his government would prefer not to enter into or tangle with the Vatican maze of red tape.

Another place in Vatican City you won't have a chance to visit is the "business district," or "downtown," which is located to the right of Saint Peter's Square and is reachable by entering through the Saint Anne Gate. This gate is supervised by Swiss Guards wearing blue uniforms instead of the usual colorfully striped ones. The roadway from the busy Saint Anne Gate leads past the tiny parish church to the post office, the car pool and the garage, the pharmacy, the press office, the offices of *L'Osservatore Romano*, (see section on the Vatican Daily Newspaper), and the supermarket. No one can enter or buy anything in the Vatican supermarket unless he has a special identification card. Prices on each item are usually lower than in the rest of Italy and Rome. Whiskey for instance, is one third cheaper than in the world outside, since there is no customs tax on it. Half of the shoppers in the market are civilians who live and work in the Vatican, and most of the rest are civilian friends of the Vatican whose families are historically close to the Church. The remainder of the shoppers are the clerics who are permitted to nudge their way up the queue to the cash register without having to wait their turn, if they are only carrying a few items.

At the apothecary across the street, there is not so much as a doorplate to identify it. Well stocked with pharmaceuticals, the pharmacy does not sell charcoal for barbecue or tennis balls (the way American drugstores do), but it does carry many products not available in Italian pharmacies like Swiss saccharin or a German anti-herpes drug. Nearly 6,000 prescriptions are filled each month. The shelves of the ''Pope's Drug Store,'' which is manned by trained pharmacists from Italy, Spain, and Australia, do carry talcum powder, toothpaste, and patent medicines — in addition to cosmetics and perfumes.

Located in the same building are living quarters of the Fate Bene Brothers who staff the pharmacy and the outpatient clinic of the Vatican Health Service, which was set up in 1953. Vatican employees and pensioners who participate in the plan, to which they make a monthly contribution from their paycheck, receive free medical and dental care and prescription drugs without charge. Going back to the year 1277 when Pope Nicholas III named a ''Pontifical Herbologist'' to supervise all the pharmacies of Rome and keep an eye on the pope's health, the Vatican pharmacy must be the oldest drugstore in the world, although it is one that most people do not even know exists.

Vatican City has 41 streets and avenues, 23 squares, and 14 courts. Up until the end of 1942 when a committee of cardinals issued a new city map, the Vatican had no street signs at all because many of the streets were unnamed. Among the names are ten saints, twelve popes, one painter (Perugino), and one composer (Palestrina)—and one street is called Avenue of Sports because of its tennis courts. On his daily rounds the Vatican mailman doesn't pay any attention to addresses because he knows who is who and who lives where.

You do not ordinarily hear very much about the Vatican post office, but it's there. It dates back to the fourteenth century when pony-express types of riders used to carry pontifical messages to all parts of Italy. Located just inside Saint Anne's Gate, the Vatican's main post office handles about two million letters a year, more than six million postcards, and over 15,000 packages. Generally speaking, its PO is efficient and reliable—and many Romans have come to learn that if they go to the trouble of mailing a letter on Vatican grounds, delivery will be faster and safer. Annually, the Vatican post office shows a profit, but this comes mainly from the sale of special commemorative stamps and the issuing of Vatican coins and medals. Dealers, collectors, and the general public usually buy out the stamps and the coins in short order. In only one instance did the Vatican post office oversubscribe itself on the printing of a postage stamp; that was during the Holy Year in 1975 when nearly a million unsold Vatican stamps of Pope Paul VI were burned. In all cases with each new issue, the Vatican just does not announce how many stamps are printed, but the number is kept to a limit so as to give the stamps a future value among philatelists.

Not very far from the post office is a converted palace called the *Floreria,* which is the junk shop of the Vatican—filled to brimming with all the things the Vatican does not need anymore but does not want to throw away. In this Vatican attic, indeed a sacred warehouse, you find portable thrones no longer used, dinner services from the time the Vatican used to entertain, the busts of forgotten cardinals, an array of fans from Persia (they used to wave over the pontiff's portable throne before the days of air-conditioning), some badly done statues of the Virgin Mary, so many carpets that all count has been lost, gilded chairs for dignitaries, coaches adorned with gilded door handles and equipped with a single throne as the back seat, and all the abandoned furniture of dead popes, such things as rickety bedside tables, wobbly stools, and brass beds—all of them neatly labeled with the names of their past owners. There is also a large collection of very bad paintings, many of them gifts from all over the world to the papacy. Notable among these is a painting that hung in the famed Vatican museum for over a hundred years. Presented to Pope Pius IX by Queen Christine of Spain in 1850, the painting, *The Mystic Marriage of Saint Catherine,* was attributed by art experts to the seventeenth century Spanish painter, Bartolomé Esteban Murillo. Not long ago the so-called Murillo masterpiece was found to be by a Vatican art expert a ''counterfeit beyond any doubt'' and was dumped away in the *Floreria.*

The people who actually reside inside Vatican City number no more than 750, and of these fewer than half have Vatican citizenship. No one is born a Vatican citizen, but all cardinals are automatically citizens even if they live off the grounds. More than 3,000 people work at the Vatican, where no private enterprise is permitted.

With a population that is more than 95 percent male, Vatican City does not have a residential section as such. Yet it has more telephones in proportion to its population than any other nation or city on earth. There are 50 palaces and office buildings all over the grounds, and many of these provide apartments for the folks who make Vatican City their home. Though living within the walls may seem like something glamorous, such is not the case: both the Saint Anne Gate and the Arch of the Bells entrance close at 10 P.M. and the Bronze Doors at 9 P.M. There is, however, a Swiss Guard on duty who will let Vatican citizens in until 11:30, after which they require special written permission. At 6 in the morning all gates reopen. As for entertainment, except for television there is no form of commercial entertainment available. Because the State of Vatican City is not run along democratic lines, with the pope having a final say on all matters, there are many regulations imposed on people which have to be abided by (such as the ban on hanging out the laundry).

The main building in Vatican City is the Apostolic Palace. With more than 1,400 rooms (overlooking 20 courtyards), the Apostolic Palace is a conglomeration of interlocked buildings built, for the most part, during the Renaissance. It is believed to be the world's largest palace, matched only by the Dalai Lama's palace in Tibet. The pope has a 19-room apartment on the top floor facing Saint Peter's Square (on the right hand side as you face the basilica). His private office is commodious, and its three windows are seldom covered by curtains; when the sun shines and gets too strong, the inside shutters are drawn. The papal work chamber measures 60 by 40 feet, the walls are panelled in blond wood, and the floor is carpeted. About five feet away from the door is the pope's work desk. Whenever John Paul wants to make an appearance from his office, he will invariably go to the middle window which is draped in gold damask. On the lower floors are the apartments of the Cardinal Secretary of State and the rooms for many of the permanent papal staff.

An almost unbelievable statistic about the Apostolic Palace, which covers 440,000 square meters, is the fact that it has nearly a thousand flights of stairs. To go, for instance, from the Bronze Door to the offices of the office of the Secretary of State on the third floor, there are 294 steps. It takes a good 10 minutes to make the trip. Again from the Bronze Door to the Pontifical Antechambers on the second floor takes at least eight minutes, and six minutes to reach the Anteroom of the Secretary of State on the first floor. There are three stairs leading up from the Courtyard of Saint Domaso to the third floor, and there are 190 steps to each of them. The Papal Staircase of Pius IX has 127 steps and the Royal Staircase 137 steps. Quite a few of the spacious rooms are divided into two floors which communicate with each other by interior stairs. (Puff-puff!)

Perhaps one of the most unusual rooms in the Apostolic Palace is a high-ceilinged chamber that is lined from floor to ceiling with steel filing cabinets, shelves, and drawers. With its librarian's ladder standing like a sentinel, the room looks like the inside of a lawyer's library. Under an electric lamp in one corner of the ''world's most macabre library'' sits a priest who has one of the most unusual jobs anywhere, a job that very few people ever hear of. His work largely consists of sending tiny boxes and envelopes to addresses in all parts of the globe.

The drawers, cabinets, shelves, polythene bags, and large (bulging) envelopes are stuffed with the relics of early saints and martyrs, and these can be slivers of bone, ashes, bits of clothing, and other saintly items associated in one way or another with the life and passion of Jesus Christ. Custom dictates that a relic must be enclosed in every altar of every Catholic church in the world. Because churches and chapels are inaugurated every month somewhere in the world, the priest-librarian keeps busy filling envelopes with pinches of dust or varied fragments of bone which are then sent out in registered letters.

The Vatican's attitude towards relics is a strange one; its stance on the subject is simply that it prefers not to bring it up. Church officers are aware that most of the relics are not authentic, but there is a firm opinion in the Vatican—not excluding those of every pope who has ever presided, including the present incumbent—that a relic does the faithful good since it gives them inspiration when praying. Unimportant to the Vatican is whether its carefully kept records show that in various parts of Italy there are four ears belonging to Saint Procopius or nine breasts belonging to Saint Eulalia. Some of the relics are an embarrassment to the Vatican, such as the Holy Foreskin of Christ. This was removed from His body at the age of eight weeks when he was circumcised in the Temple and is preserved in a spherical crystal reliquary—on public display in a church in a small village 45 miles north of Rome. It might be mentioned that there is a rival Foreskin to be found in Italy's Abruzzi region, but this one is not universally accepted, not even by the Vatican.

How "authentic" are these relics? For one thing the Vatican classifies them as "primary relics," "secondary relics," "tertiary relics," and so on. Though many of the relics have been the subject of acrimonious discussion by Vatican cardinals of the past, as to whether they are counterfeits or not, bishops, priests, and other theologians continue to hold them in ecclesiastical esteem, not to mention that they are given the greatest veneration by Italian worshippers. Even though hard-and-fast documentation is no longer possible, the Vatican generally does not discourage public attention to them.

Such an item is one of the nails allegedly used to crucify Christ. For this there is some evidence backing its authenticity but no "positive proof" that would be acceptable, say, in a court of law. The nail in question, which is to be found in a circular, glass-enclosed silver casket on display in Rome's Santa Croce in Gerusalemme Church, is about five inches long and unpointed. About a quarter of an inch before the end it tapers off in thickness to a blunt tip. Also in the same church are several other relics — three wooden splinters from the Cross (kept in a gold and silver reliquary) and a fragment of the tobacco-colored, worm-eaten nameplate placed on top of the Cross on Pilate's orders with the Latin inscription, "NAZARENVS RE . . . ." Nearby in a metal frame that looks like a hand mirror are two thorns from the crown placed on the head of Jesus. Ash-gray in color, the thorns are about an inch and a quarter long.

Even though the Vatican keeps very good records of its relics everywhere in the world, it is not possible to count or even guess how many there are, in view of the fact that there are nearly 2,000 saints in the Catholic calendar. The Vatican quickly destroyed the relics of one saint, not long ago, when Church archeologists discovered that her ribs, unearthed over 200 years ago in a catacomb and preserved in the Vatican since then, turned out to be the bones of a big dog.

Inasmuch as there are, literally, hundreds of thorns taken from Christ's crown, the multiplicity of such relics everywhere remains for the Vatican a rather thorny question (the pun is herewith intended). What do you do when you know that there are three heads of Saint John the Baptist, one in Saint Mark's in Venice, another in Damascus, and still another in Amiens, France; 28 thumbs and fingers belonging to Saint Dominic; two bodies of Saint Sylvester, one in Rome, the other near Modena; two bodies of Saint Luke, in Venice and Padua; and more than 150 nails from the True Cross?

Many of the listings in the Vatican relics library, however, are single items for which some kind of authentication is provided in the files. These would include, for example, such things as the right arm and hand of Saint John, the head of Saint Catherine of Siena, the full bodies of Saint Lucia, Saint Maximus, Saint Urio, Saint Felicity the Virgin, and Saint Julian. Saint Julian himself brought a huge number of relics from Jerusalem, including a part of Saint Matthew's leg, a tooth from Saint Mark the Evangelist, the skull of Saint James the Less, the Holy Sponge which was offered to Christ's lips, some hair from the Virgin Mary, a jar full of earth from Golgotha (soaked with the blood of Christ), and the jawbone of Saint Anthony, to mention a few prominent ones. The jawbone, by the way, lies in a bejewelled case in the Basilica of Saint Anthony, and what invariably astonishes visitors from abroad is how Italian worshippers behave in its presence: many people push and shove in order to kiss the case, rub their babies against it, fondle it with their hands, or vigorously slide lottery tickets over it.

One conspicuous relic, viewed by millions of people each year, is the so-called Throne of Saint Peter, which in fact was one that the saint could never have used. This discovery was made in November 1968 after Pope Paul VI ordered that a Carbon-14 dating test be made on the wood used in the big wood-and-ivory chair. A seven-man team of scientists at Rome University examined the ancient throne, encased in bronze and placed above the altar of the cathedral of the apse of Saint Peter's. Sworn to secrecy, the scientists submitted their report to the pope in which it was stated that the carbon tests showed that the wood dated from several centuries after the birth of Christ (Saint Peter was crucified in Rome either in 64 A.D. or 67 A.D.). The Vatican has not pronounced on the matter. Three relics are by the Throne: the lance that pierced Christ's side, wood from the True Cross, the veil used by Veronica to wipe the face of Christ.

Saint Peter's Basilica covers nearly 430,000 square feet, enough for a half dozen football fields—making it by far the largest church in Christendom. The marble-studded nave floor, by the way, has bronze lines embedded into it to demonstrate how much smaller certain other big churches in Europe are by comparison. Saint Peter's has nearly 500 columns, over 430 large statues, 40 separate altars, and 10 domes. No other church attracts so many people as does the basilica, and upwards of 10 million people a year visit. Just to maintain the church and Saint Peter's Square runs to approximately $2,000 a day. This does not include unforeseen expenditures that mass crowds might bring on. Take the case of the Vatican's 800 black raincoats . . . .

Let's go back a little bit and explain that on the doors of the basilica there are two conspicuous signs posted in five languages telling worshippers and tourists that they must be dressed properly in order to preserve an atmosphere of reverence. Women are not supposed to wear mini dresses, walking shorts, or sleeveless dresses, while men cannot go inside wearing shorts. Four ushers are in charge of enforcing the Vatican's fashion dictum, and almost daily they get into wrangles with some lightly clad visitors who object strenuously. One usher, after a fist fight with a German woman's escort, had to be hospitalized. Vatican administrators tried another tack: they decided to station a nun at the door to stem the tide of modern deshabille from swamping the major temple of Roman Catholicism. That was during the summer of 1972, and Sister Fiorella did her job conscientiously. After three months of coping with more than 20,000 women wearing garb that was tabbed as immodest, the hardy nun could not take the stress anymore and had to withdraw. Now the Vatican came up with still another idea: it issued long, black plastic raincoats that were lent free of charge at the entrance to women in miniskirts and men in shorts. Eight hundred such ponchos were acquired from a Milan firm for $2,000, and the Vatican thought it had solved the problem, except for one thing: the 800 black raincoats disappeared within a week. Filched as souvenirs.

Saint Peter's Basilica

BECAUSE EMPEROR CONSTANTINE (280–337) was firm in his intent to include Saint Peter's original memorial shrine in the foundation of his basilica, there were quite a few snags right from the beginning. These had to do with the so-called "Red Wall" that separated the shrine from a Christian cemetery (which was near Caligula's and Nero's Circus). What Constantine had in mind was that the memorial to the martyr be part of the foundations of the basilica's apse.

Soon after the year 313, workers started to level the terrain in such a way that the shrine could be covered with slabs of marble walled in with wood, which would then be covered again in marble on the outside. With four columns standing at the corners of the old tomb, the shrine was lit up by a large golden candelabra that looked like a crown. It had more than 50 lights and four large, finely decorated candlesticks. Consecrated in 326 amid pompous ceremony, the basilica was opened with splendiferous magnificence, thanks to Constantine's lavishness. Not generally known is that so devoted was Constantine to the job that he himself shoveled 12 pails of earth and personally carried them.

In front of the ancient basilica was a broad square portico decorated with mosaics, built under Pope Simplicius (464–483), which had the name, "Paradise."

The area measured 164 feet by 154 feet, and in the center there was the pool of water that had been used for blessings at the foot of the four Ionic columns supporting a bronze grill with figures of peacocks (a symbol of the immortality of the soul). The marble basin, decorated with a mythical winged beast that in Christian symbolism represented the two-fold nature of Christ (divine and human), poured forth water from a large bronze pinecone (also used as a symbol of Christ). During the course of history, over many centuries, the portico served as the burial place of popes, emperors, and other important personages of the era.

Essentially, the facade of the church was simple, adorned only with a mosaic of Christ surrounded with the 12 Apostles. The five doors in the facade were interrelated with the five internal naves. These were the Porta Judicii, reserved for funerals; the Porta Argentea, so-called because silver covered it; the Porta Romana, with its victorious symbols; the Porta Ravenniana, which referred to the Trastevere, and the Porta Guidonea, named after the guides who took pilgrims on tour. Divided into five naves, the basilica's interior comprised a mammoth hall with 88 Corinthian columns. Standing higher than the ones at the side, the columns of the central nave—which were three times the width were crowned by a rectilinear beamed construction, over which the arched windows had been placed. The colonnades of the aisles on the side were brought together by smaller arches. As for the roof, it consisted of a double slope having a triangular recessed face as its central nave and a single sloping roof on both sides that covered the lateral aisles.

There was quite an impressive contrast between the intricately inlaid and ornate floor and the basic character of the architectural structure. With both walls housing 24 frescoes from scenes of the Old and New Testaments, the central nave came to an end in a triumphant archway at the precise spot where the altar was. The apse (entirely decorated with mosaics of Saint Peter in his role as the Church's principal leader) lay behind the transept, and both it and the transept were shut off by an iron grill and twisted columns. Bernini, years later, used these for his Loggia over the Reliquary.

As a place for continuous pilgrimages, Saint Peter's Basilica during the Middle Ages drew people from many nations who came to pay their respects to the very place where the body of the Prince of the Apostles was buried. Through a hole in the marble slab which was part of Saint Peter's tomb, visitors could peer at a gold cross weighing 150 pounds that Constantine had given as an offering. As was to be expected, over the centuries that followed, each and every pope left some kind of mark to memorialize his pontificate. In most cases that was done either by restoring a part of the structure or by embellishing it. The most significant of these was the raising of the floor level by Pope Gregory the Great and the consecrating of a new high altar by Pope Calixtus II.

Curiously enough, the barbarians who invaded did not take anything from the ancient basilica, despite the fact that it had all kinds of precious metals and stones. The Saracens who came in 846, however, did carry off a lot, including Constantine's gold cross. The basilica, nevertheless, kept being restored with newer and newer splendors, not only because popes themselves undertook such endeavors but also because the populace contributed en masse. Altogether, a thousand years went by in which the history of Rome itself was closely tied to that of Saint Peter's where quite a few dramatic and violent events were to take place.

The destruction of the ancient basilica and the start of a very long undertaking to construct the present one began in 1452 when Pope Nicholas V made plans for a restoration. After he called in Bernardo Rossellino, there began a steady line of architectural activity. What Rossellino planned was to employ the entire area of the old Basilica and construct a portico that would go right into the new church. It would still retain the five naves width, but now it would be in the shape of a Latin Cross that would terminate in an apse and be crowned by a dome. In 1455, however, when Pope Nicholas died, the restoration came to a halt, and his successor, Pope Pius II, only put in a new loggia for benedictions and did some work on restoring a facade. During the reigns of four subsequent popes —from 1464 through 1503—reconstructions of any kind were stopped. It took a man like Pope Julius II, who reigned from 1503 to 1513, to become committed to the drive of constructing a new basilica. Julius II was attracted to the grandiose nature of Bramante's plans, which may have originated from an idea of Leonardo da Vinci many years before, and these included a church based on a central axis in the form of a Greek Cross, with apses at the end of the arms. As a kind of linking element, a square building with an internal dome and an external belltower stands between one apse and another. This would, in effect, mean that the great tower that would stand at the central meeting point of the four arms would be surrounded by four minor ones.

Bramante began the work in April 1506 with the enthusiasm of Julius II to shore him up. But the Pope's death in 1513 and Bramante's a year later brought on an interruption so that of all that had been planned, only the four great central arches, the supporting pillars of the dome and a part of the corner supports of the hemisphere were done. Fortunately, Bramante had the foresight to call in Raffaello to carry on the project, but after Bramante's death, Raffaello brought in both Giuliano da Sangallo and Fra Giocondo da Verona, and a new plan evolved that differed markedly from the Bramante one. Instead of a square basis, the plan was changed to a rectangular one—which was done by removing the Greek cross idea and putting into play a Latin Cross. Though the plan met with papal approval, Raffaello died in 1520, and the plan, judged to be too costly, was dropped when Antonio da Sangallo the Younger was put in charge of the project which he directed from 1535 to 1546 with the assistance of Baldassarre Peruzzi. Seeking to find a simpler and less expensive solution for Raffaello's earlier plan, Sangallo planned a consolidation of the structures that Bramante had left and added apsidal bays and restored towers. Among other things, the Sangallo plan would have had the dome supported on two concentric drums with a lantern flanked by small crowning columns.

When Sangallo died, Michelangelo came into the picture, having been nominated by Pope Paul III as the Vatican Architect for Life. Almost without hesitation Michelangelo went back to the Bramante plan based on the Greek Cross with five domes, but he would simplify it internally by removing the bell tower. Inasmuch as Michelangelo believed the dome would draw the visitor nearer to God, he paid this aspect the greatest attention. But by the time Michelangelo died in 1564, only the drum had been done, and since Vignola, who took over the reins, made no changes in the Michelangelo idea, the dome was finished between 1586 and 1593, with Giacomo della Porta putting on the last touches. The latter also raised the curve of the dome by eight meters, thereby increasing the slope of the curves. Dalla Porta, with the help of Fontana, then constructed the lantern.

Now there followed an open competition, called by Pope Paul V, to work out further plans for the basilica, and at the request of the commission of Cardinals and also the pope himself, it was decided that the plan would change over to the Latin Cross when Carlo Maderno won the competition in 1606. His plan was to provide for the broadening of the basilica facade, an external architrave surmounted by a low attic and statues that would not impede the view of the Michelangelo Dome. He also extended the atrium and provided it with five doors that corresponded to the five naves of the church. To Michelangelo's nave he put in three new arches with lateral chapels. In spite of his sensitive precautions, Maderno came under heavy criticism mostly because he had changed some of Michelangelo's plan, but in the final analysis, his solution turned out to be viable. Thus on November 18, 1626, after almost 120 years of labor, the new Basilica of Saint Peter's was consecrated by Pope Urban VIII.

The Atrium of Saint Peter's Basilica

ENTERED THROUGH five openings which correspond to the five doors of the basilica, the atrium is a noble monument to the religious taste of seventeenth century church decoration. It measures approximately 23 feet by 44 feet by 65 feet. Under Pope Leo XIII, the floor was remodelled in 1888, replacing the one that Bernini had designed. A recent addition to the floor is the inlaid coat-of-arms of Pope John XXIII in polychrome marble, as a memorial to mark the opening in 1962 of the Second Vatican Council. Giving added splendor, the vault is supported by 20 marble columns in various colors. The work of Ambrogio Buonvicino, the scenes are from the Acts of the Apostles, dominated by the coat-of-arms of Pope Paul V. The atrium's walls are divided by Ionic columns and six pilasters; above the entrance one can see tympanums on which are cherub heads that were carved by Borromini while still in his youth. Notice the important inscriptions between the doorways and also the busts of 30 martyred and canonized popes which are near the top of the walls.

Leading from the atrium built by Carlo Maderno (1608–1612), are five large bronze doors to the basilica — the two at the extreme right and left take you into the lesser naves and the three in the middle to the central nave.

The first door on the left was done by the artist, Giacomo Manzù, a good friend of John XXIII — who, in fact convinced Manzù to finish the door after many years of vacillation. Executed in the style of a refined form of classicism, the door is called "The Door of Death" because it depicts the many ways a person can die while carrying out its theme of the Ascension of Christ and the Assumption of the Virgin. Manzù used his best persuasive powers to convince Pope John to include him kneeling (he's seen in profile). The most recent door is the next one that was done in 1977 by Luciano Minguzzi and carries the title, ''Door of Good and Evil.'' Known as the Porta Mediana, the third door was commissioned by Pope Eugenius IV and done by Antonio Averulino (''Il Filarete''), a Florentine humanist. Dating from 1445, the work has its main theme done in narrative form since the artist was steeped in the classics. When first made, the door was 11 feet wide and 19.6 feet high, but it was enlarged in 1619 in order to fit the new basilica. All of the carved figures are in bronze, and the frieze around the panels deals with mythological elements, animals, fruits, and the like. The larger panels, however, display reliefs of Christ, the Virgin, Saint Paul, and Saint Peter. Others show the martyrdom of the two ''Princes of the Apostles.'' Pope Eugenius IV is shown, by the way, kneeling before Saint Peter.

In the small panels, you view important events from the reign of Eugenius, which include the visit that Emperor John VIII Palaeologos had with the pope. Also the same emperor is seen at the Council of Florence. Then there is a scene of the coronation of Emperor Sigismund of Luxembourg. Included also is the handing over of the formularies of the faith to the Abyssinian Embassy. In the middle section the story is related of how the artist came back to the city atop a donkey. Dominating the top of the doorway is a bas-relief by Bernini of Saint Peter meeting with a group of Christians from Jesus. As the product of the artists's own internal meditation, Door Number Four (by Venanzo Crocetti) concerns itself with the Seven Sacraments.

The last door on the right is the Porta Sancta, which is usually walled up and is opened up personally by the pope every time there is a Holy Year. In 1950 during the Jubilee, the Catholics of Switzerland offered a gift to the Vatican of a bronze door which was the work of Vico Consorti. Eventually, this was attached to the reverse side of the Porta Sancta inside the basilica. A mosaic of the ''Navicella,'' the work of Giotto, is above the central entrance of the Atrium. Commissioned by Cardinal Jacopo Gaetano Stefaneschi in 1298, the door was once in the portico of the old basilica and then housed in various locations until Pope Alexander VII ordered it put where it now stands. Since the mosaic has had to undergo innumerable restorations, a large part of its original character has been diminished. There is a scene of Christ walking on the water to calm the fears of the astonished Saint Peter, an idea that goes back to Byzantine times.

With its variety of different structural and ornamental elements, the atrium still offers a homogeneous and organic whole, as it extends for the entire length of the facade. At the far right is Bernini's statue of Constantine; at the other end is a statue of Charlemagne on horseback done by Cornacchini in 1725 against a mosaic background by Adami.

A central view of the interior of Saint Peter's Basilica. *(Photo by Carlo Piccolo)*

The Interior of
Saint Peter's Basilica

IN THE FORM OF a Latin Cross, the insides of Saint Peter's Basilica give the impression of being one vast nave. Such is not the case. Vast as it is, indeed. As put into effect by Maderno, the architectural plan is along the lines laid down by the Council of Trent with decorations added by Bernini. The interior gives you, immediately upon entering, the impression of unlimited size. The interior's overall length is 611 feet with a width that spans 82 feet. Each of the side aisles, 20 feet wide, are 250 feet in length and end at the pilasters of Saint Andrew and Saint Longinus that lead into the great area into which the circle of the dome is inserted. From this spot, the three apses begin, forming the head of the Latin Cross around the dome.

By keeping the main nave free of altars and monuments, the harmony of architectural decoration is maintained. Altars and monuments are positioned in the side aisles, in the chapels, and along the walls of the transept and apse. Altogether there are 45 altars, 25 monuments, 11 chapels, and 10 minor domes. When you plan your visit, it is best to divide the interior into five sections, as we will do here on these pages.

As a beginning, you should give an overall look at the main nave with its four arcades supported by pillars in pairs with pilaster strips. To lighten the enormity of the pillars the upper part of the niches houses statues of the Holy Founders of Religious Orders. Attached to the first two pillars are two large holy water basins done by Agostino Cornacchini, dating from the eighteenth century. The huge cherubs holding the antique yellow marble shells were carved by Francesco Moderati. The figures on the pavement run the entire length of the church, but it is the large disc in red porphyry that is a historical curio: it once stood before the high altar in the ancient basilica. On this disc stood some 20 emperors, from Charlemagne to Frederick II, who were crowned by popes.

Your tour starts with the right-hand nave. This corresponds with the Porta Sancta, above which is the mosaic of Saint Peter (the work of Ciro Ferri in 1675). Notice that the roof of the side aisles is determined by three oval domes, one for each of the bays onto which the side chapels open up. In the first chapel is Michelangelo's Pietà — which is now protected by bullet-proof glass. The oval dome serving as a roof has three frescoes executed expertly by Giovanni Lanfranco, and they depict the Triumph of the Cross and angels caressing the symbols of the Passion, its theme being the salvation of mankind achieved by the sacrifice of Christ.

Michelangelo's Pietà is part and parcel of this strain of devotion. Commissioned by Cardinal Jean de Villier in 1498, the Pietà was done by Michelangelo when he was 25 years old and had just arrived in Rome. Combining a human theme with a divine vision, the Pietà has a symbolic quality. Typical of Leonardo da Vinci is Michelangelo's use of pyramidal construction, which is the basis of the structure — but in the Pietà this is done in such a way that is reminiscent of Gothic art and techniques. Yet never forget that the Pietà has its own absolute individuality that is imbued with a soul capability of being reunited in trance or ecstasy and suggests what a work of art is to be. Notice that the Madonna is very large in size, enabling her to take into her lap not only the Christ figure but also the whole of humanity which, too, suffers. Michelangelo intentionally did the disproportion between the head and the body and gave her face the finest detail to show the traditional purity of the Virgin. In her silent sorrow she cradles the body of her Son in the folds of her garments; His body, on the other hand, shows no sign of His martyrdom, and His death is highlighted solely by the abandonment of the way He lies in His mother's mantle.

Now move down the right aisle. You come to the monument to Queen Christina of Sweden (1625–1689), completed in 1702 by

Giovanni Theudon and Lorenzo Ottoni from a design by Carlo Fontana. The queen is shown in the bas-relief while she was making the conversion to Catholicism in 1655. On the opposite wall is a monument to Pope Leo XII shown as he is giving the ''Urbi et Orbi'' benediction in 1825, a Jubilee Year. Portrayed among the cardinals present is Cardinal Mauro Cappellari, later to become Pope Gregory XVI—it was he who commissioned this work from G. Fabris in 1836. The Chapel of Saint Nicholas of the Crucifix is next, designed on an oval plan by Bernini. There are many relics preserved here. Since the elevator that popes use to get down to the basilica is at this spot, the chapel necessarily is not kept open to the public.

The next chapel is named after Saint Sebastian who in a large mosaic by P. Cristofari shows the martyrdom of that saint. The body of Pope Innocent XI is beneath the altar, placed here after his beatification. On the chapel's right is a monument by Pietro Canonica dedicated to Pope Pius XI. Opposite is a monument to his successor, Pope Pius XII, known as the Pope of the Second World War, done by F. Messina. The subject of the mosaic is also the decoration of the dome. Two more monuments facing each other are those of Pope Innocent XII (on the right) and of Countess Matilda Canossa. The marble group has Pope Innocent seated between Charity and Justice. Designed initially by Bernini in 1635, the Matilda of Canossa work displays her with a sceptre in her right hand and the keys and the papal crown in her left hand—this is to symbolize her defense of the papacy. Matilda was the Tuscany ruler who supported Pope Gregory VII during the eleventh century in his conflict with the Empire. The sarcophagus containing the bones of Matilda was the first one of a woman to be placed in Saint Peter's. (There are six women buried in Saint Peter's whose tombs still exist).

Closed by an iron grille, the Chapel of the Most Holy Sacrament has Borromini decorations which deal with the Eucharistic Mystery. The sumptuous tabernacle on the altar is in gilded bronze and designed by Bernini. At the sides are two adoring angels. Representing the Holy Trinity, the altarpiece is by Pietro da Cortona, and the altar (right) is a mosaic copy of a

Domenichino painting. It shows the Ecstasy of Saint Francis. In back of the Sacrament Chapel is the monument to Pope Gregory XIII in white marble that G. Rusconi carved in 1723. The pontiff is shown between the symbols of Religion and Magnificence, while the sarcophagus on which the statue rests bears reliefs that report on the reform of the Julian Calendar. Two statues of Religion and Justice, by P. Antiche, flank the marble urn. When this aisle comes to an end, there is an altar with the mosaic of the Communion of Saint Jerome from a painting by Domenchino, found today in the Vatican Art Gallery.

The Gregorian Chapel, named after Pope Gregory XIII, is where Michelangelo starts his wide passageway around the outside of the pilasters supporting the cupola. There is an urn inside the altar in which the mortal remains are contained of the Greek Father of the Church, Saint Gregory of Nazianzus, Patriarch of Constantinople from 330 to 390 A.D. On top of the altar stands a twelfth century work of the Madonna of Succour, which was taken from the old basilica. Give a good look now to the altar of Saint Jerome before you go into the main aisle.

It's here, at the intersection of the nave and transepts beneath the cupola, that you find the well-known bronze statue of Saint Peter sitting on his throne. Sitting upright and dressed in a Roman robe, with one key in his left hand and with his right hand raised, he is giving a blessing, done in the Greek style. Now look at the feet, which project a bit over the edge of the pedestal —both are shiny and worn down, especially the right one. For more than six and a half centuries, thousands of pilgrims have planted a kiss on either the right or left foot or held their rosaries and other devotional objects against them. On important feast days the faithful stand patiently in long lines to touch or kiss the feet in reverence to the apostle. How this statue was created was for a long time a mystery that was cleared up in this century through technical and chemical analysis, and it was determined that the artist was Arnolfo di Cambio of Florence, the same master who created the interior of the cathedral in Florence. The powerful statue was struck in 1300. Far above the statue is a mosaic portrait of Pope Pius IX, which Pius had put there personally in 1871 when he celebrated his 25th year as a pope, the same number of years that Saint Peter was the bishop of Rome from 42 A.D. to 67 A.D.

From above the cupola there usually falls a rather bright light, coming down in shafts directly upon the Confessio, which has reference to the tomb of the martyr. This is the spot where faithful Catholics came to profess the same religion that the martyr died for—hence the tomb of Saint Peter. There are two marble staircases that go to a semicircular open crypt that Maderno constructed during 1600. A gilded gate opens into a niche with the Byzantine mosaic of Christ in the background. This niche bears the nickname, ''Niche of the Sacred Pallia,'' for the gold-crusted eighteenth century box where the pallia are contained (pallia are those narrow white stoles which popes bestow on new archbishops and are kept at Peter's tomb as a symbol of the close link between Rome and the local churches). You may notice an unusual lack of symmetry inasmuch as the Niche of the Pallia is not directly aligned with the middle part of the gateway. Also the longitudinal axis of the church does not run precisely through it but a bit to the right. Behind this is the so-called ''Wall G,'' in which the bones of Peter have been hidden since the time of Constantine.

Set into the floor, there is a round grating through which you can peer into the heart of Saint Peter's church, into the Chapel of Peter. In effect, the entire basilica is a vast reliquary built over and around this tomb. At this point, one must be aware of several things: at the intersection of the two lines that cross the building, the horizontal line starts at the obelisk outside and leads across the Confessio to the apse, and the vertical line begins in the depths of Peter's tomb and leads across the papal altar to the summit of the cupola. These two lines make up a cross, the main symbol of the Catholic religion.

Made from a big block of white marble, taken from the Forum of Nerva and consecrated by Pope Clement VIII in 1594, is the Papal Altar itself. In keeping with custom in early churches, the altar faces east to the rising sun. The canopy of gilded bronze, supported by four massive, twisting bronze columns, enshrines both the altar and the tomb below, a Bernini masterpiece that he labored on for a full decade. Art experts maintain that this marks the triumph of the baroque style over the plain appearances of the Renaissance. The twisted bronze columns are suggestive of the ancient marble columns that surrounded Peter's tomb in the Constantine Basilica, which were decorated with vine shoots. The baroque columns here are done with olive leaves. Seen buzzing around the canopy are swarms of bronze bees, the heraldic symbol of the royal Barberini family, this particular touch commissioned by Pope Urban VIII, a member of the Barberini clan. Because there was a scarcity of bronze, the pope commanded Barberini to remove the bronze beams from the Pantheon to be used on the bees. Since not even the barbarians committed such an act, the Romans came up with a famous quip that still lasts today: "What the barbarians did not do, the Barberini did!"

The last and greatest work by Michelangelo, according to many experts, is the cupola above the canopy. It descends on you as the paternal hands of God the Father protecting the tomb of the First Vicar of Christ. Resting on four very large pentagonal pilasters, the dome soars above you. In the niches of the four pilasters are imposing marble figures of four saints carrying the emblem of a relic conserved and venerated in Saint Peter's. The saints are Saint Longinus carrying the lance that pierced Christ's side (done by Bernini in 1639); Saint Helena bearing a fragment of the Cross she accompanied to Rome (done by Andrea Bolgi in 1639); Saint Andrew, younger brother of Peter, carrying an oblique cross on which he died crucified (done by Frans Duquesnoy in 1640); and Saint Veronica making haste to put on display the cloth on which Christ had left an imprint of His bloodied visage. From the Confessio three transept areas of the same length branch out to symbolize the Trinity. Enter the right-hand transept and you are in the place where the First Vatican Council of 1869–1870 took place, an assembly of 700 bishops. In the apse of this transept, which is 148 feet long, is the altar of the martyrs Processus and Martinianus. In the mosaic above, the subject deals with the martyrdom of Saint Peter's two jailers whom he converted and then baptized. Nicolas Poussin's mosaic, done in 1630, is to the left and it treats the martyrdom of Saint

Erasmus. In the passageway to the Gregorian Chapel, to the right, is an altar dedicated to the Christian Orient. Saint Basil the Great is depicted on the altarpiece as he converts the Aryan Emperor Valens in 372 A.D. The altar contains a crystal urn with the body of Saint Josaphat, the archbishop of Kiev, who was killed in 1623 by Russian Orthodox fanatics because he was loyal to Rome.

In the corridor that goes to the Chapel of Saint Petronilla, further on to the left, is an altarpiece in mosaic, done as a copy to a painting by Giovanni Lanfranco in 1628.

On the opposite side is the tomb of Pope Clement XIII, executed by Antonio Canova. There are two magnificent lions — one is sound asleep and the other is quite awake — guarding the tomb's entrance. In back of them are the allegorical figures of Religion and the Genius of Death. There is a story behind this: on the day the tomb was consecrated, the sculptor (Canova) disguised himself as a beggar and mixed with the public to hear what they were saying about his work. The ''beggar'' was given a few coins by Prince Rezzonico and ordered to leave the church.

At this point you reach the Chapel of Saint Petronilla, about which there is also a story to tell. In the Catacombs of Domitilla a sarcophagus was unearthed during the eighth century that had an inscription on it, reading: ''Dearest Daughter Petronilla.'' Since many thought that the name Petronilla was derived from Petrus, a legend came about that Petronilla had been the daughter of the Apostle Peter and had died a martyr. In order to have her rest near the remains of her ''father,'' Petronilla's bones were taken to a mausoleum next to the ancient Basilica, and it was given the name of La Rontonda di Santa Petronilla. Then when a new church was to be put up, the relics of Petronilla were deposited in this altar. Guercino painted an altarpiece for it in 1623 to depict the burial and glorification into heaven of the young saint, but the painting was taken to the Capitoline Museum and replaced here with a mosaic copy done by Pietro Paola Cristofari, who was the Vatican mosaics workshop's first director. Beneath the floor are also buried both Pope Sixtus IV and Pope Julius II and other members of the Della Rovere Family. Ironically, Julius II, who laid the foundation stone for the new church and who was supposed to have his own mausoleum with a commissioned funeral monument by Michelangelo, is buried here in plain earth without any tombstone since Michelangelo never finished the work.

Between the Saint Petronilla altar and the tomb of Pope Clement X (which has a marble relief done by Leonardo Leli in 1675 showing him in the act of opening the Holy Door) there is a door that leads to the archives of the Saint Peter's administration office. Unknown to most visitors, the thick walls of the church house a secret labyrinth of corridors, spiral staircases, and recesses through which church officials and the work staff of Saint Peter's make their way (anybody would get lost if he ever got into that maze). In time, you enter the apse where two wide steps of porphyry now take you to the symbolic chair of Saint Peter. With a casing of gold and bronze for protection, the wooden chair is believed to be that of Peter. But in actual fact it was a throne that Emperor Charles the Bald (823–877) brought with him for his coronation in 875 and which he then gave to the pope as a gift. As the throne became rickety over the years, Bernini enclosed it in a new covering of bronze in 1666 and placed it high over the altar in a colorful setting of clouds, rays of light, and angelic figures. Below are the statues of four Fathers of the Church—two from the west (Ambrose and Augustine) and two from the east (Athanasius and John Chrysostom). Bernini intended this to convey the idea of the collegiality of the bishops with the pope, a thought that came out only at the last Vatican Council under Pope John XXIII. In also another way Bernini was ahead of his time when he represented the idea of the infallibility of the pope 200 years before it became dogma in 1870. How did he accomplish this? He did it by using a dove with open wings in the center of the window, as if to declare that the Holy Ghost illuminates the pope when he speaks from the throne and defines a dogma. All the ingredients of baroque art are found here, architecture and sculpture, gold and glass, marble and bronze and light and shadow—Bernini's way of giving visible form and honor to the doctrine.

Over on the left is the monument to Pope Paul III who lies in an antique, priceless black marble sarcophagus. At the base are two seated allegorical female figures; the woman on the left personifying Justice was originally nude but then was covered in a penitential tunic of metal. Representing Wisdom, the other figure remains naked—no longer young and beautiful but a wise old woman. With the help of Michelangelo, this monument was done by Guglielmo Della Porta over a long period. The tomb of Urban VIII (the great patron of Bernini) is on the right. It was Bernini who set up this monument to show his gratitude to the pope for his supportive endeavors. Later on, this monument became the model for all baroque funeral monuments. You see for the first time in art a winged skeleton who is canceling the name of the deceased, while the Barberini Family bees are seen resting on the altar, a bit confused and tired.

Go left now from the apse and around the two pilasters of the cupola, and you will come up to the tomb of Pope Alexander VIII which is made of onyx and polychrome marble. Now you are close to the Chapel of the Column which refers to the particular fresco of the Madonna that had been painted on a column for the old basilica before it was placed here. The altar contains the mortal remains of three popes—Leo II, Leo III, and Leo IV. To the right is the altar of Saint Leo I the Great who was responsible for saving Rome from the invading Huns. An impressive marble relief by Alessandro Algardi, done in 1650, depicts the historic meeting in 452 A.D. between Attila the Hun king and the pope.

The tomb of Pope Alexander VII is to be found atop the door that goes from the church to Piazza di Santa Marta which is inside Vatican City. The art of baroque came into full maturity during Alexander's term in office. Under him Bernini created Saint Peter's Square, and to him he dedicated his last output. The winged skeleton of Death, appearing again from behind a heavy curtain of Sicilian jasper, is turning over an hourglass to demonstrate that the pope's time is up. Once again there are two female figures to portray Charity and Truth, and behind them you can see the heads of Justice and Wisdom. The Truth figure was also nude once, but when Pope Innocent XI inaugurated the monument, it was covered after he made a quip about the ''naked truth perhaps being too pleasant to onlookers.''

It is time now to reach the left-hand (southern) transept that Michelangelo himself built, which was then used as a model for the northern one. The apse has three altars, and in the central one are the bones of the Apostles Judas Thaddeus and Simon. Above the altar on the left is a mosaic copy of Guido Reni's painting of Peter being crucified upside down (the Reni work is currently in the Vatican Pinacoteca). The last altarpiece dedicated to the life of Peter is to be found in the next corridor. Done by Pomariancio in 1607, it recalls the incident in which Sapphira and her husband Ananius drop dead at Peter's feet because they lied to him. On the opposite side is a passageway that leads into the Sacristy and the Saint Peter's Museum. The next tomb is of great interest because it is that of Pope Pius VII and was done by a Protestant artist hired to work in Saint Peter's—Bertel Thorvaldsen, a pupil of Canova. Typical of neoclassical art, this format of white marble carries its message in a cold, academic way.

In the Clementine Chapel (started by Michelangelo)—it gets its name from Pope Clement VIII—stands the altar to Saint Gregory I the Great, which is to the right of the Pope Pius VII monument. Besides his military conquest that gave Rome its freedom, Gregory made his mark by sending out his missionaries to England to bring on multiple conversions. The Clementine Chapel also features a mosaic copy of The Transfiguration of Christ on Mount Tabor based on Raffaello's last work. He died in 1520 while putting the finishing touches to this painting, and on his death it was placed at the foot of his bier. Though Napoleon stole this painting and took it with him to Paris, the Vatican Pinacoteca managed to retrieve it where it is now on exhibit.

Two facing monuments on the path towards the exit show (on the left) a relief portrait of Vienna turning back the invading Turks in 1683—an event that threw cold water on the Islamic threat to Christianity and Europe. On the other side rests the body of Pope Leo XI, who was in office a short time, only 27 days. He was the fourth and the last of the Medici popes. The tomb was done by Algardi, known to be an enemy of baroque excesses and a big rival of Bernini. The relief art has two scenes from the life of Leo XI while he was the papal delegate in France, during which time he received King Henry IV's repudiation of Protestantism in 1593. On the oval dome of the Chapel of the Choir, which is closed by Borromini's iron grill, are some Old and New Testament scenes done in stucco. There is a marble shield to say that the grave of Pope Clement XI is underneath the paved tiles.

The bones of Saint John Chrysostom, the Patriarch of Constantinople from 350 to 407, are inside the altar, which houses a mosaic copy of Pietro Bianche's Immaculate Conception painting done in 1740. The diamonds in the halo are not real, since they were removed and placed on exhibition in the Museum of Saint Peter's.

The only tomb in the upper church that was originally in Old Saint Peter's is that of Pope Innocent VIII which can be seen directly across from the Chapel of the Choir. In the cast by Antonio del Pollaiolo, done in 1498, the pope is seen twice. Above, and for the first time in the history of art, he is seated on the throne wearing the tiara and holding a lance that makes reference to the holy lance of Longinus. The pope is surrounded by the allegories of the four cardinal virtues, which Pollaiolo had expanded well on his monument of Pope Sixtus IV. Below, the pope is lying on the funeral casket. On the opposite side is the standing figure of Pope Pius X that Pier Enrico Astori made in 1923. An unusual aspect here is that the tiara on his head is the last time that any pope will be depicted on a funeral monument that way—from Pope Pius XI onwards, the pontiff is seen wearing the bishop's mitre.

The Chapel of the Presentation is now at the right. The mosaic copy here is of the Virgin Mary as a young girl (based on a 1622 painting by Francesco Giovanni Romanelli). Legend has it that her parents took her to the Temple in Jerusalem to be educated as a temple virgin. The bronze-covered body of Saint Pius X lies in the altar itself; over in the right-hand corner of the chapel is the monument to Pope John XXIII. In 1970 Emilio Greco did a bronze high relief on which he cited John's acts of mercy and his opening of the Vatican Council. At the left of the altar is Pietro Canonica's monument to Pope Benedict XV, who is shown kneeling. The background motifs make allusions to World War I and its nightmares, a fact that plagued him during his reign.

Above the entrance to the roof are two angelic children using the sceptre and crown as toys. This is part of a monument to

Mary Clementine Stuart (1702–1735), the granddaughter of the Polish King John III Sobiesky, who was largely responsible for saving Vienna from the Turks. Mary went down in history when she married King James III, the son of the last Catholic king. Making his home in Rome, James III lived in exile from England. Mary's sarcophagus describes her as ''Queen of Great Britain, Ireland, and France,'' but in point of fact, she never once visited these countries and was essentially a monarch with nothing to reign. The sepulcher is by Filippo Barigioni, done in 1745 in the late baroque style. In honor of her two young sons and their father, Canova sculpted a monument which stands opposite that of the last Stuart queen. In the style of an antique pagan stele, it shows two figures of the Genii of Death standing on either side of the doorway of the tomb and mourning over the end of the royal Stuart line. The baptistry constitutes, in essence, the end of your visit to the basilica.

Built in 1695, almost two centuries after the foundation was laid, the baptistry is the work of Carlo Fontana a nephew of the man who, 100 years before, had erected the obelisk in Saint Peter's Square and finished the cupola. The porphyry basin you see is ancient and at one time served as the sarcophagus of the German Emperor Otto II who died in 983. This chapel is rife with mosaics that were done in the eighteenth century representing three types of Baptism—by water, by desire, and by blood. Special attention should be given to a remarkable centerpiece (from a painting by Carlo Maratta) that shows the baptism of the Infant Jesus.

Saint Peter's Museum

ARRANGED ALONG modern lines in 1975 and housing treasures gathered up in the course of many centuries many of them charitable donations—the Art and History Museum of Saint Peter's should not be overlooked, no matter how pressed for time you may be. You'll find it at the end of the left-hand side nave beneath the monument of Pope Pius VIII where there is a winding corridor. This corridor, which lists on a large tablet the names of the 147 popes who are buried in Saint Peter's takes you to the sacristy, and next to it is the door to the Museum. Though overly rich in exhibits, the Museum would be presenting even much more, but it was plundered by various invading enemies over the centuries, the last ones being the French Army which stole everything it could before leaving in 1814.

A most important column greets you in the very first room. Venerated as the "Holy Column," this piece of twisted white Parian marble is said to have come from the Temple of Solomon in Jerusalem, and it was while leaning against it that Christ preached his Sermon of the Temple when he cast out the male-factors. Originally, this column had been one of 12 surrounding Peter's Tomb in the old Basilica. In the next room is a copy (made in the Museum of Mainz in 1974) of the old wooden throne (made in the Carolingian court's art school in Metz) that was a papal throne for hundreds of years. The 18 plates of ivory on the front lower part of the chair represent 6 monsters and the 12 labors of Hercules. Across from the throne is the so-called "Dalmatic of Charlemagne," a tunic the Emperor supposedly wore during special ceremonies and liturgical rites, but in fact the garment is Byzantine from the eleventh century. The oldest item in the Museum is a gift to Rome from Emperor Justice III, who died in 578, a cross on which a portrait of him and his wife is on the back.

The gorgeous tabernacle in marble in a chapel next to this room, done by Donatello in 1432 and 1433 during his sojourn in Rome, contains an old image of the "Madonna of the Fever," often called up to cure cases of malaria. The mold of Michelangelo's Pietà, which Francesco Mercatali cast in 1934 is in the same chapel. Had it not been for this excellent copy, it might not have been possible to restore the original Pietà inside Saint Peter's after it was damaged by a half-crazed vandal in 1972. In the next room the impressive Sixtus IV monument commands your attention immediately. Artist Antonio del Pollaiolo has the pope lying in state garbed in his ceremonial dress. Surrounding him are seven panels with bas reliefs that represent the three theological virtues—Faith, Hope, and Charity—and the four cardinal virtues—Prudence, Justice, Fortitude, and Temperance. In an outer circle the artist gives us the Seven Arts of the Trivium and Quadrivium—grammar, rhetoric and dialectic, arithmetic, geometry, music and astronomy. Taught at that time in the universities, these arts (together with a relatively new one, perspective) prepared the way for philosophy and theology.

The following room is the one with the painted wooden frame in which the veil of Veronica was kept until the eighteenth century. The nearby Cyprus casket of rock crystal originally served as a home for the spearhead of Longinus' lance. A series of very precious silver candelabra from the fifteenth to the eighteenth centuries follows, together with a pair of illuminated sixteenth century music scores for the Julius Chapel, named after Pope Julius II who had this choir put together in 1513 for doing liturgical chants in Saint Peter's. To the left in the Sacrament Chapel is a kneeling white angel with imposing wings which is a clay model of the bronze angel of Bernini—mark how clever lighting brings out the expression on the face, making it even better than the completed one.

Next comes a gallery housing a considerable number of chalices, reliquaries, monstrances, and vestments. The famous eighteenth century tiara that is studded with precious stones and that is placed on the head of the Saint Peter statue inside the Church each year for the Peter and Paul observance day is kept in this gallery. One of the truly great art treasures of the Museum is found in the next-to-the-last room: the sarcophagus of Junius Bassus, a Rome prefect who died in the year 359 after becoming a convert to Catholicism. Finely worked and polished in Parian marble, the sarcophagus has a front section that is divided into ten high-relief panels with scenes from the Old and New Testament that refer to suffering, death, and redemption. A striking scene of Christ has Him in the role of a young hero who is squatting on a throne between Peter and Paul while his feet rest on the vault of heaven, as the god Uranus stretches out over His head like a sheet. On the side of the sarcophagus are the pagan god and harvest scenes. Art specialists consider this sarcophagus a most important artwork because it clearly shows the transition from paganism to the new Christian movement.

The Cupola

FROM THE BAPTISTRY it is now time to visit the Cupola. Either you take the elevator to the right of the baptistry or you trudge up 145 steps on a spiral staircase to the top. If you opt for the latter, then you have a chance to read on the way up the many tablets that commemorate the Holy Years and the visits of important personages to the Vatican. During the latter part of your climb, you will notice in a few spots some big links of a chain. In their own way these links give evidence to one of the very few times that Michelangelo goofed: he had not accurately estimated the yielding point of the drum so that not long after the cupola was finished, cracks began to form in the walls; in order to consolidate the lower edges of the cupola, a gigantic iron chain had to be especially made and affixed.

Most tourists who reach the top, which is 148 feet from the ground, get the impression when they come out on the roof that they are suddenly on the moon. With unexpected dips and holes (corresponding to the skylights), a sloping and irregular floor, and various kinds of protruding domes of cupolas and lanterns covered in lead, you almost feel you've been transported to earth's only satellite. Between Bernini's massive travertine statues of Christ with Saint John and the 11 Apostles, you get a wondrous bird's-eye view of the city. Atop the roof you find souvenir shops and rooms where you can enjoy a coffee or drinks.

But no matter what your impressions are, it's Michelangelo's great cupola that commands your attention. On either side of it are two smaller cupolas built by Giacomo Della Porta which were not meant to have any reference to the interior of the church; they were placed there for the sole reason that they would provide "company" for Michelangelo's big cupola and enhance its majestic size. At night the big cupola is lit up by strong spotlights to a brilliant white.

From up there you get a magnificent panoramic view of Saint Peter's Square down below and the eye-grabbing Via della Conciliazione (which many Romans say is a work of art itself), not to mention the nearby Castel Sant'Angelo and its impressive bridge across the Tiber River. Running in a parallel line to Saint Peter's is a reddish brick building, rectangular, that was once intended as a fortress to defend the Vatican from attack, but inasmuch as Pope Sixtus IV sought to combine military exigency with religious themes, he converted one floor of the fortress into a special pontifical chapel, and it got its name from Sixtus, becoming known as the Sistine Chapel (which is dealt with in depth in another part of this book). Looking towards the south you see the Square of The First Roman Martyrs, which was the site of Nero's Circus and in whose center the obelisk originally stood at a spot that is indicated on the ground. You also get a view of the whole Vatican City, with its government offices, railway station, gardens, towers, radio masts, museums, and the "downtown" business section with its supermarket, pharmacy, bank, and what have you.

There are a mere 16 steps that lead from the roof to the interior of the cupola, and now you are suddenly in another world indeed. The bust of Michelangelo, a copy of Daniele da Volterra's original, stands at the entry point of the staircase. Do read the inscription below the bust, because it quotes Pope Paul III (1549) in which he explains that Michelangelo did not seek anything in return for building Saint Peter's—"He worked out of pure love and special veneration for this Basilica."

Follow the dimly lighted semicircular corridor to the inner part of the cupola, at which point you look down into the basilica at a height of 173 feet from the pavement. The estimated diameter of the cupola is more or less around 140 feet, and it is, in fact, just a bit smaller than the one in the Pantheon. Here, at last, you get a wonderful closeup of the cupola mosaics, which are shored with the words Christ spoke to Peter: "You are Peter and upon this Rock I will build my church." Below are the four evangelists

depicted in medallions that are 27 feet big. If you want an idea of
how big the thing is, bear in mind that the pen Saint Mark is
using measures 4.9 feet in length. Above the six circles with holy
popes and Fathers of the Church are Christ and Mary, John the
Baptist, Saint Paul, and the Apostles. Even further up are the
angels Seraphim and Cherubim. And God the Father with his
arms reaching out in the act of blessing the world that has been
created is at the very peak of the lantern. Every one of these blue
and gold mosaics was done during the sixteenth and seventeenth
centuries from the sketches of Giovanni Guerra, Cesare Nebbia,
and Cavalier D'Arpino.

Over a period of 22 months, from July 1588 to May 1590,
both Domenico Fontana and Giacomo Della Porta, working nonstop with a team of 800 men on a day and night shift, built the
vault of the dome. It must be made clear that Michelangelo was
not inspired for this cupola by the one in the Pantheon, but by
Brunelleschi's cupola for the Duomo in Florence. Note that the
outer vault of the cupola is not hemispheric as it is in the interior
but is raised some 18 feet above the inner vault, somewhat like a
gothic arch. No one is quite sure whether this is what
Michelangelo intended or not, but experts are still arguing over
that one. One thing is certain, it is this slight upward swing that
gives the cupola a special beauty that is unique. In the Vatican
Museums there is a copy of Michelangelo's wooden model,
which he made during 1558–1561, and it shows the same profile. Some experts, however, maintain that the model may have
been altered also.

Sixteen large windows let in the light that fills the cupola. On
the outside are 16 double Corinthian columns, and on the plinth
above them there were supposed to be the statues of 16 prophets
that artist Antonio Corradino made clay models for. Since the
stone was considered to be too heavy, the statues were never
made. Above the columns are garlands of pear branches and lion
heads—which is intended as a reminder of the Sixtus V emblem
because he was the one who commissioned the work. The columns are continued with 16 vaulting ribs that taper off near the
top and conduct the eye to the lantern, which is surrounded by

double columns in the Ionic style, topped by 16 candelabra that have no function other than decoration. Between the two spherical vaults of the cupola, a narrow spiral stairway of 302 steps goes directly to the lantern. Up there from a narrow balustrade, you get the very best of all possible views of Rome, and you note how many large and small domes dot the city in an attempt to imitate the big one at Saint Peter's. From the east the Sabine Mountains are visible, the Alban Hills in the southeast, and in the southwest the Tyrrhenian Sea comes into prominent view. It was possible in the past to walk up a rather steep staircase to a bronze orb that could accommodate only 16 people for the most spectacular view of Rome of all—but for security reasons this stairway was shut down. Saint Peter's workers have to use a ladder today to get up there.

The Sacred Grottoes
of the Vatican

FEW PEOPLE KNOW that under the Saint Peter's Basilica lies still another church, the Sacred Grottoes of the Vatican. In the past this vast area underneath the basilica was so dark and damp that anyone who visited had to do so with a flashlight or a candle. The present day basilica's floor was built about 10 feet above the first one, the Sacred ''Caves,'' which was the burial place for a number of high-ranking personages. During a 15-year period that stretched from 1935 to 1950, the Grottoes were equipped with electric lights and converted into a lower church. But it needs to be said that the lighting down here is not glaring but kept deliberately low so as to respect the ancient air of mysticism.

By following a low and narrow semicircular corridor that passes along the primitive apse of Constantine's church, you can wend your way along quite easily. To the right stands a chapel inaugurated in 1981, called the Chapel of the Three Patron Saints of Europe, Cyril, Benedict, and Methodius. Then you see a group of chapels dedicated for the most part to those churches behind the Iron Curtain, the so-called ''Churches of Silence.'' Included among these are the Polish Chapel with the image of the Black Madonna of Czenstochowa, the Irish Chapel with a modern mosaic of Saint Columban, a Chapel for the Czechs (this one contains a stone coffin for Cardinal Beran, the archbishop of Prague who died in 1969). There is also a fresco of the Madonna della Bocciata, so named because it underwent a defacing by an inebriated soldier with a bowling ball. The newest Chapel is for the Lithuanians.

The semicircular corridor leads to a gilded gate behind which is the Chapel of Saint Peter, at one time called the Clementine

Chapel. In the form of an inverted cross the Chapel is in memory of Peter who was crucified in a downside up position. The sixth century altar was only recently covered in precious malachite. In back of this altar is an iron gate through which you observe a white marble wall with dark red stripes of porphyry. This wall is the old rear wall of the funeral monument that Emperor Constantine built over the earthen grave of Peter.

Recalling the style of the triumphal arches in the Roman Forum, the magnificent marble frieze on the outer wall of the Saint Peter Chapel is by Matteo del Pollaiolo, a major Renaissance artist and the first deliberately to imitate this style. It was Pope Sixtus IV in 1474 who ordered the frieze for the marble canopy of the high altar of the ancient basilica. The five high reliefs of the work deal with the life and martyrdom of Peter and Paul. Across the way from this chapel is the burial vault of Pope Pius XII whose support of the excavations eventually led to the finding of Peter's tomb—thus Pius is buried as near to it as possible, as was his request.

Before long you come to an underground basilica that is divided into three naves below pilasters. The one along the outer wall contains several tombs: (1) Pope Pius XI is buried in a white marble coffin positioned in a niche that is full of shiny mosaics. It was this pope who was one of the two signatories to the 1929 Lateran Treaty between the Vatican and the Government of Italy (Mussolini was the cosignatory), a treaty that brought about the new State of Vatican City. (2) King James III of England (who died in 1776) and his two sons (Cardinal Henry, Duke of York, who died in 1807, and Charles Edward, Duke of Albany, who died in 1778) are buried here. On the sarcophagus rests an iron crown which symbolizes the exile of the king. (3) Pope Innocent XIII, buried in the next tomb, reigned from 1721 to 1724 and was one of three popes from the Conti family. (4) Then comes the tomb of Pope Urban VI (1378–1389). (5) Following directly is the granite sarcophagus where the only English pope in history was buried, Pope Adrian IV (1154–1159), who in 1155 crowned Frederick I (nicknamed Barbarossa because of his red beard) as Holy Roman Emperor. Also buried here are three important

Germans—Emperor Otto II, who was crowned king in Aachen at age 6, Holy Roman Emperor in Saint Peter's at age 12, and died at age 28; his nephew, Pope Gregory V, the first of five German popes, and Father Ludwig Kaas, who was the director of the excavations and reconstruction of the Grottoes. The tenth century mosaic in the center portrays Christ between Peter and Paul, but Peter is not seen carrying his usual two keys but three keys. This apparently is to symbolize the three powers of the church—to minister, to teach, to govern. Other opinions on this hold that the keys represent the Church as militant on earth, penitent in purgatory, and triumphant in heaven.

Closed by a large glass window, in front of a marble arch is an area from which you can see directly into the Confessio and the Niche of the Pallia. This niche is directly above the original earthen grave of Peter. And to the right is the wall that contains his remains. Although it used to stand in front of Peter's Tomb, the kneeling marble statue of Pope Pius VI is now placed at the opposite end of the middle nave. When he died in 1799, as a prisoner of Napoleon in France, he was taken back to Rome and his body placed next to Peter's tomb in an early Christian sarcophagus. That sarcophagus is the first one to the left in the third nave. Next to it on the altar is the stunning marble relief called The Madonna of the Orsini Family, sculpted by Isaia da Pisa in the fifteenth century. The tomb of Pope John XXIII (now called the Pope of Vatican Council II and ecumenism) is in the northern nave. He lies in a sarcophagus on top of which is a relief of a Madonna and Child with two angels, a Madonna that has motherly peasant facial features. Near John's tomb are the graves of two queens: Queen Christina of Sweden, whose impressive monument is upstairs in the upper basilica, and Queen Carola Lusignan-Savoy who was the last queen of Cyprus. After being expelled from her island, she spent the remainder of her life at the papal court with her Greek-Oriental retinue.

Go down a few steps at this point and you come to the tomb of Pope Benedict XV whose reign in office embraced World War I. Artist Giuliano Barbieri effectuated a number of clever openings under this tomb so that a visitor can look directly down into the antique cemetery. The tomb that follows is that of Pope John Paul I, who died in September 1978 after only 34 days in office but who nevertheless managed to win the admiration of people all over the globe. His sarcophagus is in gray marble with two Renaissance angels at the corners. Across are the tombs of Pope Innocent IX and Pope Marcellus II, to whom Palestrina dedicated his well-known Missa Papae Marcelli. On the floor of the next niche is the travertine tombstone of Pope Paul VI, who died in 1978. Since it was his strong wish to be buried in a plain earth grave with no flowers or candles, there is just a relief on the wall of a previously existing fifteenth century Madonna and Child.

As you turn the corner, you see the new Hungarian Chapel. Go on ahead and on your left are the tombs of Pope Innocent VII, Pope Nicholas V, and Pope Boniface VIII (who in 1300 announced the very first Holy Year). Sculptor Arnolfo di Cambio has depicted him lying on his deathbed above a marble sheet that is finely pleated. Nearby is a frescoed Madonna by Lippo Memmi which he did during the fourteenth century. By turning left you reach the base of two columns and part of the outside wall of the old basilica, still in its original place. This alone gives you a clue as to the massive size of the Constantine structure. There is also a part of the high wall that was put up in 1538 by Antonio da Sangallo to separate the old building from the new edifice that was going up behind it. As you reach the exit, there is a niche in which you find Saint Peter in a seated position, lifesize. The interesting story behind this unusual marble statue is that it is an old Roman copy of a Greek original of a pagan philosopher. It befell to Nicolo de Longhi in 1565 to take this statue and transform it into Saint Peter, and he did this by placing a new head on it with a halo and a curly beard. Then instead of a scroll that the original had in the left hand, the artist replaced the hand for a new one that held the keys of Peter. Now in a few short steps you reach one of the Vatican courtyards.

The Excavations
Beneath Saint Peter's

SINCE CONSTANTINE wanted his basilica built on the very spot
of Saint Peter's tomb, it was believed (correctly!) that Saint
Peter's Basilica stands on top of the bones of Saint Peter. Underneath the basilica are the Vatican's Sacred Grottoes, and underneath them are the excavations that, commissioned in 1939 by
Pope Pius XII, brought to light the Necropolis from 1941 to
1949—which you can inspect. Running some 230 feet, they are
23 feet under the present church and can be visited by first getting permission from the Vatican's Excavation Office (Ufficio
Scavi)—not a very difficult proposition, by the way. If you solicit
the assistance of a local priest in your city before you go to Italy or
a priest in Rome, the way will be paved for you with not much
fuss. Before you actually go down below, do read up on how the
centuries-old mystery of Saint Peter's Bones was finally unraveled
by a woman and a mouse (yes, a mouse!). Agatha Christie could
not have composed a better, more intriguing detective story.

The Story of Saint Peter's Bones

The story began with the crucifixion of Peter in Nero's Circus
and his burial on the Vatican hill. Centuries and centuries went
by and not until May 1942 did any kind of official announcement
come from the Vatican as to where indeed Saint Peter's bones
were buried. On May 13th of that year Pope Pius XII announced
on the radio that the bones of the first Roman pontiff, the first
Bishop of Rome, had been found. Then towards the end of 1950,
Pius once again spoke on the subject in his Christmas message:

53

The excavations under the Altar of the Confession, at least as regards the tomb of the apostle, a search on which we set our heart from the very first days of our pontificate, and their scientific study have been happily concluded. The essential question, then, is whether Peter's tomb has now really been found. To this question, the final conclusion of our studies provides an answer — a very clear Yes. A second question subordinate to the first one regards the relics of Saint Peter. Have they been found? On the edge of the sepulcher have been found the remains of human bones which, however, cannot be proved with certainty to belong to the body of the apostle.

Fully 18 years later, Pius' successor, Pope Paul VI formally let it be known that the bones of Saint Peter had indeed been found. In a public declaration on June 26, 1968, Paul VI declared: ''New and very patient and very accurate inquiries have been carried out: the relics of Saint Peter have been identified in a manner which we consider convincing.''

Quite frankly, Pope Paul on this day was not being thoroughly honest, for he led the world to infer that the Peter's bones he had talked about were the same bones that Pope Pius had talked about in 1950, when in fact two different sets of bones were actually involved. The first ones that Pius had talked about turned out to be, after thorough inspection, not those belonging to Peter. No complete or clear announcement, however, was ever made about this. The two papal announcements, as welcome as they were to the Christian world, did not indicate at all the series of absolutely incredible blunders the Vatican committed, the truly fantastic detective work and superb piece of scientific detection by a stubborn woman who would not take No for an answer, and the tiny mouse which came to the rescue when all seemed lost. Let it all be told now.

Three months after becoming pope in June 1939, Pius XII — eager to resolve once and for all the mystery behind Saint Peter's bones — asked Monsignor Carlo Respighi, who held the office of Secretary of the Pontifical Committee for Sacred Archeology, to institute a formal attempt to uncover Peter's tomb underneath the main altar in the basilica. Although the Curia was very much against any kind of excavations underneath the altar because of the stupendous weight of Bernini's bronze and marble canopy that embraced the general area, Pius pushed his weight around on this one and took the full responsibility for any consequences. He even promised that if the sum of money set aside for the excavations ran out, he would have the work continue with money he would take out of his own pocket from a personal bank account he still had under his family name of Pacelli. Still the Curia fought him and sought to block the diggings, but in the end Pius got his way and the shovels began.

In 1940 four archeologists, three Italians and a German Jesuit, were given the job that was to run for about nine years, and they were assisted by a team of the Vatican's best carpenters, ironmongers, plumbers, masons, and electricians—known inside the Vatican as *sampietrini*. These workers were under the direct supervision of Monsignor Ludwig Kaas, a somewhat easy-going German whose inefficiency almost proved disastrous during the course of the work. Two blunders that Monsignor Kaas committed were his failure to keep a proper day-by-day logbook of the work and his failure to take photographs of the work under way. Monsignor Kaas was also responsible for the lack of coordination between his crew of workers and the four archeologists. But his biggest blunder was yet to come.

The archeologists—Antonio Ferrua, Enrico Josi, Bruno Apolloni-Ghetti, and Engelbert Kirschbaum—discovered that substantial portions of a monument known by historians to have been built by Emperor Constantine to honor Saint Peter had been used as the basis upon which to build Saint Peter's Basilica, with the main altar being placed on the site of the monument itself. Incorporated into this monument was a much smaller, somewhat primitive monument built earlier, a small niche dug into a brick wall, flanked by two small marble columns supporting a slab of travertine and resting on another slab which covered a hole in the ground that had been cut away to look like a trench. Although the archeologists spent almost nine years getting down into Peter's original tomb, when they finally reached it, it was empty.

But close to the tomb was a small collection of human bones that had been placed in a small arch, and these were taken away by Monsignor Kaas, placed into a zinc box, and eventually put behind lock and key in his office. As luck would have it, Monsignor Kaas allowed one of the archeologists, Father Kirschbaum, to take a photo of a fragment of a humerus and a femur. The bones remained in Monsignor Kaas' cupboard and would have probably remained there forever, if Pope Pius had not one day just happened to have seen the two photographs taken by Father Kirschbaum. Pius asked his personal physician, Dr. Riccardo Galeazzi Lisi, to look at the bones and tell him what he thought of them.

Even though more than 80 percent of the bones were missing for any kind of meaningful reconstruction of a skeleton, Dr. Galeazzi Lisi arrived at the conclusion that the bones belonged (1) to one man, (2) to an elderly man, and (3) to a man of sturdy build. This fit Peter's description quite well. There was only one fly in the ointment—subsequent examination of the bones revealed that they actually were the bones of two men and a woman. But in the meantime Pope Pius had already announced in 1942 that the bones were of Peter. So in his 1950 announcement he simply said the bones ''could not be proved with certainty'' as belonging to Peter, letting the world infer what it wanted.

It is at this point that an incredible series of events follow in which a woman—Dr. Margherita Guarducci, then a professor of Greek epigraphy at the University of Rome—intruded into the history of Peter's bones and became a legend in her own right within the Vatican itself (one of the few women ever to do so).

She had read in 1952 in a Roman newspaper an article on Antonio Ferrua, the Italian Jesuit who comprised one of the quartet of the Vatican archeology team. What caught her attention in that article was a casual reference to Father Ferrua that an inscription had been found on the wall, inside the recess, which had Greek letters that read: PETR on one line and ENI on the other line. Since she was an expert on Greek inscriptions, she asked the Vatican if she could study this carefully. As was to be expected, Professor Guarducci was repeatedly turned down by Vatican bureaucrats. Rebuffed but undaunted the woman successfully managed to get an appointment to see Monsignor Giovanni Montini, then Substitute Secretary of State, who was later to become Pope Paul VI. With Monsignor Montini's help, Professor Guarducci got a private audience with Pope Pius and convinced him she should take a close look at the inscription. In May 1952, the double-locked section of the secluded excavations were opened to her, but alas and alack, the PETR and ENI inscription were nowhere to be found. When she sought out Father Ferrua, he assured her he had personally seen the letters himself and bemoaned the fact that they had not been photographed.

What had happened to the inscription?

It took Professor Guarducci years of persistent hunting, but eventually she discovered that Monsignor Kaas had stored away —once again in his cupboard—a tiny chunk of plaster from the wall that came unstuck. Guessing that this piece could very well have the Greek letters on them, she sought to get Monsignor Kaas to let her look at it. He refused. There was nobody who could get the headstrong monsignor to change his mind. So back to Monsignor Montini went Professor Guarducci who once again went to see the pope who then ordered Monsignor Kaas to comply. Sure enough, there were the elusive letters. It took her six years of intensive study of the faded graffiti to solve the riddle of what the early Christians had scratched on that wall. She did this mostly by using enlarged photographs of the graffiti and studying them almost daily in her home and office.

Professor Guarducci then made a most revealing discovery. After considerable study on the spot (for now she had been given access to the excavations anytime she wanted), she deciphered an inscription written in the form of $P E$. With the help of her sister Maria, she poured over the strange criss-cross of signs and letters in the grottoes beneath the altar and compared them with those in the catacombs inside Rome and near Rome. She and Maria found significant repetitions and meanings, and now a special line was beginning to take shape.

During the second century, the Christians who had gone underground because of the systematic persecutions, developed a mystical code of their own. They had symbols such as the Greek chi rho—a combination of the first two Greek letters of the word Christ to form a P . Similarly, early Christian worshippers and pilgrims used the Latin letters P and E for Peter, M for Mary, and T for the Cross. These were often inserted in the names of the worshippers and those they wished to commemorate. Thus, if a Christian's name was Paolo, beneath the P in that name, an E was drawn in to signify Peter's crucifixion. If the Christian's name was Claudia, then this name was written with a Greek X fused with the P, making the chi rho and indicating Claudia's devotion to Christ.

Dr. Guarducci found that the PE symbol in various combinations occurred again and again in the crypt beneath the confession altar. It dawned on her that Peter's name was not spelled out and that this was why none of the archeologists was able to find it. Yet, there it was, in monogram form at the foot of the P to make it look like a key — thus, E . She further concluded that the letters underneath could be an abbreviation of the Greek word, ''*Ernesti,*'' which when put together with the monogramic letters would mean ''Peter is buried here.''

Unknown to her, the Vatican workers, in demolishing a segment of Constantine's wall, uncovered a horizontal slit in the wall next to the graffiti. When they made it bigger, they discovered a small recess behind it in the form of a rectangular box, lined with marble slabs that had been bricked in. The archeologists put down in their notes that the recess was empty, ''except for the remains of organic matter and bones, mixed with earth, a strip of lead, two small skeins of silver thread, and some coins dating from the tenth century.''

As luck would have it, one day in September 1953, Dr. Guarducci was on her knees studying the graffiti on this wall with a magnifying glass, and a foreman of the *sampletrini,* one Giovanni Segoni, was standing nearby watching her. She asked Segoni if the excavators had found anything else in the recess, besides the objects already known about. Much to her surprise, Segoni said there was indeed some other stuff (yet another box that Monsignor Kaas had squirreled away), a wooden box in a damp cellar in front of the chapel of Saint Colombanus. Segoni led Guarducci to the box, and inside was the most incredible assortment of objects, consisting of many human bones, some bones of cats and dogs, ancient coins, tiny shreds of woolen cloth with golden threads, and the almost complete skeleton of a mouse.

It was not fully clear why Monsignor Kaas had not reported these objects to any of the four archeologists when the diggers had uncovered them; he apparently had stuffed them into a box, forgot to label them, made no record of them in a ledger, and took no photographs. These objects at first did not indicate in any way that they might be the bones of Peter, partly because the animal bones would hardly be mixed up with the remains of the saint and partly because of the coins and other objects that were not of the era of Peter. Guarducci, nevertheless, routinely submitted the bones to an anatomy expert in Sicily, Professor Venerando Correnti of Palermo University. After several years of study, Professor Correnti reported that the bones comprised a nearly complete set that belonged to one person and those bones were of an old man. His report also showed that the age of the man was between 60 and 70 years and the height between 163.6 and 167.9 centimeters.

With this information in hand, now Professor Guarducci began to think that these bones could be those of Peter. She surmised that when Constantine's workers opened Peter's original tomb, they found his skeleton covered in earth, and in order not to damage the relics, they picked up the whole lot and placed both the earth and bones intact inside Constantine's monument. What baffled Guarducci, however, were those animal bones, 29 in all. Further examination by Professor Correnti, helped now by Professor Luigi Cardini of Rome University, identified the bones as those of a hog, a rooster, an ox, and sheep. The remaining 19 bones belonged to one animal, the mouse.

But there was something very special about the rodent's bones. Unlike the other which were yellowed and encrusted with earth, the mouse's bones were very white and clean. The riddle Guarducci faced was: What was the meaning of all these animal bones that were mixed with those of Peter that had been so carefully hidden and protected inside Constantine's monument? For most of a summer Guarducci wrestled with this question and could not come up with a solution. Now she decided to bring the question to some of her professional friends in academia, especially archeologists who had had a lot of experience digging in the Rome area. She asked them if they ever had occasion to find animal bones mixed in with human bones, and one of her friends said that such cases usually indicated that a body had first been buried on farm land, among the carcasses of dead farm animals, and then later disinterred and reinterred together with the farm soil and the animal bones.

Slowly the pieces to the jigsaw puzzle seemed to be falling into place. Guarducci learned that the body of the martyr had first been buried in a simple trench on a farm until Constantine decided to move it to a safer and more sumptuous place. And there the whole collection remained for 16 centuries. Professor Guarducci undertook still further scientific tests. Experts were consulted on the other materials found inside the recess. Soil analysts reported that the earth found in the recess very likely came from the soil in which the first century tomb was dug. Chemical analysis showed that the cloth in which the bones were wrapped had a fine plate of gold, other threads were made of pure gold, and some of the linen showed traces of having been gold-plated. But perhaps the most important fact from the chemists was that the wool had been dyed with a real purple which in Peter's time was the most expensive dye and was reserved for royalty and high Church dignitaries.

There still remained one stumper. What about those coins from the tenth century? How could coins from the tenth century be inside a recess that had been, supposedly, never opened since the days of Constantine the Great (288–337 A.D.)? The bones of the little mouse finally solved the question and gave Guarducci her final clue as to the authenticity of the bones of Peter. Since the bones of the mouse were whiter than the other animal bones and since there was a lack of earth encrustations on the skeleton, the mouse had obviously infiltrated into the recess after it was built and perished there. With his wriggling to get into the recess from above, the mouse (Guarducci surmised) helped some of the coins, which were very thin and small in diameter, to slip into the tiny space. Coins were apparently thrown onto the church floor by pilgrims, and the janitors of the basilica swept these into receptacles —but a few of them managed to slip into the cracks in the floor unnoticed and gradually worked their way downwards over a century or so.

After nearly 10 years of painstakingly slow detective work, Guarducci had finally solved a mystery that had plagued the Vatican for centuries. But in so doing, she upset an ecclesiastical applecart that meant a big embarrassment for Vatican officials. For centuries the Saint John Lateran Church in Rome had kept the ''skull of Saint Peter'' in a silver container, to which millions of believers had gone to pay homage. Guarducci's final report made it plain that this was a false relic. When Pope Paul VI announced that Saint Peter's bones had been discovered, no mention was made of the skull. Nor was any mention made of Margherita Guarducci.

The entry to the excavation site is from the south side of the Church. First you go through three rooms that contain remains of Constantine's building until you reach the outside walls of the ancient basilica. Then by going a few steps downward, you are immediately in the necropolis, one of the largest in old Rome. On two sides of a narrow alleyway there are 22 funeral chambers with frescoed walls, mosaic and marble floorings, windows, and entrance doors. Most of the families buried here were members of Rome's middle class—merchants, civil servants, and professional people. From the various symbols, you infer that quite a few of the mausoleums were pagan in origin—besides which you find Greek and Roman gods mixed with oriental and Egyptian deities. As time went on, some of the families were Christian. Some of the tombs go back to Peter's time.

At the lower, east end of the street, the first mausoleum has a marble slab over the door that gives the name of the deceased and his age, social standing and other pertinent information. This procedure was used for nearly all of the other burial sites. This first mausoleum, from the second century A.D., was Popilius Heracla's who, according to the written words on his grave, ordered his heir to build him a funeral monument. On the right are the Mausoleums of Marcia and that of the Egyptians. The latter got its name from the mural painting of Horus, the Egyptian god of death. Inside both of these are sarcophagi decorated with Dionysian scenes evoking everlasting happiness. Now comes the Mausoleum of the Caetennii in which a Christian woman, Aemilia Gorgonia, is buried. She is portrayed next to a fountain where she is filling an amphora with water. Apparently, the religious idea put across here is taking water from the fountain of perpetual life, which symbolizes Christ.

The adjacent mausoleum, largest in the necropolis and perhaps the most beautiful, belonged to the Valerii Family. In various kinds of artwork are seen different cults. Two heads are drawn in charcoal in a wall niche. One of them is believed to be Christ and the other is Peter, since the scrawled words refer to him. Because Peter is being asked to pray for the people buried here, it indicates that the person who wrote them in the Year 300 A.D. believed that Peter's tomb was in the immediate vicinity. In the tiny area between two pagan tombs is a Christian sepulcher of the third century. This one is of special interest because it has all the early symbols of Christ—the Good Shepherd, the Mystical Fisherman, and Jonah. Covering the entire ceiling are mosaics showing vine branches, another Christ symbol. Christ is portrayed rising to heaven and surrounded by sun rays.

As the underground street makes a right turn, you reach a long narrow wall called the "Red Wall" (from the red color on the surface). Behind it you follow a tight path that goes upwards to other funeral chambers. To reach the front of the "Red Wall," you climb up an iron staircase that takes you to the next level. By following some arrows, you will in time come to what is called "Wall G," which has had a hollow space knocked out of it and is covered on the inside with five fine marble slabs, looking like an urn without a lid. By looking through this irregular shaped opening to the inside of the marble urn, you will see whitened bones. These are the relics of Saint Peter.

The Vatican Gardens

CONTRARY TO expectations, the papal gardens, now open to sightseers in groups of about 30 who make the rounds under the wing of an official guide, are fairly accessible to anyone who is eager to visit. To get in on this visit to the world's oddest speck of land, you report to the Vatican Tourist Information Office on the left side of Saint Peter's Square (adjacent to the public toilet facilities) and join one of the groups which start out in a mini-bus at 10 A.M. During the height of the tourist season, you are advised to report a day or two in advance and get your tickets ahead of time, if you don't want to be shut out. Between the first of March and the 31st of October, the tours are on Monday, Tuesday, Thursday, Friday, and Saturday (Wednesday is always set aside for papal audiences), and during other times of the year the tours go in only on Tuesday, Thursday, and Saturday. Ticket prices are 8,000, 9,000 or 16,000 Lire, depending on which of the Vatican Garden tours you pick — that is to say, some of them attach a visit to the basilica or a visit to the Sistine Chapel with an art expert who takes over as your second guide. The tours are given in Italian, German, French, and English — and when there are many people signing up who opt for English, often a special bus is set aside just for them. It may leave an hour later.

Once boarded onto a mini-bus, you are taken through the Arch of the Bells, which is supervised by the inevitable, stern-faced, halberd-bearing Swiss Guards, who wear Michelangelo's striped red, yellow, and blue uniforms (with leg of mutton sleeves), and from there you are escorted mostly on foot (except for brief hops aboard the bus) to various quarters of the Vatican Gardens. It is an inimitable experience as you first go in and breathe a kind of otherworldly atmosphere in a backstage area that seems to be suspended between heaven and earth.

63

The bus makes its initial stop in the first piazza, the Square of the First Roman Martyrs, and on descending you are shown a marble disc sunk in the tiny square. On this spot stood an obelisk of Nero's Circus where thousands of Christians met death in combat with lions, tigers, and other beasts. To the left, shaded by dark cypress trees, is a small burial ground known as the Teutonic Cemetery, which goes back to the Year 799. It is believed that Constantine filled this enclosure with earth from Calvary. Many prominent Germans and Swiss who had something to do with Vatican history are buried here. The guide takes you through this cemetery for a brief visit. Around the inner walls is a Way of the Cross in ceramic. On the far side in the building there is an interesting collection of Christian antiquities. Still on foot, your next stop after passing through two arches is Saint Marta Square, one of the Vatican's largest. Of the two buildings on the left, one is for offices and apartments, while the other is a 300-bed ''hotel'' run by nuns catering to pilgrims. (Individuals cannot book rooms here at all.) At the top of the square is the Vatican courthouse, and just beyond that, to the right, is Saint Stephen of the Abyssinians Church, the oldest church in the State of Vatican City. Founded by monks in the sixth century, the church was used by Charlemagne when he worshipped in its crypt. Inside the church's thick walls is the tomb of a monk who died in 1740 at the age of 107.

Following a road that goes uphill from the church, you come to the Mosaic Studio, responsible for most of the mammoth mosaics found inside Saint Peter's. This laboratory, which was set up in the early part of the eighteenth century, has a supply of colored stones that is kept in a long corridor lined with nearly 30,000 boxes that hold over 20,000 different tints. As the largest collection of stones anywhere on earth the studio has stones that are colored by a formula no longer in existence, and some of them are over 200 years old—the blue ones and the red ones have yet to be duplicated. Next to the workshop there is a showroom where some of the stones can be purchased. There are also three exhibition rooms, of which the middle one is the best. A customer can ask the studio to make a reproduction of a famous painting, and it will be shipped forthwith to any corner of the globe. Some of the finished mosaic works are for sale for prices that range from $10 up.

Practically facing the mosaics labs is the rear of the Vatican Railroad Terminal serving what is doubtless the shortest railroad in the world, being measured in feet rather than miles. Put up by Mussolini as a gift and comprising one of Vatican City's curiosities, the candy-colored station (constructed in pink, green, and yellow marble) has often been described as one of the most beautiful RR terminals in Europe. A double-track spur enters the pocket-sized domain through a pair of big iron gates that draw open slowly. Although passenger trains rarely depart from the station, freight trains do come in regularly with tax-free goods, food, and other necessities. These are stored in the high-ceilinged waiting room. The last passenger train to have left the station carried Pope John XXIII in October 1962 on a 400-mile trip to the historic shrine town of Loreto to offer prayers for the Ecumenical Council. Incidentally, several of the walls of the station still show shrapnel pockmarks from an aerial bombing in 1942—the only time Vatican City was hit during World War II.

From the station as you walk up a slight incline, you arrive at the Palazzo del Governatorato which is the seat of the Governor of the State of Vatican City. The ground floor is composed of offices, as well as the plush office of His Excellency the Governor (who is, currently, Bishop Paul Marcinkus, an American prelate from Chicago). Up on the next floor is a special apartment for illustrious guests, and two smaller suites for whenever more than one VIP is staying over for a night. These guest rooms are stately and quite modern, with furniture that was made expressly for the rooms, enriched by some antiques and copies of paintings by Lorenzo Lotto and by Gabriele Bella. On the same floor are seven reception rooms, one of which is an elaborate dining room. The principal reception room is called The Throne Room, and on its ceiling there is a decoration that recalls the peace treaty between the Vatican and Italy, the 1929 Lateran Agreement. The small anti-chamber is dominated by a precious mirror made in Venice by seventeenth century glassblowers. In a wing of this floor, along a wide corridor, is an apartment for a woman visitor, which is

Swiss Guards posted at the Bell Arch Doorway in the Vatican Gardens. *(Photo by Irene Rooney)*

A garden and fountain will greet you as you approach the Ethiopian College. *(Photo by Irene Rooney)*

The Viale al Quadrato in the Vatican Gardens. *(Photo by Irene Rooney)*

The Vatican Railroad Station. *(Photo by Nino Lo Bello)*

serviced by a chambermaid nun when occupied. Once you go down to the ground floor, it is possible, before leaving, to visit the new Church of Santa Marta, which is annexed to the Governor's palace by a beautiful portico.

Back onto the bus at this point, you are turtled uphill along Ethiopian Seminary Avenue to Marconi Road and the Vatican radio station, designed by Marconi and supervised by him until his death. Said to be the world's most powerful, the Vatican Radio complex also includes a compound some 13 miles outside the Vatican City itself where modern equipment and supplemental studios are to be found and which transmit programs emanating from within the Vatican itself. Vatican Radio reaches nearly every country and broadcasts programs in some 30 languages. A new Vatican Television Center, which was started in 1983, is now underway. Crammed in a few rooms, it has ten employees who put on tape everything Pope John Paul II does in public. The television center also does a brisk business of selling videotapes of the pope during his appearances, especially those of talks given to audiences (these are the ones most requested by people present on such occasions). Note: See chapter on the Vatican Radio in the addenda.

When you disembark the mini-bus now, it is the last time you see it, for the rest of your tour will be done on foot. At this point, which is the highest spot on Vatican Hill, you get an on-the-ground glimpse of the hideaway tower apartment Pope John XXIII loved so much. Because the structure is battened by Rome's breezes, which sometimes can get rather blowy, the structure is known as "The Tower of the Winds." This was the place to which Pope John would often hide from his office in the Apostolic Palace "on the other side of town" with a pair of binoculars, spending many a relaxing hour looking at what was happening on the streets of Rome. And what was the pope looking at? He loved to watch kids playing on the sidewalks, housewives hanging out wash, or automobiles weaving in and out on the streets. The Tower of the Winds, located near the West Wall, is today used by the Vatican as a private apartment for visiting dignitaries. While renovations were being made in the papal quarters a few years ago, Pope John II used it as his temporary office and personal quarters. But today the Polish Pope never goes there at all when he wants to unwind, nor does he make use of the Vatican Gardens that John XXIII loved so much. They are, in fact, never visited by the present pontiff who has other preferences for whatever spare time may come up, usually a sport endeavor.

The road flanking the Leonine Wall leads to what looks like a grass tennis court (and used to be) but is now the Vatican's "airport," which John XXIII once referred to as "our helicoptorum." The landing plot was used by both President Eisenhower and President Johnson when they left Rome after a Vatican visit. Usually overlooked is the fact that beneath the Vatican heliport are two subterranean reservoirs containing about 1.6 million gallons of drinking water piped in from nearby Lake Bracciano.

Overseeing every quarter of the world's tiniest city state is Michelangelo's titanic dome of mighty Saint Peter's Basilica. Within the shadow of the colossal edifice that even MGM could not have conceived, everything you now see and do is food and calories for your camera. Your guide will decide up which lane or down which alley you walk, but in the end you will be enraptured and mesmerized by all that you see. This includes the Vatican Woods and Gardens (the most beautiful part of Vatican City and manicured year-round by a green-thumb staff of 20 workers). Indeed, it is a marvelous place to relax and meditate. Amid dozens of marble angels are towering trees (some of them, alas dead from Rome's big February 1986 frost, shadow-blessed footpaths, flamboyant cannas ranged against green laurel hedges, cauliflower patches, plants rooted in oversized ceramic jars, and fountains of all shapes, some with lilies afloat in mossy pools. Two fountains are especially noteworthy: one is the Eagle Fountain from which the waters flow down to the fountains in Saint Peter's Square, and the other is the seventeenth century Galleon Fountain which has each of its 16 cannons shooting water, as do some of the masts and the little boy in the prow blowing a spray through his horn.

To ensure an adequate water supply, Pope Pius XI had 9,300 irrigators installed, connected to 55 miles of pipe lines. At the pope's request, by the way, the irrigation system was equipped with some rather special gadgets—trick devices that can squirt jets of water at an unwary visitor. Whenever in a playful mood, Pope Pius loved to drench new cardinals whom he took for walks along the pebbled pathways. Because the jets no longer work, the guide can only point out some of the dry nozzles.

Among other sights that you will reach in no necessarily pre-planned order are a reproduction of the Lourdes Grotto with the original altar brought from Lourdes in 1958 (The Centenary Year), the Ethiopian College and its chapel done in Abyssinian style for the liturgy of that rite, the shrine of the Madonna of the Guards of Genoa (a sailor's Madonna), a bench made of frag-ments of sculpture that Pope John XXIII frequently used to rest on whenever he took walks (which was often).

There are two villas nearby. One of them is the Casina of Pope Pius IV, an enchanting example of sixteenth century architecture with delicate reliefs, mosaics, shell work, and statuary that are exquisite. Pope Pius XI enlarged this villa in many ways and made it the seat of the pontifical Academy of Science. The other villa is not far from the New Pinacoteca building, and it has an Italian garden in front, which is a most eye-arresting attraction. This is the Casina of Pope Leo XIII with its impressive massive tower not far from the bronze statue of Saint Stremonio among the cedars.

A major curiosity for all visitors is the Vatican prison, which because of lack of use, mostly serves as a storehouse. More like a hotel room than a jail cell, the Vatican prison has two lockups with hot and cold running water and beds with soft mattresses. Through the bars, one looks out at the dome of Saint Peter's, the Vatican Gardens, and a splashy fountain. Were there any pris-oners today, they would enjoy good heat (when needed) and tasty food (prepared by the same cook-nuns who make meals for the Swiss Guards). Other services to a detainee would include a daily copy of L'Osservatore Romano (the Vatican semi-official evening newspaper), a deck of cards, and a radio. (The convicted papal assailant, Mahmet Ali Agca, who is serving a life sentence, remains in solitary confinement for security reasons in an Italian prison.) Only two inmates have been known to serve time in the Vatican prison: one was a cleric, Monsignor E. P. Cippico, who had been involved and convicted of illegal money traffic; and the other was a man caught stealing coins in Saint Peter's. Using a stick with a piece of soap stuck on the end, he moved from altar to altar (rosaries in hand) and extracted coins from the offerings boxes (the crime occurred in the 1930s). He received a sentence of six months, primarily to spare him what would have been a heavier penalty from the Italian courts.

As you continue your guided tour, you begin to notice that most of the people busy with their chores are not clergymen but ordinary laymen. These are the citizens of the State of Vatican City, and they are the gardeners, mechanics, painters, bricklayers, carpenters, bakers, policemen, firemen, and office workers (with their wives and families) who keep the Vatican City machinery functioning. Curiously, there is no private ownership of real estate in the Vatican City; the some 1,100 citizens have their quarters assigned to them. Rents are very low, usually about 4 percent of one's income, and citizens are not charged for electricity or telephone services. The local mail delivery within the borders of the diamond-shaped enclave is par-plus efficient, since the postman knows who all the people are. If you happen to hit it right the day you visit, you may even be amused by a unique method of delivering a letter—in some instances the Vatican mailman places an envelope into a basket that has been lowered from the top floor on a string, and said basket is then hauled up.

What also amuses many visitors—and this was true of my group everytime I took the tour—was the gasoline pump near the Vatican governor's building. The Vatican uses the Exxon brand. Be that as it may, the Vatican would never let Madison Avenue exploit the fact several years ago, during the time of the so-called tiger campaign, that the pope had a tiger in his tank.

The Vatican Museums

OFTEN LOOSELY and erroneously referred to as ''The Vatican Museum,'' the art treasures of the Vatican—a vast and unique collection of works from all ages and of many cultures up to the present day—are to be found in ten pontifical museums, all housed within the Vatican Walls in a complex of buildings that connect with and to the Apostolic Palace where the pope lives and keeps his office. Hence, the proper designation is ''The Vatican Museums'' so that the small letter ''s'' is given full play.

If there is one word to describe the Vatican Museums, it is O-V-E-R-W-H-E-L-M-I-N-G! A colleague of mine once quipped that if you wanted to tour the entire ''show'' (his word), you would need a motorscooter or a pair of well-oiled roller skates. Tourists who enter the Vatican Museums are handed a folder suggesting they not try to cover everything in one visit. Taking up quite a sizable chunk of Vatican City geography, the Museums house the world's largest collection of ancient art, another 55 rooms of modern art, one of the best Etruscan collections anywhere, an extensive library of precious old manuscripts, an astounding array of maps and tapestries, a Missionary-Ethnological Museum, a museum of pontifical carriages, the Raphael Rooms, the Borgia apartments, one of the finest Egyptian collections in Europe and, of course, the Sistine Chapel with the work of that superstar, Michelangelo. There is all this and much more, to coin a phrase. There's even an enticing, superb practical joke by Michelangelo (about which more later). If you can spare the time, the Vatican Museums are a most rewarding experience.

The priceless works and objects in the Vatican Museums are protected by a closed-circuit television setup and an electronic alarm system that allow attendants in a control room to monitor key locations on more than two dozen TV screens. There are

72

over a hundred roving plainclothesmen and women roving as "tourists" in the Museums. The net result of such precautionary measures is that the Vatican Museums have never had a theft.

The beginnings of what eventually was to become the Vatican Museums are now found in the ancient statuary which Pope Julius II (1503–1513) had collected and put on exhibit in the courtyard of the Palazzetto del Belvedere, a tiny palace that had been erected by Pope Innocent VIII. Julius II commissioned Bramante to connect it with the Vatican Palace itself by means of a long corridor. As other popes came to the throne, additions were made to the collection, and during the reign of Pope Pius V, the layout of the Belvedere Court was completed. By adding a second corridor parallel to the original one and linking it to a building at the far end, the stage was set for the various museums to grow. But it was during the eighteenth century that several popes, imbued with the collector's instinct, began to buy up Greek vases and other antiques and art works in special areas. One pontiff, Clement XIV (1769–1774), set up a new museum with a large floor span and ordered the remodeling of the Palazzetto del Belvedere, which had to be completed under the rule of Pope Pius VI, his successor.

But it was Pope Pius VII, ruling for 23 years from 1800 to 1823, who made purchases of numerous old sculptures. Considered one of the most enlightened popes ever, Pius VII (Barnaba Chiaramonti) enriched the collections in many ways and also ordered the building of the Braccio Nuovo, which is the link between the two parallel corridors of the Vatican Library. During excavations and important art discoveries at Cerveteri and Vulci between 1828 and 1836, new purchases were made by the Vatican so that the Museo Gregoriano Etrusco was inaugurated. Pope Gregory XVI (1831–1846), taking advantage of materials already in the possession of the Capitoline Museum and with items from Hadrian's Villa, sought to acquire whatever was available, at any price, in his effort to start up the Egyptian Museum.

Since then the Vatican Museums have gone on growing and growing, getting richer and richer in content as a result of many purchases and of some unusual discoveries which were made in and around the State of Vatican City itself. In 1970, while Pope John XXIII was at the helm, notable expansions were made when he added to the collections by bringing in many art objects and works that had been in the Lateran Palace. Visitors today who go into the Vatican Museums get the impression that it is "disorganized"—and to a certain extent this may be true. In spite of the fact that the halls are not continuously numbered (they have names), that the main entrance to the museums is "irrational," and that a visitor often has to take long walks to visit one gallery or another or to get to a certain corridor to view some of the principal works of art, there is nothing in the world to compare with its massed cultural and historical relics.

The Vatican Museums and Galleries, the entrance to which is on Viale Vaticano, offer an immediate surprise when you enter. You are confronted instantly with a monumental double spiral staircase that could easily slip by you, meaning that the stairway that goes up is different from the stairway that goes down. Although you can take a convenient elevator to go up, it is worth your while to use the double-spiral stairway going up *and* down. There aren't many places in the world that have such a set of stairs (the only other one I know of is inside Vienna's Musikverein, which is primarily a concert hall). These stairs do not really take you "upstairs," in that sense of the word, because they lead you to an upper level of the Vatican Hill from which you walk to a tiny vestibule where you can get a good look at a great collection of early mosaics from various places in and near Rome.

From the vestibule you go into a courtyard that leads to a rather modern building that is the Art Gallery (Pinacoteca). The entrance on the left leads to the Sculpture Galleries (called the Pius-Clementine and Chiaramonte Museums). Most of the sculpture is Greek (Before Christ) or Roman (first three centuries Anno Domini). In the first hall is the famous Greek Cross which has two very large porphyry sarcophagi that are for Constantine's mother and daughter, Saint Helena and Constanza.

From the vestibule you go into a courtyard. Because the galleries surround the courtyard with eight sides, you can go from one room to another by criss-crossing the courtyard. For tourists who are in a hurry and prefer to do a quick tour of the Vatican Museums—which means jogging and even running (not recommended)—keep in mind that on the far side of the courtyard you can go through a lobby with an unforgettable piece of sculpture—the so-called Belvedere Torso, done by an Athenian artist of the first century B.C. Tourists can give a close inspection to this supreme masterpiece by revolving it on its base. Here's a tip: to get your best view of this unusual statue, have someone turn the torso while you position yourself down a bit on a set of stairs.

The administration of the Vatican Museums has set up a color-coded plan of four itineraries, of which a visitor is supposed to choose one. According to a folder given out to all entrants (in English, Italian, Spanish, German, and French), if you take Route A-Purple, which lasts 90 minutes as you take your time casually walking along, it will lead you to the Sistine Chapel—the star attraction of the Vatican Museums. Route B-Beige will take you up to three hours and also covers the Etruscan, Missionary-Ethnological, Gregorian Profane, Pio Christian, and Historical Museums, as well as the Borgia Apartment, before leading you to the Sistine Chapel. Route C-Green does the job in some three and a half hours, and in addition to all the stops included in the Purple plan, it covers the Braccio Nuovo, the Room of the Aldobrandini Wedding, the illuminated manuscripts of the Vatican Library's Sistine Salon, the Pinacoteca, the Chapel of Nicholas V, the Pio-Clementine, Chiaramonti, and Egyptian Museums, and the rooms of Raphael, as it keeps you on a line towards the Sistine Chapel. All-embracing is Route D-Yellow, which will take a minimum five hours or even all day, but it touches all the main features of Route A-Purple, Route B-Beige, and Route C-Green—while you are on the correct path to the Sistine Chapel. Note that whichever route you opt for, it will take you to the Sistine Chapel.

Along the way there are signs/arrows indicating the pathway to the Sistine Chapel, but when and if you do indeed get "lost," a nearby watchman will set you straight. One final footnote: if you choose the quick tour (*repeat*—not recommended), this is carried out by way of a one-way traffic route that is put into play on most days of the week, especially during the summer months, to avoid bottlenecks of throngs going in counter-directions or attempting to go through the same narrow doors.

Herewith follows a comprehensive guide description of each of the Vatican Museums. The order in which each museum is listed here is, arguably, the best one to follow so as to eliminate the possibility of inadvertently leaving one of them out or getting yourself ''hopelessly lost'' in one of the most intriguing mazes on the face of the earth.

[Admission to the Vatican Museums is 5,000 Lire (roughly about $5.00). During the summer, the hours are from 9 A.M. to 5 P.M., but during other times of the year, the time is from 9 A.M. to 1 P.M. The Museums are usually closed on Sundays and holidays but are open on Mondays, unlike museums in Italy which are closed every Monday. Although cameras were not permitted in the past, these are now allowed, but you cannot use flash bulbs or tripods.]

Beato Angelico's Life of Saint Nicholas. *(Photo by Carlo Piccolo)*

The Egyptian Museum

FATHER L. M. UNGARELLI, who was one of Italy's first Egyptologists, was given the honor of arranging the Vatican's Egyptian Museum which had been founded by Pope Gregory XVI (1831–1846).

Room number I is principally intended as an introduction to Room II, which recreates the setting of a tomb of the Valley of the Kings. As you enter, you see a reconstruction of a look-out turret for the deceased—a gimmick to enable him to see who has come to visit his tomb. The walls bear commemorative and funerary carvings, and on the back wall are two statues of Sekhmet (seated) who is the goddess with the head of a lion.

Room II is indeed a touristic delight. It is a reconstruction of an underground tomb of the Valley of the Kings. At the left-hand side are three large, dark gray to black stone sarcophagi which ordinarily would command immediate attention, except for the fact that there are five mummies present that are the real thing. Under plexiglass, two of them are on view in two half portions of a wooden mummy case. The Vatican makes a point of this exhibit by reminding visitors that (a) they are not works of art, and (b) they are human bodies that, though dead, "must command the respect of the living." Vatican labs, with their advanced procedures of restoration and preservation, have seen to it that the mummies are devoid of all kinds of worms, eggs, and other disinfestations, besides which special oils are used to stop any more deterioration of the bodies. The back wall has Canopic vases that contain the internal organs of the dead person that were removed before the body was mummified. On the painted wooden coffins are delicate markings that reproduce the magic formulas and passages from the *Book of the Dead.*

Retaining its original nineteenth century decorations, Room III houses Roman works from the second and third century A.D., all inspired by Egyptian art. Most of the art is from Hadrian's Villa, while the others are from the Temple of Isis in the Campus Martius. In Room IV is an unusual wooden coffin which is painted on the inside as well as the outside. This one originally belonged to Queen Hetep-heret-es and was repainted and then reused during the Ptolemaic period. It is now restored to its original state. At the doorway that leads to Room V are two statues of the goddess Sekhmet.

Room V, a large semicircle, has many showcases holding restored wooden coffins. The statue of La Bella, though of a later era, still shows the grace and delicacy of Egypt's classical sculpture. There is also a remarkable item—the throne of a lost statue of Pharaoh Ramses II. In the center of the room is a colossus of Queen Tuia, mother of Ramses II, near which is a headless statue of a dignitary. Across from it is a sandstone head (with traces of paint on it) of a pharaoh of the eleventh dynasty (2,000 B.C.) Next come three large pink granite statues (Ptolemaic period), of which one is unfinished; the male figure is Ptolemy II Philadelphus who ruled from 258 to 247 B.C. Along the wall across from the windows are many showcases that exhibit mummy cases.

The Chiaramonti Museum

DESIGNED BY Donato Bramante, the long corridor to your right which connects the Apostolic Palace with the Belvedere Palace (in those days the pope's summer residence) is the Chiaramonti Museum which is divided into 30 different segments and which houses just under a thousand pieces of ancient sculpture. Taking its name from its founder (Pope Pius VII, whose family name was Chiaramonti), the museum has changed very little since its original setup (1807–1810) by Antonio Canova. Of this gallery with its hundreds of exhibits, it should be said that there aren't many people who have the time to give to it (a pity!)—so what most visitors do is to walk rather quickly past it all, glancing to the left or to the right and stopping if something especially catches the eye. One item that certainly captures attention is the blindfolded horse turning a millstone with the help of the hind parts of another horse treading in the opposite direction.

The pieces on display include portrait statues, statues of gods, pagan altars, architectural ornaments, urns, and sarcophagi. In the lunettes are paintings by artists commissioned by Canova "to commemorate the impulse given to the fine arts by Pius VII." To celebrate the papacy of Pius VII, Luigi Agricola did the lunette in Bay XLI on the left to show the seventh year of the pope's reign, which lasted from 1800 to 1823. (The walls on both sides are divided into Bays, each of which has been ascribed a Roman numeral—which will be used here not in chronological order but in the order which will be convenient for a tourist to follow.)

Bay I has the sarcophagus of C. Junius Euhodus and of Metilia Acte with an inscription that dates back to 161–170 A.D. The scenes shown are from the myth of Alcestis who was prepared to die in place of her husband, Admetus. On the sarcophagus, the heads of Alcestis and Admetus are actually portraits of the deceased. Bay II is the bust of Hephaestus, identified by the conical felt cap. This is a Roman version of a famous statue by Alcamenes from 430 B.C. In Bay VII are fragments of reliefs of Aglaurids and Horae. The three female figures dancing toward the left are the Aglaurid sisters, known as the dispensers of the evening dew. This piece of art was found on Rome's Esquiline Hill and is a Neo-Attic copy of a fourth century B.C. model. On the floor of Bay X is a funeral monument to the miller P. Nonius Zethus. This is a block of marble with notches for cinerary urns. At the sides of the inscription the reliefs indicate strongly that the deceased was both a flour merchant and a miller. Bay XI has a superb head of Cicero that is from the Renaissance.

The funerary statue of Cornutus as Saturn is in Bay XII, with an inscription that says, "Here am I, Cornutus, sorrowful, with my eight beloved children." The figure, which is covered with a mantle and is carrying a sickle in the right hand, is surrounded by little boys holding various fruits. This is a typical representation of Saturn, the lord of the so-called Golden Age. Another Roman Imperial Age work is the Statue of Ganymede with Eagle in Bay XIII. One of the museum's high points is to be found in Bay XVI which houses the colossal head of Athene, apparently made in anticipation of a statue that was going to be done later in other materials. Particularly noteworthy are the restored eyes which recreate the vivacity of her gaze, so characteristic of ancient works. It is believed that the model for this Roman copy, done at the time of Hadrian, was the fifth century B.C. Phidias Athena Promachos.

Dominating Bay XXI is a statue of Tiberius, who was Emperor of Rome from 14 to 37 A.D., and he is seated in a way that was frequently done for statues of Jupiter. Also featured in a seated position is a fragmentary relief of Penelope in Bay XXIII. Dated approximately 450 B.C., this fragment belongs to a Boeotian funerary relief. Bay XXIX displays two colossal heads—one of Augustus (who died in 14 A.D.) and the other of Tiberius (who died in 37 A.D.). In Bay XXXI on the wall is a relief of the Three Graces, based on the same subject of the Acropolis in Athens where a cult had sprung up in the name of the Graces. The original to this dates back to about 470 B.C., but the copy goes back to the first century B.C. For a remarkable statue of Hercules, pay special attention to Bay XXXVII where the great hero is seen leaning on his club, a lion skin over his left forearm. This one belongs to the school of Lysippus in the fourth century B.C. On the floor of Bay XLIII is a statuette of Ulysses, which is part of a group from the Cyclops episode. In this Roman work (inspired by Greek models) the hero is offering a drink to Polyphemus.

[Note must be made of the Lapidary Gallery to which only scholars or people with special permission are admitted. Request for such permission can only be done by a registered letter—which may or may not bring on an answer, the Vatican bureaucracy being what it is. Easily one of the richest and most important on earth, the collection was begun by Pope Benedict XIV, added to by Pope Pius VI, and enlarged considerably by Pope Pius VII. Housed in this gallery are more than 3,000 Christian inscriptions on a wall at one side and pagan inscriptions along a wall on the opposite side.]

Braccio Nuovo

THE SO-CALLED New Wing, or Braccio Nuovo (as it is called in Italian) has a number of exhibits that warrant your attention. Pope Pius VII had decided in 1806 to build this new wing, but the pope's plan could not be executed until 1817, when the sculptures that Napoleon had taken to Paris with him were returned. Though the wing was planned by the Roman architect, Raffaele Stern, who died in December 1820, it was Pasquale Belli who assumed the responsibility and supervised the construction. In 1822, the Braccio Nuovo was opened officially amid considerable pomp, but the main topic of admiration were the displays of ancient mosaics from the second century A.D. that relate the adventures of Ulysses. These were taken from the excavations near Tor Marancia on the Via Ardeatina.

The New Wing does not use a Bay Roman Numeral numbering system, and the visitor is virtually on his own. To your right is a Statue of Silenus cradling the Child Dionysus in his Arms, a Roman copy of a Greek original from around 300 B.C. In the fourth niche on the right there stands what many experts consider to be the best statue of any Roman Emperor. It shows Augustus, who ruled from 31 B.C. to 14 A.D. The emperor is shown addressing his soldiers; in appearance he is very regal and is holding a staff of authority. This masterpiece was found in 1863 in Livia's Villa on the Via Flaminia. On Augustus' armor are many relief decorations.

The central scene of these decorations deals with an event that happened in 20 B.C. when a Parthian, King Phraates IV, returned the Roman insignias lost by Crassus in 53 B.C. The whole universe is seen witnessing the peace offering. In the scene is Caelus wearing his woolen mantle, and in front of him are Dawn and Dew. Down further is Tellus, the Roman earth goddess, and at the sides are Apollo holding a lyre and Diana holding a torch. At the sides of the central scene are two seated female figures, personifications of the Provinces of Dalmatia and Germania. The figure of Cupid on a dolphin is present providing a support to the leg of the statue; this is an allusion to Venus. The bare feet are symbolic of the heroic treatment of the subject. This copy was doubtless made for Livia after Augustus' death.

An interesting statue of Emperor Titus in a toga presents itself, interesting because the toga was the civilian dress of a citizen in Rome. Now comes a head of Julius Caesar placed on a bust that doesn't belong to it. The piece has been so frequently reworked that hardly anything of its original surface remains. Originally standing in the first court of Constantine's Basilica of Saint Peter, the two peacocks in gilded bronze, which are symbols of astral immortality, are probably from Hadrian's mausoleum. Just before you enter the Vatican Library appears a bust of Pope Pius VI (founder of the New Wing) that was done by Antonio Canova, another supreme masterpiece in marble.

On the other side of the gallery is the eye-grabbing Statue of A Wounded Amazon, the bronze original of which dates back to 430 B.C. Not far away is a Roman copy of a bronze original of a statue of Demosthenes, who was an enemy of the Macedonians and who died in 322 B.C. Commanding almost immediate attention is the stunning Colossus of The Nile, found in 1515 in the area of the ancient temple of Isis and Serapis. As a dispenser of blessings, the river god is identified by the crocodiles and the sphinxes. The 16 boys depicted are believed to be an allusion to the level of the Nile when it floods, thereby fertilizing the region surrounding it. Based on a Hellenistic original, this work is marked by some good reliefs that depict quite well life on the banks of the Nile. With a hairstyle that is typical of the Flavian era, the statue of Julia (daughter of Emperor Titus) stands opposite that of her father. By all rights, this work should be carefully inspected from all angles.

Identified by the helmet, shield, and serpent, the statue of Giustiniani Athene is a Roman version from the second century

A.D. of a Greek bronze (fourth century B.C.). An oddity in art is to be found in the togated statue of Emperor Claudius, who ruled from 41 to 54 A.D.; the head and the body do not belong to each other. Now you face one of the most admired works of antiquity, a statue by Praxiteles of a resting satyr (this is a copy). The portrait head of Lucius Vero (who died in 169 A.D.) is affixed to a statue of an athlete. The athlete's body, strictly on stylistic grounds is probably a copy of an original from the fifth century B.C. by Myron. As for the spear-bearing statue of Doryphorus, this is a Roman copy of a bronze original from 440 B.C. by Polyclitus. Tradition has it that Polyclitus created this work to exemplify the principles he set out in his theoretical work, the ''Kanon.'' Of this representative piece of art, the Vatican says: ''The expression and attitude are simple and clear, yet conceived with supreme art. One leg carries the weight, while the other is relaxed; one arm is in action, while the other is at rest. Action and inaction alternate and merge in this figure, down to the smallest details.''

The Pio-Clementine Museum

THE ENTRANCE HALL of the Pio-Clementine Museum, with its ancient sculpture, is the only one of its kind in the world, a square vestibule in which appear the busts of both Pope Pius VI and Pope Clement XIV, the two men responsible for this unusual array—much of which was acquired through the purchases of the Fusconi and Mattei collections in 1770.

The sarcophagus of Lucius Cornelius Scipio the Bearded One, who was consul in 298 B.C., is in the niche in the left wall. Archaic Latin verses constitute a eulogy of the deceased, together with a description of his career and achievements. Regarding the shape of the sarcophagus, one sees immediately the Greek-Hellenistic influence. This precious item in gray tufa was taken from the Scipio Tomb on the Appian Way.

Over on the other side in the window space is a base with scenes from Trojan and Roman legends, the so-called Casali Altar. Within the wreath of oak leaves on the front, you are informed that the monument (so says the inscription) was dedicated by Ti Claudius Faventinus. On the front are reliefs of Mars and Venus and on the back the legend of Romulus and Remus. The sides contain Trojan myths.

Now follows the Cabinet of the Apoxyomenos. Found in Trastevere in 1849, the Apoxyomenos by Lysippus is a Roman copy from the first century A.D. of a bronze original, circa 320 B.C. As the athlete is returning from the gymnasium, he is holding in his left hand a strigil with which he is wiping off both the dust and the sweat from his right arm, while gazing wearily into the distance. Although this is supposed to be a depiction of a victor, actually it shows the athlete overcome by fatigue *after* his moment of glory. The idea of Lysippus, according to Vatican art experts, is to portray people not as they are but as they appear during fleeting moments. This piece of art is unusual in that it displays that Greek artists Before Christ were capable of subtleties that came into art in large measure after the birth of Christ and especially during the Renaissance.

In the Vestibule, actually a small room, is the Bramante Stairway built by Pope Julius II during the first part of the sixteenth century. This odd staircase is constructed so that a Vatican VIP could ride up to the palace doors on a horse. (You can visit this spiral staircase only on request.) Based on the principles of Vitruvius, the columns on hand are of three types — the first part is Tuscan, the second part is Ionic, and the third part is Corinthian. So named because of the water spouting from its guns, the Fountain of the Galley was executed by Carlo Maderno for Pope Paul V and placed there during the papacy of Clement IX. On the opposite wall is a relief depicting an ancient warship. Nearby is the Statue of the Nile in gray marble — once again the river god is shown with his own symbols: a sphinx and a crocodile. There are also heads of wheat to symbolize fertility. During the eighteenth century the statue was completely restored by G. Sibilla. On the wall are mosaic panels showing arena scenes that are quite good.

Originally square in shape, the so-called Octagonal Court — which is the internal court of the Belvedere Palace — is the heart of the Pio-Clementine Museum. While he was still a Cardinal (Giuliano della Rovere), Pope Julius II placed his ancient statues here, including his famous Apollo Belvedere named after the palace. It was Julius II who got the rights to the Laocoön group. The court came to its present octagonal shape when Pope Clement XIV contracted with Michaelangelo Simonetti to build a portico.

Above the entrance is a frieze with Dionysian procession showing Bacchus and his followers returning from a banquet. This is a late Hellenistic work from Campania. Against the wall is a fragment of a relief depicting an attendant leading a large bull. In the exhibit named Cabinet of the Apollo we see the Roman copy in marble of a Greek bronze that was struck around 320 B.C. and that stood in the Agora of Athens. The hands were made by

Giovanni Angelo da Montorsoli in 1532, but they were removed in 1924. The god called "He-Who-Strikes-Home-From-Afar" is holding a bow in his left hand as a symbol of his role as avenger. In his right hand he once held an arrow that he had taken from his quiver. Emphasizing his radiance is the cloak draped over his shoulders and left arm. Homer said of this piece: "Thus the gods dispose that poor mortals must live in anguish, but they themselves are not touched by pain." Johann Joachim Winckelmann, however, really had the final say about the Apollo: "Of all the works of antiquity that have escaped destruction, the statue of Apollo represents the highest idea of art."

A statue that has been in the Vatican since 1536 is the Reclining Statue of a River God (the so-called Tigris) from the second century A.D.. Nearby you see the partial reconstruction of the Fountain of the Tigris, which was arranged by Michelangelo on one of the corners of the Court itself. A few feet away is a sarcophagus giving light to a battle between Greeks and Amazons, made around 170 A.D.—which during the Renaissance period served as the basin for the Fountain of the Tigris.

Special attention, of course, must be given to the Laocoön from the first century B.C., dug up in 1506 on the Esquiline Hill. (The strange word Laocoön is the name of a priest who, together with his sons, is being attacked by various snakes because he has apparently offended the gods.) The statue was found by a grape farmer, Felice Fredi, near the Baths of Titus and the Colosseum, and it created an unprecedented sensation because it was the first time a Greek original had been discovered in Rome. Pope Julius II, deeply impressed by the find, knighted Fredi and assured him of a pension for life. Of this statue, Pliny the Elder—who died in the Mount Vesuvius eruption in 79 A.D.—said that it was the work of three sculptors (Hagesandros, Athanodoros, and Polydoros). He had seen it before it was to become lost, and at the time declared that it was to "be preferred to all other works of sculpture or painting."

Certain missing parts, like the right arm, were restored by sculptor Giovanni Montorsoli with the advice and assistance of Michelangelo. The latter was very impressed with the Laocoön,

The Apollo Belvedere is one of the most famous works in the Vatican collection. *(Photo by Carlo Piccolo)*

and it is known that he studied it frequently and intently, praising the ancient masterpiece as a standard of quality. The statue has become one of the most admired works of art by the experts, and poets have written inspired verses of praise about it. Missing for some 400 years, the lost arm was found by an Austrian archeologist, Ludwig Pollack, in the work studio of a stonemason, and he gave it as a gift to the Vatican. That happened at the turn of the century, and it was not until a few years ago that the Vatican finally got around to removing the ''fake'' limb and restoring the statue's original right arm. When the so-called ''Pollack arm'' had been put back into place, one of the Vatican's top experts said: ''It is incomprehensible how human art can create anything so great and natural.''

Locked in the coils of two serpents, Laocoön and his two sons are caught on the steps of the altar. As he vainly tries to tear away from the snake's head that is ready to bite him on the hip, the Trojan priest's chest rises and swells. Meanwhile, the other snake has already sunk its teeth into the younger son who collapses in agony; at the same time the older son tries to get himself free from the serpent's coils.

For a full account of the event, Virgil described it in detail in the Aeneid II: in brief, the story goes that Laocoön, skeptical of the wooden horse that the Greeks had left behind, warned his people about it and to show his disdain threw his spear at it. So angered was Athene by this insult that she sent the snakes to kill Laocoön. But the Trojans paid no attention to Laocoön and pushed the wooden horse into the city. The statue was commissioned by the emperor in the second half of the first century A.D. and done in Rome. The flexed right arm, by the way, was discovered only in 1905 and was replaced onto the statue during the restoration of 1957–1960. A curiosity is that Montorsoli's old reconstruction has been preserved in the plaster cast nearby because the Vatican believes its merits as a work of art and its importance in history give it a special status.

The Statue of Hermes is a Roman copy from the time of Hadrian of a Greek original in bronze from the fourth century B.C. Found near Castel Sant'Angelo, the statue is shown with a traveling cloak over the left shoulder. Going a bit further on the left is a sarcophagus with a battle of Amazons. Penthesilea is dying of her wounds as Achilles with a headpiece looks on. Across the way are the fragments of a big bath-shaped sarcophagus which shows bevies of fighting animals on both sides. The statue of Venus Felix by Praxiteles has a head that reminds you of the young Faustina of about 170 A.D. Going on a bit further, you observe to the left a sarcophagus of a condottiere (mercenary) which shows mercy being given by the victor to the loser—this is supposed to be one of the great Roman virtues.

The Cabinet of Canova is a time stealer indeed. Napoleon (whose sister Pauline was sculpted by Antonio Canova for Rome's Borghese Palace) was a great admirer of the Italian sculptor ("because he can make hard marble look like soft flesh . . ."), and he took all of Canova's works back to Paris with him. Pope Pius VII purchased three of them from the French Government in 1800 and placed them on exhibit here. These included Perseus Triumphant With the Head of Medusa, the Bacchic sarcophagus in the shape of a bath, and the boxers Kreugas and Damoxenos. The story behind the two pugilists is that they were engaged in a boxing match in Nemea. Damoxenos unfairly stabbed his adversary in the stomach several times and killed him. The referee disqualified Damoxenos and declared the dead Kreugas the victor.

The Animal Room houses a collection prepared by Pope Pius VI that will hold the attention of anybody who likes animals. Most of these exhibits are by the artist, Francesco Antonio Franzoni (1734–1818), who did such an extensive restoration job, with considerable free expression, that today most art experts consider them to be Franzoni's own works. Franzoni reflects an impressive skill in capturing the charming animals, and one of them in particular is the camel's head. All of the animal mosaics are delightfully mixed in with vegetables, not to mention a particularly amusing work of a rooster and a cat. The Statue of Meleager shows him as the hero of the Calydonian Boar hunt with a dog and boar's head. The north wing to the right features a Mithras group showing the killing of a bull (symbol of procreation) by the Persian god Mithras. Seen are a scorpion, a serpent, and a dog trying to prevent the sacrifice. This is from the second century A.D. On the wall are two panels of a mosaic with land-scapes from Hadrian's Villa, and not far away is an unusual sculpture of a crab in green porphyry, an extremely rare stone.

Once an open loggia on the lower floor of the Belvedere Palace, the Gallery of Statues was built by Jacopo da Pietrasanta and in 1776, after being enlarged, was joined to the Room of the Animals, an improvement that required the removal of a chapel that Andrea Mantegna had done up in frescoes. The Statue of Sleeping Ariadne, which was once thought to be that of Cleopatra, shows the woman who had been dumped by Theseus as she awaits the divine appearance of Dionysus. This is a copy of a Hellenistic original from the second century B.C. and is held in rather high esteem by connoisseurs. Serving as a base to this statue is a sarcophagus that has a scene with several giants (both of them have serpent-like legs) fighting with gods, though the lat-ter are not in the picture. This is a late second century A.D. work.

On display are two ornamental candelabra from Hadrian's Villa, on the bases of which are figures of gods in relief — Jupiter with a sceptre and thunderbolt, Juno with a sceptre, Mercury with a ram, Mars with a helmet and lance, Venus with a flower, and Minerva with a parade helmet and shield. Across the way, on the right, is a statue of Hermes, a second century Roman version of a Greek original from the fifth century B.C. He is holding a lyre and has wings cropping out of his hair. The Eros of Centocelle displays marks on the back where his wings once were before removed and lost. Not far away to the left is a statue of a resting satyr, a copy of a famous fourth century B.C. original by Praxiteles.

On the right side of the gallery are a head and torso of a water deity from the Hellenistic period. There is a charming work of the God Apollo in bronze (Roman copy of a Greek original from 350 B.C.) portraying him blissfully absorbed in a simple game that is certain to be an allusion to Apollo's struggle with Python the monster.

A work that originated from a competition among artists around 430 B.C. is the Statue of the Wounded Amazon by Phidias and dedicated to Artemis of Ephesus. The great Greek dramatist, Posidippus, who died in 250 B.C., is shown in a seated portrait statue. The face has been remodeled so that it does not quite resemble the original from 250 B.C. anymore. This work was found from the excavations of the Viminal Hill in Rome, together with the so-called Menander, a seated portrait statue. Here too the head has been extensively remodeled but up to now no authoritative identity has been made by the experts as to whom the head represented.

The Room of the Busts (divided into three sections and indicated by Roman numerals) begins with the portrait group of Cato and Portia, found in a tomb during the latter part of the first century B.C. Between the windows are votive offerings of the sick, with prayers for recovery or for grace received. Section I also has the head of Julius Caesar, the head of Augustus (with a crown of thorns), the head of Titus, and the head of Trajan, on the lower shelf. On the upper shelf are a head of Emperor Antinius Pius and busts of Marcus Aurelius, Lucius Verus, Commodus, and Caracalla.

Section II displays a head of Caracalla as a child; this was made around 193 A.D. as a portrait of the future heir. There is also a bust of a boy dressed as the commanding officer of an army. The boy, who was assassinated in 218 A.D., is thought to be the son of Emperor Macrinus. On the side opposite the window on the lower shelf is a head of Menelaus with a parade helmet. This is a copy from the time of Hadrian. The upper shelf has a basalt bust of Serapis, which is a copy of a cult statue by Bryaxis in Alexandria during the fourth century B.C. This syncretic deity embodies Osiris and Apis and Jupiter and Pluto. Section III has a statue of Jupiter Verospi. It got its name after the Verospi Palace where it had been formerly on exhibition. Seated on a throne, Jupiter is holding a sceptre in his left hand and in his right a thunderbolt. This work is in gold and ivory and is after a third century A.D. cult statue, made after 85 B.C. In front of this statue is a celestial globe with stars and the zodiac.

Given the name, Cabinet of the Masks, this collection in the tower-like buttress from the Belvedere Palace became part of the Pio-Clementine Museum in 1780. The floor decorations, which are four panels of an ancient mosaic, comprise representations of masks — three of which are theatrical masks and the fourth an idyllic landscape with grazing animals. The panels were found, together with the mosaics in the Room of the Animals, in 1779 on the site of Hadrian's Villa near Tivoli. The ceiling of this room was painted by Domenico de Angelis who used mythological scenes as his theme — the Judgment of Paris, the Awakening of Ariadne, Diana and Endymion, and Venus and Adonis.

If you start at the right and proceed counter-clockwise, you begin this row with the Statue of the Crouching Venus. Getting ready for her bath, she is shown crouching under a spout of water. This is a Roman copy of a famous third century B.C. work by Doidalsas of Bythnia. The next statue is a copy of the famous cult statue carved by Praxiteles in the mid-fourth century B.C. This statue of Venus of Cnidos does not capture any of the high artistic standard of the original. Famous in its day, this work constitutes the first example of a cult statue in which the Goddess of Love appears nude. Her clothes are lying at the side of the bathtub, and Venus appears quite unaware of anyone watching her. The next work, Group of The Three Graces, a Roman copy of a late Hellenistic work, has a special charm because of the interplay of variation and repetition. Finally: the Statue of Satyr in red marble, taken from Hadrian's Villa.

The ceiling frescoes in the Room of the Muses are the work of Tommaso Conca and show Apollo, the Muses, and poets forming a thematic link with the statues that are on exhibit here. In 1973 the Belvedere Torso from the first century B.C. was put into this room. The muscular figure is seen seated on an animal skin spread over a rock. The figure is likely that of Hercules, but some experts believe it could also be either Marsyas or Skyron. After this statue was found in the fifteenth century, it was kept in the Colonna Palace and then moved to the Belvedere garden during the papacy of Clement VII. Renaissance artists admired this work very much, as did Michelangelo. The artist is Apollonius.

Against the walls are seven statues of Muses and one of Apollo, which were excavated near Tivoli in 1774. Over on the right are Thalia to portray comedy, Melpomene (tragedy), Clio (history), and Polyhymnia (mime and song). On the room's left are Erato (love songs), Calliope (heroic songs), Terpsichore (dance), and Apollo Citharedos, who was the master of the Muses. From other excavation sites are Euterpe (flutes) and Urania (astronomy).

Portraits of famous Greeks (Roman copies) are also to be found in this room, and they include a small bust of Sophocles, which was discovered in 1777 in the Conservatory of the Mendicants garden, and the head of Epicurus, the philosopher founder of the Epicurean school (he died in 270 B.C.). On the opposite side are Euripides (who died in 406 B.C.) and Plato (who died in 347 B.C.). Both Socrates and Homer are included in the lineup. Over to the other side of the room you encounter Aischines (famous orator and adversary of Demosthenes), Antistenes (the founder of the Cynic philosophical school), Pericles (shown with Corinthian helmet of the army commander), Periander (son of Cypselus, tyrant of Corinth), and Bias (a contemporary of Croesus and one of the Seven Sages).

Known as the Round Room, this domed chamber with the height of some 22 meters holds a Pantheon inspired work by Michelangelo Simonetti. Built about 1780, the Round Room has floors that are decorated with old mosaics from Otricoli. The scenes include a battle between Greeks and centaurs and marine animals with nereids and tritons. To the left of the entrance there is a niche that holds the Statue of the Genius of Augustus (in a toga). A fold of this toga covers the head, and in his left hand is a cornucopia. If you proceed counter-clockwise, you come across a colossal head of Jupiter of Otricoli, which is a Roman copy of the Greek interpretation of Zeus from the fourth century B.C. Then you reach a colossus of Antinous. Together with an ivy wreath, there are a pinecone on his head and a mystic cist near the left foot. There follow a statue of a goddess restored as Demeter—a work from the year 420 B.C.—and a colossal head of Hadrian, taken from his mausoleum. The Round Room has a large porphyry basin and a black and white mosaic floor showing mythological figures. All around are statues and busts against the walls and various saints and emperors.

Found near the Theatre of Pompey in 1864, the colossus of Hercules in gilded bronze had been struck by lightning and buried right on the very spot. Covering its grave, where it had been carefully buried, stone slabs carry an inscription that gives the history of the work. The slabs also show Hercules' club, his lion skin and apples of the Hesperides. Now comes a colossal bust of Antinous who drowned in the Nile River in 130 A.D. After his death, Emperor Hadrian deified him. Additionally, there is a statue of a goddess, the so-called Hera Barberini—which is a Roman copy of a late fifth century B.C. Greek work usually attributed to Agorakritos. Then come a statue of Claudius dressed as Jupiter, a statue of Juno Sospita (doubtless a cult statue of the second century A.D.), and a colossal portrait of Plotina, wife of Trajan. Because of the size of the portrait, it is believed the work was executed at the time and on the occasion of her deification in 129 A.D.

Designed in the form of a Greek cross (one with four equal arms), the Greek Cross Room was built during the papacy of Pius VI in 1780. As you approach the room, the passage is flanked by two Egyptian-style statues serving as architectural supports. These were modeled along the styles used for the Pharaoh or Osiris types. This red granite work from the second century A.D. comes from Hadrian's Villa. The central part of the floor shows a sumptuous mosaic, the bust of Athene.

In the right wing is a sarcophagus of Constance, the daughter of Constantine. She is honored with a relief that shows cupids harvesting grapes, two peacocks, a ram, and another cupid with a garland of flowers. Now comes a statue of Augustus from Otricoli (he ruled from 31 B.C. to 14 A.D.) which is based on the Diomedes model of the fifth century B.C.. In the left wing you can find a sarcophagus of Saint Helen (mother of Constantine), an early fourth century A.D. work. The scenes depict victorious Roman cavaliers and prostrate barbarians in chains. The heads have been extensively restored. It is believed that this was not constructed for Helen but for her husband. The sculpture of the tomb of Helen does not come across as particularly feminine, for it shows Roman horsemen, prisoners, and wounded or dead soldiers, whereas Constance's tomb is representative of a grape harvest, with children stamping on the collected grapes.

Along the sides, near the exit, are two reclining sphinxes in reddish gray granite, and in the floor between the sphinxes is a colored mosaic with a basket of flowers. This is a modern copy of a second century A.D. original found on the Appian Way and now standing in the vestibule that leads to the Pio Christian and Gregorian Profane Museums.

The Nile. *(Photo by Carlo Piccolo)*

The Etruscan Museum

FOUNDED BY POPE GREGORY XVI in February 1837, the Vatican's Etruscan Museum keeps on display many of the artifacts that were unearthed during excavations (private) done in necropolises of Southern Etruria, which is now part of Italy's Latium Province. Forming an integral part of this stupendous collection is a most important collection of vases, as far as the history of ancient ceramics is concerned. The Etruscan Museum occupies the first floor of the Belvedere Palace and of the building annexed to it by Pope Pius IV, so that if a tourist wants to visit the Greek and Italiot Vase Collection, which is housed in four separate rooms, he must retrace his steps and enter the semicircular room through the so-called Room of the Bronzes (see later reference).

Room I of the Etruscan Museum is devoted to monuments of various kinds. Gathered here are sarcophagi, urns, sculptures, reliefs, inscriptions, artifacts from ancient cities like Palestrina, Orte, Cerveteri, Chiusi, and Vulci from the sixth to the first century B.C. One thing all these artifacts have in common is the material with which they were made—varieties of tufa or travertine or sandstone which Etruscan sculptors and stonecutters preferred because it was easy to cut. Its aesthetic drawbacks were cleverly hidden by the artists of the time, but the inevitable deterioration of this soft stone is always apparent, because the cover-up stucco work is now almost completely gone.

Visiting the room clockwise, you come across sarcophagi which are decorated in various ways with various figures. The first one, called limestone sarcophagus with polychrome relief, has a representation on the lid of the deceased. The two decorated sides of the coffin give good evidence of a funeral procession. This late fifth century B.C. Etruscan work was found in a chamber tomb with painted walls in Cerveteri.

97

On the front of the next sarcophagus is shown the last voyage of the deceased, a magistrate. He appears on a chariot preceded by two figures in toga bearing fasces (a symbol of authority for Roman magistrates). The inscription on the top gives the name and the age of the dead man—with instructions as to how to bury him. This item was unearthed in Tuscania and comes from the third century B.C. The nearby tufa sarcophagus with representations of the slaying of the Niobids shows an excellent battle scene involving centaurs. On the right side Achilles is shown with the body of Hector. This particular stone coffin was found with 26 other second century B.C. sarcophagi in a dynastic tomb in Tuscania.

Flanking the left side of the window is the bilingual stele from Todi, a rectangular sepulchral slab in travertine that has text in both Latin and Gallic, written in a special alphabet derived from Etruscan. It makes mention of the construction of a tomb of a certain Ategnatos, son of Drutos, by his younger brother, Coisis. Not far away to the right of the window is a sandstone statuette (bare breasted) of a female figure. This is very likely a statue of an Etruscan female demon, known as Lasa. It is considered one of the most delightful creations of Greek-inspired Etruscan sculpture (third/second century B.C.) because of the delicacy and acquiescence of the girl figure who is a member of the underworld.

Just opposite the window are, on the left, nefro (a local variety of tufa) busts of horses, which were in front of a tomb at Vulci, emphasizing the funeral and the trip to the underworld. Right are two lions (also from a Vulci tomb), which are from the late sixth century B.C. and were once used to guard the entrance to a tomb. It is assumed by experts that this gives evidence that the Etruscans believed in the continued existence of the person who died.

Room II is called the Regolini-Galassi Tomb. The artifacts on show here were found during the excavations of the necropolis of the Sorbo in 1836 and 1837 by General Vincenzo Galassi and Alessandro Regolini, the archpriest of Cerveteri (hence the name). The material in this room comes from nine tombs built within four neighboring mounds. The richest part of the collection comes from the oldest and central tomb and is exhibited in the large showcase along the wall across from the windows.

In the showcase marked A are housed the findings from the main tomb, which dates back to the mid-seventh century B.C., and it provides some of the most complete information that has yet come to light on Etruscan civilization. During this period, Etruscan cities, especially the coastal cities like Cerveteri, had many prominent monuments that displayed a fine artistic expression. The material in this tomb testifies to good trade contacts Cerveteri had with countries in the Mediterranean Sea and the Aegean Sea and shows remarkably the influence these areas had on Etruscan art. Exhibited in the showcase, the objects are laid out according to the approximate position archeologists found them in the tomb. It is known that the tomb had two occupants —a woman of noble birth and a man of equally high rank. A third occupant was also in the tomb, but because he/she was cremated, there is considerable uncertainty about this person.

The woman owned a number of jewels and precious ornaments, some of which were woven into the cloth of her garments. Especially attractive is the very large gold fibula like a safety pin with a foliated bow and a disc catchplate. Her gold jewelry was made by incredibly gifted virtuosi, the artists demonstrating their craft in filigree and granulation work. Their refinement is found nowhere else in the antique art of the Mediterranean, for it is the ultimate in creative endeavor. The fibulas, pendants, and earrings decorated with animals and the necklaces were struck with thin gold leaf, exhibiting mechanically precise coils of wire and tiny grains of gold. All this was done with unbelievable preciseness and soldered on as if by a breath of air. Lending a particularly exotic note are the stretches of gold wire that are eight-one-hundredths of an inch thick and grains of gold that are six- or seven-one-hundredths of an inch in diameter.

The man is shown in bronze lying on a bed, a rare example in this medium, since this type was usually made in stone. He was no doubt a high-ranking warrior because of the number of parade shields that apparently belonged to him.

Inside the tomb were also found a number of vessels that suggest foreign materials. The silver jug with the gold-plated handle is from Cyprus. The silver gilded cups are decorated with Egyptian-style motifs. The small silver amphora with engraved double spiral is a good example of a local form. One of the most important pieces in this display is a pear-shaped inkwell which has an inscribed alphabet on the base and some graffiti on the sides. Experts have testified that this type of writing was introduced to the Etruscans in the late eighth century B.C. by the Greeks who had colonized southern Italy.

In the showcase marked B are the findings of the so-called Giulimondi Tomb on the Via Braccianese which was excavated in 1906. Among the many artifacts particularly noteworthy are two globular perfume jars and various ovoid perfume cups. Taken as a whole, the contents of this tomb, which is thought to date back to the seventh century B.C., is the oldest part of the collection. Showcase C, containing finds from the Calabresi Tomb, has several interesting chalices with ribbon handles and conical bases and an ampulla with two pictures of horses and a handle in the form of a charioteer. This showcase also contains a red-earth cinerary urn with a rich oriental decoration.

Room Number III, generally referred to as the Room of the Bronzes (see the reference at the end of the first paragraph of this chapter), keeps on display all the bronzes, statues, and votive offerings picked up from early nineteenth century excavations. Except for a few objects, the exhibits are in chronological order.

In Showcase A are two vases in the ancient form of the biconical ossuary made of Villanovan clay and showing Greek ceramic influences. This is from the seventh century B.C. The showcase keeps on exhibit hands in bronze plate, decorated with small gold studs. Made from a single sheet of bronze, the hands were closed at the wrists and slightly folded over at the edges of the long fingers. Apparently this piece of ancient art comes from Vulci, as it appears to have certain affinities with the bronze masks found on some Canopic vases done with early Etruscan experiments in sculpting the human figure in bronze. Also included are eleven raised ornaments with heads of lions and of Acheloos, a mythological figure, later a river god with the horns and ears of a bull. The examples on exhibit are from a chambered tomb in the necropolis of Mount Quaglieri, Tarquinia, and are magnificent samples of late sixth century B.C. Etruscan bronze-work. They bear a strong affinity with the terra-cotta master-pieces of Veii because they show a simplicity of style, precision of line, and carefully stylized details.

Within the layout of Showcase B are several bronze statuettes of seated boys. There is also a statuette of what is called a haruspex (Etruscan priest), whose job was to examine the guts of animals in order to ''understand'' the will of the gods. This fourth century B.C. figure wears a tall skin hat which had to be tied under the chin to stop it from falling off during the ceremony —which would have been considered an ill omen. Showcase C displays fourth century B.C. headpieces with embossed caps that represent the hair and ears of a silenus (an ancient Greek mythological deity with a horse's ears and tail on a human form).

The bronze mirrors exhibited in Showcase D are decorated in the back and give evidence to a significant class of Etruscan handi-work. One mirror has a scene of Aurora abducting a young hunter; this is considered a rare relief technique and is from Vulci, circa 470 B.C. In the same showcase is a collection of a woman's toilette articles, and on one handle is an embosssed decoration depicting a battle of Amazons, which clearly shows Hellenistic influence.

Showcase E holds a good array of candelabra, which are deco-rated with mythological figures, drawn from the world of dance and the world of the gymnasium. These examples are mostly from the fifth century B.C., while others are from the fourth cen-tury B.C. A rich series of bronze articles are on hand in Showcase F. These come from a chamber tomb near Bolsena and date back to the middle of the second century B.C.

The final item in the Room of the Bronzes is to be found in the center of the room, the Mars of Todi, cast in several parts. It is one of the few large-sized Italiot bronzes that have survived. The Italiots were Greek inhabitants of ancient Italy, and the Italiot bronzes were done by the Italiot potters. This one is of a young warrior leaning on a lance with his left hand and offering a drink with a cup in his outstretched right hand. The work reflects Greek influences of the second half of the fifth century B.C. It was found buried between four slabs of travertine.

Room IV, which has not been given a special name, is divided into three sections which house seven showcases. In showcases A, B, and C are materials discovered towards the middle of the nineteenth century near Bologna at Villanova. A biconical urn, typical of the cultural phases found in Etruria in the Iron Age, has a distinctive feature. It has a single handle, and wherever a second handle existed, it was deliberately broken off—remaining as one of the various ''Etruscan mysteries.''

Noteworthy of the bronze pieces are two pins with long catches made of alternating discs of bronze and amber with incised geometric ornaments. The material is mainly from Vulci and the ninth century B.C.

Showcase D contains materials from Iron Age tombs, excavated in 1817 between the towns of Marino and Castel Gandolfo. The hut urn was known to the cremators of Etruria and is a typical product of Iron Age Latium, as indeed are the vases that are decorated with mesh designs. These objects from the ninth and eighth century B.C. were also known to the cremators of Etruria. On display in Section II of Showcase E are clay mixture vases from the eighth century B.C. from Etruria and Agro Falisco. Of special interest in the center of the showcase are two vases, one decorated with engravings showing a horse, three stags, and a long snake and the other decorated with a kind of excision technique: the cavities have been filled with a red substance so as to give life to the composition as a whole. Between the handles are human figures half hidden by two four-legged animals that are probably horses. Showcase F is devoted to various types of typically Etruscan ceramic vessels that are decorated with little dotted fans, some of which are done in relief.

In Showcase G (Section III) the display constitutes a funereal monument to dying Adonis who lies on a bed mortally wounded. This carefully done scene of the young hunter of mythology explains the causes of his death (Adonis myths were a favorite subject in Etruscan representations of death). The holes in the surface were put there to insure ventilation of the clay form during the firing. The Section III room also contains alabaster and limestone cinerary urns from Perugia, Chiusi, and Volterra. The lid on the second century B.C. Volterran urn is unfinished because the artist did not have enough material, and it shows a couple reclining at a banquet. The decoration on the urn depicts the King of Pisa in Elis, dying after a chariot race he had organized for the hand of his daughter (Hippodameia). The race was won unfairly by the son of Tantalus (Pelops).

The plaque above the entrance to Room V explains why it is called the Guglielmi Room. This room was set aside by Pope Pius XI to keep the collection donated in 1935 by Benedetto Guglielmi. Divided into three sections, this room has painted ceramics, bronzes, and jewelry. Of particular interest in the Guglielmi Room is a small, late seventh century B.C. earthen pot that has graffiti on it, an Etruscan inscription that reads, *"mi Ramuthas Kansinai."* This was intended to convey the idea that the pot was speaking to the viewer in the first person, identifying itself as the property of one Ramutha Kansinai. This particular pot, together with all the other artifacts in the room, were found near ancient Vulci in several necropolises.

Room Number VI, called the Jewelry Room, which is on the third floor of the Palazzetto of Innocent VIII, has startling collections of Etruscan jewelry. Showcase A displays two earrings in gold, rock crystal, and hard stone from Vulci in the late sixth century B.C. On the lower shelf are a series of fourth century B.C. gold and silver-gilt rings with engraved and embossed elliptical settings. The top shelf of Showcase B has amber objects and a number of pendants. Pay close attention to the exquisite horsehead and the head of a silenus carrying a wineskin on his shoulders. These go back over 500 years Before Christ. The middle shelf has a layout of cylindrical earrings. Towards the back of this showcase are rings with scarab-shaped settings, with engravings like seals on the under portion.

In Showcase C you are shown several kinds of lockets that are designed to contain an amulet. A type of horseshoe-shaped earring common during the Etruscan period is on view in profusion in Showcase D which gives an idea of the various phases of development of this kind of jewelry. Two nearby showcases contain funereal diadems in gold foil, and the last showcase holds a lot of Roman jewelry in gold—with one large locket from the first century A.D. that is impressively shiny.

In the Room of the Terracottas (Number VII) there is a chest urn found in 1838 at Orte with a human head protruding from the lid, suggestive of the custom of burying corpses in tree trunks (a practice especially common in Southern Etruria). The same display cabinet features a bust of a winged horse, shown as it takes flight with its forelegs extended towards the sky. This is an early fifth century B.C. ornament found at Cerveteri. In another showcase are four terra-cotta urns, a large pointed amphora, a jug, a mirror, an amulet, a tile with an almost illegible inscription, an earthen pot, a vase, and a small jug. One of the inscriptions painted on the urns mentioned four members of the Cejcna Family, considered a very prominent family of the Volterran aristocracy.

In five successive showcases can be found a large collection of votive offerings from temples in the ancient city of Cerveteri. These consist of small reproductions of cult images and of representations of various parts of the body, especially heads and half heads. These latter items were apparently offered by the faithful as symbols of their piety. These heads were made with blond hair or dark hair, with or without beards. Most of these unusual heads date from the third to the first century B.C. Nearby are four slabs with floral decorations and human heads that were once attached to the horizontal beams of a temple. There are also terra-cotta pediment reliefs from Tivoli that were found in 1835 during road constructions. One scene shows an acanthus tree from which hang the hind legs of an empty sheepskin. According to a Vatican expert concerned with this room, ". . . this detail recalls the iconography of the Golden Fleece and confirms beyond all doubt that the central theme of this monument is the quest of the Argonauts . . . . The reconstruction is intended merely to suggest one way in which the reliefs might have been arranged originally.''

Included in the Etruscan Museum are four separate collections which have been placed here. They are the Antiquarium Romanum, the Greek originals, the Assyrian reliefs, and the Greek, Italiot, and Etruscan vases. Because the Antiquarium Romanum and the Vase Collection intermingle with Etruscan, Greek and Roman works, they form an integral part of the museum, in accordance with modern standards of exhibition.

Room VIII then becomes the Antiquarium Romanum, which deals mainly with Roman and minor arts of various periods. Section I houses a collection of architectural ornaments in terra-cotta from Rome and Latium dating from the first century B.C. to the second century A.D. There are reliefs depicting three of the labors of Hercules (the killing of the Nemean Lion, the killing of the Hydra of Lerna, and the killing of the Cretan Bull). These form part of the famous Twelve Labors undertaken by Hercules on the orders of the Pithia, as an act of expiation after Hercules had murdered his own children in a fit of madness. In a showcase marked D is an ivory doll with jointed limbs, originally dressed in cloth interwoven with gold. This came from a sarcophagus of a little girl found in Rome during the second century A.D. On the bottom shelf of this same showcase are several small vases in silver and silver-plated bronze. From the inscriptions, one can deduce that they were dedicated to Apollo.

Section II houses ''The Megara Cup,'' a turned vase with molded decorations on the outside. This was a special type common in central and eastern Mediterranean areas during the Hellenistic period. In the same showcase are several clay lamps, most of them dating from the first to the fourth century A.D. Both pagan and Christian examples are included. Among the artifacts on exhibit in Showcases L and M are those made of transparent polychrome glass. Some of them are from Etruscan tombs and others are Roman works. Section III has a bust from a portrait statue in bronze. It shows a cloak over the left shoulder and an extended left forearm. The partial nudity of this statue suggests that it is an idealized portrait statue, possibly of Marius or Sulla, neither of whom has been found in other portraits.

Room Number IX is the Falcioni Room, in which the frieze is part of the decoration of the time of Pope Julius III (1550–1555). On exhibit here is the Falcioni Collection acquired by Pope Leo XIII in 1898. It consists of Etruscan and Roman artifacts, most of which are from the Viterbo region. Without any logical criteria, archeological finds are assembled here indiscriminately—such as the most ancient clay mixture vases of the proto-Villanovan Age and the eighth century B.C. bucchero vessels, artifacts in bronze (like vases, candelabra and statuettes), and gold and votive objects up to the latest Roman period. These include such items as lamps, weaving weights, terra-cotta seals, and common ceramics.

Rooms of the
Greek Originals

DURING THE latter part of the 1950s, the Vatican brought together all the fragments and reliefs of the fifth–fourth century B.C. Greek statues which had been scattered all over the Vatican Museums, and assembled them on the top floor of the Belvedere Palace. These are now on view in four rooms, one of which is actually a corridor.

Proceeding clockwise, once you have entered Room I, you will come across a fragment of relief with representation of a banquet in homage to the God Dionysus. This is from the second century B.C. Analogous in theme is another relief with funeral banquet showing Hades with a crown on his head, as a sign of divinity. At his feet are a group of worshippers and Persephone. Another heroic relief shows a horseman, an altar, and worshippers — a work of art that goes back to 400 years Before Christ.

The same room also has the Head of Athene, an acrolith that originally belonged to a statue made of wood covered with precious metal leaf. Note the eyes here. The inserted eyeballs are in a gray, very hard stone, and the eyebrows are made of a thin bronze foil. Jewels are attached to the ear lobes. Since Athene was the only goddess permitted to wear a helmet, several holes on her forehead and temple show where the helmet was attached. Belonging to a cult statue of Magna Grecia, this work goes back to 460 B.C.

Other statues in this collection are three votive reliefs of three male figures, and Aesculapius on a throne with Hygeia. Because the Aesculapius cult began in Athens in the second half of the fifth century B.C., this statue is thought to have been executed around the end of that century. As a matter of fact, Hygeia's hairdo and the manner in which her head is carved would rule out the possibility of an earlier dating.

Serving as a room, the corridor that follows offers a full view of the funerary stele of a young man. In front of this stele on the left wall are three fragments of reliefs, dedicated to the Nymphs, three of whom are dancing in a circle. This one is dated 400 B.C. The corridor also houses Aphrodite leaning against a female herma crowned with a high cylindrical headdress worn by Green goddesses. There's also a figure of a seated woman with her head covered to indicate she is in mourning. This is believed to be Electra at the tomb of her father, Agamemnon, as she awaits the arrival of Orestes. Found in Taranto, this great work is from the fourth century B.C. Nearby is a very tall, thin funereal stele of a young man on a base that once stood on a burial mound. The dead youth has raised an arm in a greeting; a boy brings gymnasium articles to him. As a significant and illuminating form, this work is classic Greek from about the year 450 B.C.

Room III holds three original marble pieces of the Parthenon's sculptural decorations, done between 448 and 432 B.C. by a trio of masters: Pericles (the commissioner), Iktinos (the builder), and Phidias (the sculptor). Of considerable importance, there is a horse's head fragment from the pediment of the Parthenon. Athene and Poseidon are shown competing for domination over Attica. The heads of the three other horses belonging to Athene's cart have been preserved and it is pretty certain that this fragment must be the fourth.

From the north frieze of the Parthenon there is a fragment of a relief of a boy, representing the procession of the Panathenaea, a festival in honor of Athene. Remarkably, more than 300 men and 200 animals are included in this eye-opening frieze.

Another fragment, the bearded head of the 16th metope, is shown here. (There were in all 92 metopes of the Parthenon, showing the battles by gods and heroes to bring world peace.) It is from a piece of the south wall depicting the Battle of the Centaurs, in the center of which stands Erechtheus, a son of Earth and king of Athens, and it is his head which is exhibited here. Not far away is a small marble copy of the shield from Phidias' statue of

Athena Parthenos done in gold and ivory, and depicted on the shield is Medusa's head with snakes for hair, surrounded by battling Athenians and Amazons. There is also a rectangular slab in relief that depicts a wounded Athenian being dragged from the scene of fighting by his fellow soldiers, a copy of part of a frieze from the Battle of the Amazons decorating the outer part of Athena Parthenos' shield.

Known as the Astarita Room, the fourth chamber has various materials from a collection donated by Mario Astarita to Pope Paul VI, which constituted a second donation. The left-hand showcase has Roman glasswork, bottles, jugs, pitchers, and bowls. The right-hand one has terra-cotta votive offerings (heads and statuettes), polychrome antefixes and projected curved moldings, red-figure pottery of the fourth century B.C., black enamel pottery, and a fine example of Samnite armor in bronze laminate.

On the upper part of the staircase that leads to the Assyrian Reliefs (which are not opened to the public) are some reliefs from Palmyra, some Assyrian reliefs, Assyrian and Sumerian cuneiform inscriptions, and Cufic supulchral inscriptions. The Cufic, or ancient Arabic, inscriptions are from Egypt and are the oldest of these known; they date from the year 511 of the mass emigration.

Giovanni Benni, a student at the Istituto di Propaganda Fide and a native of Mesopotamia, donated the Assyrian fragments when he and one P. E. Botta excavated in 1842. The reliefs are from the palace of Sargon II (722–705 B.C.) at Dur Sharrukin. Most of the inscriptions are from the palace of Sennacherib, Sargon's son and successor. These reliefs and inscriptions tell the story of the military exploits of the two kings.

Now retrace your steps to Bronze Room to enter Vase Collection Rooms.

Rooms of the Vase Collection

The Vase Collection in the Etruscan Museum includes a large number of Greek vases, on the grounds that they belong alongside Etruscan antiquities because many of them were uncovered in Etruscan tombs.

Room XIII, called the Room of the Italiot Vases, contains red figure vases and painted black vases produced in southern Italy and Etruria. Most of the red figures date from the mid-fifth century B.C. to the early third century B.C., whereas the black vases go back to the first century B.C. Most of the items in one showcase testify to the fact that many Italiot potters drew their inspiration from the theater while decorating vases. Especially important are the works of one of the greatest vase painters in history, an anonymous potter from Campania who was active about 350–325 B.C. and who executed superb scenes by actors. Two of the best deal with the grotesque hairstyles of actors who are busy burlesquing mythological characters and one of Zeus wooing Alcmene, wife of Amphitryon while Hermes is watching the entire proceedings.

On the walls of Room XII (the Hemicycle) is a set of frescoes by an anonymous artist which illustrated works that were done in the time of Pope Pius VI (1775–1799). Three showcases are noteworthy in this room: in Showcase A is an Attic black figure wine jug, the work of a well-known prolific painter of vases, one of the last and most skillful painters to use the so-called black figure technique. His lavish use of additional colors is a device employed by him to force the limits of the then widely used two-color method, which gave an austere aspect to any work of art.

Both red and black figure decorations dominate Showcase F. Around the time of 530 B.C. Attic vase-painters started to abandon the technique of black figures on natural grounds, in favor of red figures painted on a black background, a change that was to lead to a significant evolution in the art of vase-painting. In Showcase F there is one of the great masterpieces of Attic ceramics, signed by the potter, Exekias. On the front of this amphora is a scene of Achilles and Ajax laying down their arms and playing a game called morra.

The Astarita Room (Number XI) is named after the man who donated the ceramics collection, Mario Astarita, who gave it to Pope Paul VI in 1967. All of the exhibits in this room are worthy of close attention. In various showcases are to be found a Corin-thian hydria and miniature-like cups of Tleson and of Sakonides. The most important nucleus of the collection is the red-figure ceramics, highlighted by outstanding examples of the ceramist decorator Oltos and the potter Kachrylion. In one showcase is a large late-Corinthian crater, on the front side of which is por-trayed the mission of Odysseus and Menelaus to effectuate the return of Helen. This scene reverts to a famous epic tradition used widely in both painting and poetry.

Room X, which is often referred to as the Room of the Sundial because of the many astronomical instruments it contained (in-cluding a sundial), once served as an observatory for Cardinal F. S. de Zelada, secretary of state under Pope Pius VI. The cardinal lived in this room until 1801 before it was turned over to the Vatican Museums. The vases on display here are the oldest to be found in the Vatican and consist mainly of Greek and Etruscan black figure ceramics.

Showcase B contains a jug with oriental style bands displaying series of panthers, bulls, deer, herons, and sphinxes. The ivory-colored background on this jar is studded with rosettes formed by a circle of points around a central point. Made in Corinth about 630 B.C., this jug was responsible for the ceramist being given the nickname of "Painter of the Vatican 73" by the author of a pub-lication on painted antique vases of the Vatican.

There are some 50 examples in Showcase D of Cerveterian hydria (water jugs with horizontal side handles and a vertical back handle), the product of a school certain to have also made temple paintings. Several of these were executed by an Ionian Greek master who emigrated to Cerveteri and worked there for most of the second half of the sixth century B.C. His best work is a vase portraying Heracles in the act of slaying the giant shepherd Alkyoneus in his sleep.

In Showcase E is an entire class of vases that owes its name to the Scythian costume of the archers on the shoulder of the vase. But today this type of vase is without a doubt attributed to a Vulci workshop active between 550 and 525 B.C., a period when Etruscan art came under the heavy influence of Greece and Asia Minor. Showcase G has a Laconian cup with Prometheus and Atlas on it. This one came from Sparta and dates back to the middle of the sixth century B.C.; it constitutes an excellent example of black figure ceramics, characterized by the large internal medallion divided into two segments.

[Room XIV, the Upper Hemicycle, unfortunately is not open to visitors, unless they can show in writing a scholarly interest in making a formal request of the museum director. The room, according to Vatican officials who would not let this writer visit, has a hydria with Apollo on a tripod. This particular work has long been considered one of the loveliest vases in the Vatican collection and was made in Athens around 480 B.C. by an artist called the "Painter of Berlin." Apollo is portrayed as sitting on the Delphic tripod as he flies over the sea.]

Room of the Biga

BEGUN IN 1786 and situated above the Atrium of the Four Gates, the Room of the Biga gets its name from the two-horse chariot in the center which is called a ''biga'' and which is illuminated by the opening in the ceiling. Completed for exhibition in this room by Francesco Antonio Franzoni, this statue is considered one of the comic oddities of all time, while nevertheless remaining an effective work of art. Franzoni was presented with two fragments of what was once a piece of art—the rump of a horse and the chassis of a carriage. For centuries the seat of the carriage had served as the bishop's throne in Venice's Church of San Marco. Using all his skill and imagination, Franzoni fashioned a remarkable team and carriage that invites all viewers to tarry. Its relief decorations (laurel branches) recall certain scenes of the chariots of the gods, Ceres and Triptolemus.

At the entrance to this room is a statue of Dionysus with an ancient inscription on the hem of the cloak folded diagonally across his chest. This is an excellent Roman copy of a Greek original (first century A.D.) done of the circle of Praxiteles in the late fourth century B.C. that requires a hard look. Elsewhere are five children's sarcophagi depicting cupids competing against each other in a circus cart race. The interpretation behind this artwork is that the race is a symbol of the struggle for survival, while the circus is life itself and the finishing line is the goal of life.

Certainly the most important work in the room, however, is the marble copy of the famous Discobolus (The Discus Thrower). Note the attitude of the young athlete expressing his total concentration. Another statue on the same theme makes a point of the twisting of the chest, the movement of the left leg, and the stretching of the arms. This is a copy from the time of Hadrian in the second century A.D. of a bronze original of about 460 B.C.

112

Gallery of the Candelabra

GIVEN THE NAME Gallery of the Candelabra because of the candelabra that stand in front of the pilasters, this gallery—once an open loggia in 1761—was closed in during the reign of Pius VI and divided into six sections by a series of arches and pilasters. During the years of 1883–1887, under Pope Leo XIII, the ceiling was painted by Demenico Torti and Ludwig Seitz.

Section I has a statuette of a boy tossing a walnut with his right hand, as a cloak he is carrying begins to slip from his arm, a theme that is quite typical of the Hellenistic period. In front of this statuette is a sarcophagus of a dead child, a boy who is depicted on the lid. The artwork on the front has the same boy seated on a throne, like an ancient philosopher; he is encircled by chubby little boys representing the Muses. This work is Roman, from about 270–280 A.D.

In Section II under the arch where two oil- or wax-burning candelabra stand guard is an ornamental motif of what used to be a table leg. It is a Roman copy from the second century A.D., portraying Ganymede being carried off by an eagle dispatched by Zeus. This copy is of a large bronze group done by Leochares (mid-fourth century B.C.), a spectacular work showing the eagle gently grasping the youth by his clothes to avoid harming him with his claws.

A sarcophagus with scenes from the myth of Protesilaos is in front of the next niche. On the left you see Protesilaos bidding goodbye to his wife. Then you see him dying as he lands at Troy, being the first Greek to jump from the ship. Next is a picture of Hermes taking Protesilaos to his wife, Laodamia. Accompanied by Hermes, he is ferried by Charon across the Styx to the underworld. On the right side of the stone coffin three famous penitents

113

of the time are shown—Ixion, Sisyphus, and Tantalus. This sarcophagus was found along the Appian Way at or about the second mile and is a Roman Work from about 170 A.D.

Opposite from this is a sarcophagus showing scenes from the myth of Orestes, the slaying of Aegisthus and Clytemnestra, and Orestes at Delphi. On the sides are sphinxes curled up. This Roman work is dated 160 A.D. Behind this sarcophagus is the statue of the Ephesian Artemis, a copy of the cult statue that symbolizes fecundity.

Two pairs of candelabra, discovered in the seventeenth century in the vicinity of the Sant'Agnese Church on Rome's Via Nomentana, dominate the four arches on both sides in Section III which displays on the walls 10 fragments of Roman frescoes. These come from Tor Marancia from the second century A.D. and served as wall decorations. On the right side is a second century A.D. statue of Apollo on a base that does not belong to it. Bearing the attributes in his outstretched hands, Apollo stands erect. This work, based on classical models, was made to look archaic.

In Section IV is a statuette of Victory (Nike) with the head of Athene, a head which belonged to another statue. You see Nike leaning on a trophy, with her leg on the bow of a ship that has emerged victorious from a battle. Based on a Greek model of the second century B.C., this is a Roman work of the Imperial Age. Another sarcophagus contains a scene from the myth of Bacchus who with his companions find Ariadne. The nearby Roman (160 A.D.) sarcophagus on the left depicts the massacre of Niobe's six sons and six daughters by Apollo and Artemis who are angrily shooting their deadly arrows.

Boy strangling the goose. A three-year-old boy is busily squeezing a goose's neck with both hands, trying to overcome the bird's resistance. This is a marble copy of a bronze original from about 300 B.C., attributed to Boethos by Pliny. Across the way there is a statuette of the Tyche of Antioch on the river Orontes. She is seated on a rock with a mural crown and strands of wheat in her hand; a bust of the River God Orontes is at her feet. The original of this Roman copy was made in 300 B.C. by Eutychides shortly after the foundation of Antioch in honor of the city's patron goddess. This statuette is looked upon as one of the Vatican's most valuable in its category.

There is only one statue (from the first century B.C.) in Section V, and it is of a woman athlete running. The palm branch on the support is a symbol of victory. Section VI has a Roman version of a fourth century B.C. statue of Diana (Artemis). Prominent is her belt to which she had attached her quiver full of arrows. A close look at this statue will show you that the head does not belong to it but to another unidentified statue. From the so-called small shrine of Attalus, which the Pergamenes set up as a votive offering on the Acropolis of Athens in the second century B.C., there is a copy of a statuette of a Persian soldier wearing a tiara. The theme behind the Persian soldier has to do with the Battle of the Amazons, the Battle of the Giants, and the war between the Greeks and the Persians.

Below the statuette is a sarcophagus with reliefs on the abduction of King Leucippus' daughters by the Dioscuri who are wearing their pointed headgear. The two girls are being taken away by Castor and Pollux. On the right are a woman and a warrior in flight. On the left is a bearded figure trying to stop the kidnappers, but he is held back by a young soldier. The next scene shows the wedding of the abductors and their victims. The reason that the Dioscuri frequently appear in funerary representations is that Jupiter had placed them among the stars, and therefore they were considered the lords of the astral spheres. The work is dated 160 A.D.

Gallery of Tapestries

TAKING ITS NAME from the tapestries on exhibit since 1814, the Gallery of Tapestries contains works shown as the "New School," so named to differentiate from those tapestries of the "Old School" (which can be seen in the Pinacoteca and which were woven during Pope Leo X's reign in the Brussels workshop of Pieter van Aelst from Raphael cartoons). These New School tapestries, made in the same workshop during Pope Clement VII's rule, are from designs by Raphael's students. In this Gallery are tapestries from the Vigevano workshop established in 1503 and from the Barberini workshop set up in 1627 by Cardinal Francesco Barberini, nephew of Pope Urban VIII. Events from the latter's life are depicted in the tapestries.

From the Brussels workshop can be seen: Adoration of the shepherds; Adoration of the Magi; Presentation in the Temple; Slaughter of the Innocents; Resurrection; Jesus Appears to Mary Magdalen, and Supper at Emmaus. From the Vigevano workshop: Conversion of the centurian Cornelius, a sixteenth century work by Master Benedetto.

From the Barberini workshop: Maffeo Barberini graduates from the University of Pisa, Maffeo Barberini controls the level of Lake Trasimene; Maffeo Barberini is made a cardinal by Paul V; Maffeo Barberini is elected pope and takes the name of Urban VIII; Countess Matilde donates her possessions to the Holy See; Urban VIII annexes the city-state of Urbino to the Holy See; Urban VIII begins building Fort Urban, and Urban VIII saves Rome from the plague and from famine.

116

Gallery of Maps

CONSTITUTING AN extremely important record of sixteenth century geography and cartography, the Gallery of Maps has 40 topographical maps which Pope Gregory XIII had painted in this spectacular hall between 1580 and 1583. Thirty-two of these are large frescoes on two long walls, and eight of them are smaller ones to be found at the ends of the gallery. They were done by Ignazio Danti, whom the Vatican has called one of the greatest cosmographers in history — and a look at these extraordinary maps certainly does not belie the claim.

Danti used the Apennine Mountains as the dividing line for the arrangement of the maps of the regions of Italy and of the Vatican's land possessions of the era. The regions on the Ligurian and Tyrrhenian Seas are to be found on the wall towards the Court of the Belvedere, and the regions surrounded by the Alps and the Adriatic are on the garden side of the wall. At the end opposite the entrance, on both sides of the long walls, are the maps of ancient Italy and present-day Italy, supported by a series of regional maps, each of which has the city-plan of a main city. Running some 120 meters in length and six meters in width, the gallery (covered with a barrel vault) was built by Ottaviano Mascherino in 1580; he also built the Tower of the Winds situated directly above the Gallery of Maps at the north end. This tower, by the way, was used for extensive astronomical observations that led to the adoption of the Gregorian Calendar, named after Gregory XIII.

Particularly noteworthy in a hallway that holds your attention already are the paintings on the short walls — the Siege of Malta, the Battle of Lepanto, the Island of Elba, and the Tremiti Islands. On the opposite side of this north wall are depictions of four great ports of the epoch: Venice, Genoa, Ancona, and Civitavecchia.

117

A sizable team of artists also worked together to decorate the long overhead ceiling (vault) with stucco and a series of 80 episodes from the lives of saints. Cleverly, each episode is linked geographically to the region represented below it. Ornamental embellishment elements accompany many of the maps. Both Cesare Nebbia and Girolamo Muziano coordinated the team of painters and also supplied a lot of their own art to the general appearance of the Gallery of Maps.

Michelangelo's celebrated Pièta. *(Photo by Carlo Piccolo)*

Apartment of Saint Pius V

ANOTHER INTERESTING part of the Vatican Museums is the Apartment of Saint Pius V which consists of the gallery, the two rooms to the left, and the chapel at the far end. Dedicated to Saint Michael, the chapel—originally intended for the resident laymen in the pope's household—was decorated by Giorgio Vasari and Federico Zuccari, but all that remains is the vault fresco called The Fall of Lucifer and The Rebel Angels. The gallery today keeps a series of tapestries from various periods in history and from various places—the most valuable of these being from Tournai, Belgium, which in the fifteenth century was Europe's most important center for tapestry quality and tapestry quantity.

As you enter, just above the door, are two seventeenth century friezes of the baldachin from the Barberini workshop. From Tournai are such samples (late fifteenth century) as the Episodes from the Passion, the Last Supper, Tapestry of the Credo, and the Baptism of Christ. From sixteenth century Brussels is the Coronation of the Virgin done from cartoons (preparatory sketches) of the school of Raffaello.

Another Brussels tapestry, done by Pieter van Aelst, is called Religion, Justice, Charity, and it once formed the bottom of the throne of Clement VII. It dates back to the year 1525.

The Sobieski Room and
the Room of the
Immaculate Conception

THE SOBIESKI ROOM is dominated by an enormous painting that takes up the entire north wall, the work of Jan Matejko, a Polish artist. Its subject is the victory of the King of Poland (John III Sobieski) over the Turks in 1683 outside the walls of Vienna. Matejko turned down the 80,000 florins that had been promised him for this massive work, considered his supreme masterpiece, on the condition that the painting be presented to Pope Leo XIII on the occasion of the bicentenary of the victory of Vienna on September 12, 1883. (The presentation of this painting, by the way, is shown in one of the frescoes in the second bay of the Gallery of the Candelabra.)

Each of the other paintings exhibited in this room is of nineteenth century vintage and included are Francesco Grandi's *Martyrdom of Blessed Johann Sarkander,* Cesare Mariani's *Saint Jean-Baptista de La Salle,* and Cesare Fracassini's *Saint Peter Canisio and Ferdinand of Austria.*

Located in the Borgia Tower is the Room of the Immaculate Conception where there are frescoes by Francesco Podesti. These show scenes of Pope Pius IX in 1854 proclaiming the doctrine of the Immaculate Conception.

On the side walls you see the pope wafting incense at the image of the Virgin. Another scene depicts a discussion among theologians. Between the windows Podesti has painted Sibyls, while his ceiling is rife with medallions of biblical scenes and allegorical figures. A view of Paradise is afforded above the windows.

The showcase in the center of this room will hold your attention. It displays ornately bound and decorated volumes (most of them are handwritten) that were presented to Pope Pius IX. The volumes contain the text of the papal bull of December 8, 1854, which have been translated into a large number of dialects and languages. These came as donations from kings, heads of state, bishops, provinces, and cities as a result of a proposal made by Father Marie Dominique Sire, a French priest.

Raphael's Adoration of the Magi. *(Photo by Carlo Piccolo)*

Raphael Stanze

PERHAPS THE BIGGEST drawing card in the Vatican Museums (next to, of course, the Sistine Chapel) is the series of rooms on the second floor of the Apostolic Palace that used to serve as the apartment of Pope Julius II and his successors up until the accession of Pope Gregory XIII.

These rooms, known today as the Raphael Rooms or the Raphael Stanze, constitute one of the Vatican's (and Italy's!) greatest art treasures, for which no sum of money can possibly be cited to give a market approximation of their worth. Let it be said that if such estimates were ever made in the light of a possible auction, the asking price would certainly start with at least $1 billion. As one of the Renaissance's major painters, the man known as Raphael (or Raffaello [his real name was Raffaello Sanzio and/or Raffaello Santi]), is noted for works that demonstrate the clearest expression of exquisite harmony and balance in composition. He achieved a monumentality that was emulated far into the nineteenth century.

After the death of his father, who was a painter in the court of the Duke of Urbino, Raffaello (1483–1520) entered the workshop of Perugino whose influence is evident in many of the young painter's early works. Though he died at the age of 37, Raffaello's extensive output of masterpieces left a firm imprint on the history of art. It was the work he did for the Vatican after 1508 in the pope's private apartment that marked the beginning of his brilliant career; at papal behest he took over the job from artists then much better known than himself (including his teacher Perugino). To make room for the "decorations" he and his assistants would be effectuating in the apartment, many works of art had to be erased or covered over and these included paintings by such artists as Luca Signorelli, Piero della Francesca, Bartolomeo della Gatta, Lorenzo Lott, Baldassare Peruzzi, and Perugino.

Built on a rectangular plan and covered with a cross vault, the Raffaello Rooms number four in all; originally the pope's suite included the Room of the Swiss Guards, the Room of the Chiaroscuri, the first antechamber, the private Chapel of Nicholas V, the pope's bedroom, and the Loggia. When tourists come to view the Raffaello Rooms, depending on which season of the year it is, there is a required one-way route to follow, but this route sometimes goes ''backwards'' if there is overcrowding (as happens all too frequently during the summer months, a necessity imposed by Vatican officials who make this prescription for visitors' convenience.)

Ordinarily a tour of the Raffaello Rooms begins with the Hall of Constantine, which at one time was used for official receptions and other ceremonies. Mostly decorated by Raffaello's assistants, who painted from designs left behind by the master after his death, the room carries out the theme of the Church's victory over paganism. All of the main scenes are based on allegorical figures—with popes and virtues appearing in the corners. A painting by Francesco Penni is called the Baptism of Constantine in which Pope Silvester has the features of Clement VII. The Battle of the Milvian Bridge represents Constantine's victory over Mexentius. Done by Giulio Romano, the details are taken from the reliefs on Trajan's Column—but a few of Raffaello's sketches can be seen. Giulio Romano also did two other paintings here —The Apparition of the Cross and the Donation of Rome to Pope Silvester. In the latter work Francesco Penni collaborated with Romano.

Room of Heliodorus is the second room, and Raffaello decorated this ''secret'' antechamber of the apartment himself. This room is an ambitious project, and the scope of the frescoes is to illustrate the miraculous protection given by God to a Church threatened in its faith. One sees Saint Peter delivered from prison and Attila the Hun turned away from Rome. Also: Heliodorus is driven out of the Temple. The caryatids (draped female figures in place of a column) are by Francesco Penni, and the small panels, repainted, are by Carlo Maratta. On the vault are seen the Sacrifice of Isaac, the Burning Bush, Jacob's Ladder, and God Appears to Noah.

Although Attila was rebuffed as far away from Rome as Mantua, Raffaello elected to give this event a Roman setting — so that you can see, for example, the Colosseum in the background, and also a basilica, an obelisk, Saint Peter, and Saint Paul (brandishing swords as Attila and his terrified barbarians run off). An odd aspect to this painting is that Leo X, who is seen advancing on a white mule, appears twice inasmuch as he was a cardinal (under Julius II) when the painting was begun and had become the pope when the painting was being completed.

Based on a miracle that took place in 1263, *The Miracle of Bolsena* shows a Bohemian priest who had severe doubts about the presence of Christ in the Eucharist until he saw blood pour forth from the host while celebrating Mass in Bolsena. This gave rise to Corpus Christi Day and to the construction of the Cathedral of Orvieto. Considered one of Raffaello's supreme masterpieces, this one shows Julius II kneeling before the altar with two cardinals of his retinue.

Heliodorus Driven Out of The Temple tells the biblical story of Heliodorus who was ordered by the King of Syria to filch the Temple of Jerusalem of its treasure. While sneaking out he was nabbed by two youths and a horseman and evicted from the premises. Using this particular episode, the pope wanted to make reference to his policy of throwing out any usurpers from Church territory. So as to make the message even stronger, he asked that he be portrayed in the scene. Raffaello added one of his own touches, however, and included his dear friend, an engraver called Marcantonio Raimondi, who is seen as a chair bearer in a German costume. In addition, the painter recorded the death of the Constable of Bourbon during the Sacking of Rome in a dado underneath the work, with an inscription on part of a column below the work.

Perhaps Raphael's most famous work is the one called *Saint Peter Delivered from Prison*. This shows the angel awakening Saint Peter and conducting him out of the cell past the sleeping guards. Then you see a soldier carrying a torch as he wakes up his fellow guards who show confusion. Note that the face of the apostle in this fresco is that of Julius II.

The third room bears the name Room of The Segnatura. As the library and study of Julius II, it was the first of the rooms to be decorated—and the painting is totally by Raffaello. As its theme, the painting has the three highest categories of the human spirit according to the neo-Platonic vision—the True, the Good, the Beautiful.

Depicting Theology, Philosophy, Justice, and Poetry, the large vault medallions are linked intimately to the wall paintings. So too are the works on Adam and Eve, the Primum Mobile, the Judgment of Solomon, and Apollo and Marsyas. Bramantino is the artist who did the central octagon, and the chiaroscuro items are by Perin del Vaga, which replaced the wooden panelings that Giovanni Barile and Fra Giovanni da Verona had done and which were lost during the Sacking of Rome in 1527. Do notice the inlaid, polychrome marble floor ornamented with the name of Julius II, the emblems of Leo X, and the crossed keys of Nicholas V.

The Dispute Over the Holy Sacrament shows Christ seated between the Virgin and Saint John in Paradise. Above him is God and below the Holy Ghost. Saints and Old Testament figures are contemplating over the Trinity. At the sides of the altar you see doctors and theologians participating in the incarnation of the Trinity through the Eucharist. Over on the right part are Gregory the Great (painted to look like Julius II) and Sixtus IV, behind whom stands Dante. Savonarola is also in the scene, but his head is somewhat concealed by a hood. As for the ecstatic-looking old man in Domenican costume on the far left, he is believed to be Fra Angelico. Since this fresco reveals a variety of influences (one of which came from Leonardo da Vinci), it anticipates the artist's mature style. Roman soldiers, during the Sacking of Rome, left two graffiti on this fresco, one of Charles V and of the Constable of Bourbon, and one in eulogy of Luther.

Raffaello's masterpiece, *The Cardinal and Theological Virtues* uses women as representatives of virtues. Fortitude is holding an oak branch, Prudence is observing herself in a mirror, and Temperance is holding reins. In addition, Faith is pointing to the sky, Hope is holding a burning torch, and Charity is shaking the acorns from an oak tree. In another painting Gregory IX is seen approving the Decretals Received from Saint Raymond de Penafort —these are the canonical laws. Displaying the features of Julius II, Pope Gregory is flanked by three cardinals (one of whom is Giovanni de'Medici). This work is attributed to the workshop team and not to Raffaello.

In *The School of Athens,* you view ancient philosophers and scientists chatting and strolling inside a basilica. In the center are Aristotle and Plato—the latter is pointing to the sky to indicate the world of ideas, and the former is extending his open hand between the heavens and earth. At the left is Socrates with his well-known profile, and in front of him are Alcibiades and Alexander the Great, the latter in armor. Diogenes is on the right in a supine position. Wearing a wreath of vine leaves is Epicurus, and behind him is Averroes watching Pythagoras while the latter scribbles on a blackboard. A bit further down is the isolated figure of Heraclitus (Michelangelo), and history tells us that Raffaello changed his original composition to get this figure included, despite the fact that he and Michelangelo were rivals. On the right Euclid is bending over while drawing with a compass —and on the neck of his garment are Raffaello's initials, R.V.S.M. For a self-portrait of Raffaello, look behind the figure of Sodoma in white at the extreme far right. Both Apollo and Athene serve as ''types'' for Raffaello who put them in the work. He was to make liberal use of these ''types'' in his later years.

Forthwith you come upon Parnassus. Here you note Apollo surrounded by the Muses as he plays a lyre sitting down. The blind Homer is on his right, and he is flanked by both Dante and Virgil. Sappho is seated below. On the right are a number of well-known Italian poets and writers, including the great Giovanni Boccaccio. Art experts are in total agreement regarding this painting; with it Raffaello came ''into full possession of his powers of expression.''

Once the pope's dining room, which was also used as a music room, the Room of The Incendio is the last of the rooms that Raffaello decorated on his own. He did the designs and left the executions to Giulio Romano and Francesco Penni. The frescoes in this room were done primarily to exalt Leo X by bringing out events from the lives of two other popes who used the same name—Leo III and Leo IV. The vault decorations you see that depict allegories of the Trinity were done by Perugino, and the paintings in the corners of the room are by Giulio Romano. They represent the Egyptian supports (those in the form of statues) that were found in Tivoli before 1504 (presently in the Pio-Clementine Museum).

To commemorate the concordat reached between France and the Catholic Church in 1515, *The Coronation of Charlemagne* in Saint Peter's Basilica shows Charlemagne with the features of Francis I and Leo III with those of Leo X. The story of how Leo IV put out a blazing fire in Borgo Santo Spirito by making the sign of the cross is shown in the painting, *The Fire in The Borgo.* The fire took place between Saint Peter's and the Tiber, and in the foreground you see the terrorized crowd and on the left a scene of Aeneas fleeing from Troy with his father on his shoulders, as related by Virgil.

The Battle of Ostia celebrates the victory of Leo IV (painted to look like Leo X) over the Saracens, alluding to the crusade against the Turks. Prominent among the VIPs in the retinue are Cardinal Bernardo Bibbiena and Cardinal Giulio de' Medici (on the left). Giulio Romano actually painted the fresco and possibly did the cartoons also.

Equally fascinating is the work called *The Self-Defense of Leo III*, which depicts the oath sworn in Saint Peter's by the pope to defend himself against the slander of the nephews of Adrian I. This painting alludes to the okaying of the 1516 Lateran Council's precept that a pope must answer for his actions only to God. This work was painted by Raffaello's sidekicks.

Special mention should be made here of the Chapel of Urban VIII, a small chapel richly decorated with gilded stucco and frescoes. This once served as the private chapel of Pope Urban VIII. All the work in this chapel was done by Pietro da Cortona. Above the altar you see the Deposition of Christ. The fresco above the altar was taken from the Church of San Filippo on the Via Giulia.

The Loggia of Raphael

IN 1508 DONATO BRAMANTE was entrusted by Pope Julius II
to build three arcades, but since both men died in 1514 and only
the first range of arches had been done, Pope Leo X called in Raffaello to complete the arcades—which he did by 1519, including
the decoration of the loggia which today bears his name. It was
Giovanni da Udine who decorated the ground-floor loggia and
then thoroughly repainted the top loggia (both of which are not
open to the public today). It is, however, the Loggia of Raphael
that is the most interesting and worthy of the three—this one is
open to the public most of the time. When the Raphael Loggia is
closed, for whatever Vatican reasons are behind that, visitors will
be admitted only upon written request. Scholars, by the way,
usually get priority treatment.

From the Hall of Constantine of the Raphael Stanze, you
approach the Loggia. At the end of the Loggia, through a doorway, begins a ramp originally designed to be climbed on horseback, built by Bramante, to connect the three floors of the
building to the Court of Saint Damascus. The arcades were out in
the open until they were enclosed in glass during the nineteenth
century to protect the frescoes and stucco work which today are
in bad shape—they began to break down early on, for the first
restoration was in 1560.

Reflected in the loggia decoration are Leo X's taste for antiquities. The themes of the grotesques and stucco ornamentations
are antiquaries and derive from the Domus Aurea, of which Raffaello
and his sidekicks had a good knowledge, since the master painter in
1514 had been given the job of Superintendent of Antiquities. Still
another Renaissance characteristic in evidence here is the mixture
of biblical and mythological motifs that were needed to execute the
complex decorative plan that had been set up. Collaborating with
128

Giulio Romano and Francesco Penni, Raffaello also called in Giovanni da Udine and Perin del Vaga to work on the project. Although these five skilled artists worked especially well as a team, Raffaello nevertheless got a number of other contemporary painters (like Caravaggio and Vincenzo da San Griminiano) to make minor contributions to the total job. One negative note to throw in here is that the original majolica floor that Luca della Robbia the Younger had designed was removed in 1869.

Because many of the aforementioned artists did single works, today there is considerable controversy as to the identity of the men. Vatican experts are sure that the stucco ornaments, done in the so-called Roman style are by Giovanni da Udine who employed a mixture of lime, plaster, and marble sawdust. In the pilasters of the first two bays, Da Udine took the occasion to portray himself more than once and also threw in a scene of Raffaello's studio at work in which Da Udine appears again. No one is quite sure who was responsible for the biblical scenes on the vaults, but they form what is known as ''the Bible of Raffaello,'' with the exception of the scenes in the last bay which are based on Old Testament accounts.

The 13 bays follow. Bay I has God dividing light from dark, God dividing land from water, God creating the sun and moon, and God creating the animals. Bay II deals with the Creation of Eve, the Original Sin, the Expulsion from Eden, and Adam and Eve with their sons. The building of the ark, the flood, and Noah's sacrifice occupy Bay III, and Bay IV concerns itself with the victorious Abraham encountering Melchisedec. This bay also contains God's promise to Abraham, the angels' visit to Abraham, and the burning of Sodom. In Bay V God forbids Isaac to go to Egypt, and Abimelech learns that Rebecca is the wife of Isaac. Then Isaac is shown blessing Jacob and then blessing Esau. The theme of Jacob continues in Bay VI which shows Jacob's vision, Jacob meeting Rachel at the well, Jacob reproaching Laban, and the return to Canaan.

Bay VII, which treats the information on Joseph, has Joseph relating his dreams to his brothers. Then Joseph is double-crossed by his brothers. Joseph then interprets the Pharaoh's dreams. For the Bay VIII scenes, you are treated to Moses in the Nile, the burning bush, the crossing of the Red Sea, and Moses making water spring from a rock. Moses, in Bay IX, receives the tablets of the Law. Included are the worship of the golden calf, God speaking to Moses from a cloud, and Moses giving the tablets of the Law to the people. Bay X depicts the Ark of the Covenant being carried across the Jordan, and the capture of Jericho. Joshua is seen stopping the sun, and there is the division of the land of Canaan. Dealing with David, Bay XI shows him anointed King, him killing Goliath, and his triumph. David's sin is also in the work. Bay XII concerns itself with the consecration of Solomon, the judgment of Solomon, the Queen of Sheba, and the building of the temple. And finally Bay XIII brings out the birth of Christ, the adoration of the Magi, the baptism of Christ, and the Last Supper.

About this enchanting corridor, visitors should keep in mind that for more than 300 years, the Loggia had been subjected to the worst winds and rains and to flying dirt because they were out in the open, literally. In addition, other damages were inflicted both by soldiers from Garibaldi's legions who flecked off parts of the frescoes with fingernails or bayonets and by nonthinking tourists who took the liberty of carving their names or initials onto the woodwork. Many of these damages have been repaired or retouched, though they can be detected close up. If you view them from afar, however, the general appearance is not affected.

Room of the Chiaroscuri

AS THE FIRST antechamber of the apostolic apartment, the Room of the Chiaroscuri is where Leo X used to hold the ''Secret Consistory''—the council of Cardinals who were living in Rome. Also various ceremonies, both public and private, religious and secular were held here. Curiously, this room was once known as the Room of Pappagallo (parrot) for the simple reason that as far back as the Middle Ages there was a cage with a parrot kept in the room. So as not to have the old name forgotten, artist Giovanni da Udine painted two parrots on the wall that leads to the locked room used by the Swiss Guards. The Room of the Chiaroscuri is divided down the middle by a row of columns.

The ceiling of this room was painted from a design submitted by Raphael during the papacy of Pope Leo X. The chiaroscuro figures (hence the room's name) of apostles and saints, made by the school of Raphael, were partly damaged in 1558 and were restored by Taddeo and Federico Zuccani in 1560. Further decorations were done by Giovanni Alberti and Ignazio Danti in 1582. In the center of the room is an eighteenth century model of the dome of Saint Peter's, considered a most faithful copy of the model made by Michelangelo, the last of four. Michelangelo's first model was in clay, his second, which was much larger, was in wood, the third was a clay model of the dome and drum, and the fourth was a larger wooden version of the third.

Chapel of Nicholas V

FORMING PART OF the oldest section of the Apostolic Palace, the Chapel of Nicholas V is in the Tower of Pope Innocent III. Relatively small in size (21 1/2 feet by 13 feet) and built on a rectangular plan, this chapel is covered with a cross vault. The decorations of this chapel were undertaken by Florentine Fra Angelico (Giovanni da Fiesole) between 1447 and 1451, who did some outstanding frescoes for it that deal with the lives of Saint Stephen and Saint Lawrence. These frescoes are considered the masterpieces of Fra Angelico's maturity. The embroidered front on the altar is a late sixteenth century work from the Church of San Filippino on Rome's Via Giulia. Fra Angelico had painted an altar-piece with the Deposition of Christ, but it was eventually lost and replaced with a wooden crucifix, a work from the fifteenth century Italian school. The floor is the original one by Agnolo Verrone, a Florentine marble-worker and a contemporary of Angelico.

The various frescoes on the walls and pilasters cover the following subjects: Saint Gregory the Great, Saint Anastasius, the Ordination of Saint Stephen, Saint Stephen distributing alms, the Ordination of Saint Lawrence (the figures in this fresco are portraits of the artist's contemporaries), Saint Ambrose, Saint Thomas Aquinas, Saint Stephen preaching, Saint Stephen addressing the Council, Saint Lawrence receiving the treasure of the Church, Saint Lawrence distributing alms, Saint Augustine, the stoning of Saint Stephen, Saint Lawrence before Decius, the Martyrdom of Saint Lawrence, Saint Leo the Great, and Saint John Chrysostomos.

The Borgia Apartment

NOW HOUSING some of the Vatican's collection of modern religious art, the Borgia Apartment was decorated by Pinturicchio at the behest of Pope Alexander VI whose Spanish family name was Rodrigo de Borja y Doms. Spread over the whole first floor of the Apostolic Palace and built between the thirteenth century and the end part of the fifteenth century, the Apartment was never used after the death of the so-called Borgia Pope, since succeeding popes wanted to live somewhere else. So the Apartment was used as the residence of certain cardinals, one of whom was Carlo Borromeo, Pope Pius IV's secretary of state.

In the Borgia Apartment there are rooms having special names of their own—like The Room of the Vestments, Room of the Pappagallo (also known as the Dressing Room and Room of the Secret Consistory), the Audience Room, the Room of the Pontiffs, the Room of the Falda, the Room of the Mysteries, Room of the Saints, Room of the Liberal Arts, the Room of the Creed, Room of the Sibyls, and two adjoining rooms that served as a bathroom and as a treasury.

Pinturicchio's frescoes, which he did from 1492 to 1494 with the assistance of members of his workshop, were repainted and restored in 1816 while Pius VII was in office. They were also touched up again in 1897 when Leo XIII opened the Apartment to the public. Most of the floors have been reconstructed with copies of the original ceramic tiles.

You start your tour of the Borgia Apartment with the Room of the Sibyls, situated in the Borgia Tower. Vatican history shows that Cesare Borgia (nephew of Alexander VI) had his brother-in-law, Alfonso d'Aragona, murdered in 1550 in this room. On the octagonal panels there are the astrological symbols of seven major

133

planets and the human activity they were thought to influence. Saturn is with a coach drawn by dragons. Jupiter is with hunters and a coach drawn by eagles. Venus is with lovers and a cart drawn by bulls. Mercury is with merchants and a cart drawn by deer. The Moon is with fishermen and a cart drawn by dragons.

The Room of the Liberal Arts is the first one located in the wing that Nicholas V had constructed. Having served as Alexander VI's study, it is also the room in which he dined all the time. When he died, his body lay in state here. As for the name, the room is called that because the Arts are represented in the lunettes as enthroned women, each of which is identified by an inscription: Astronomy, Grammar, Dialectics, Rhetoric, Geometry, Arithmetic, Music. The figure of Euclid, kneeling before Geometry and intent upon measuring with compasses, is said to be a portrait of Bramante. In the large central arch are some sixteenth century additions—five octagons that depict Jacob taking leave of Laban, the Angels saving Lot from the destruction of Sodom and Gomorrah, Justice, Trajan's justice, and Justice distributing gifts. The big sixteenth century fireplace, from a design by Sansovino, is thought to have once graced the inside of Castel Sant 'Angelo. It is carved in a type of hard sandstone that is found in Tuscany.

It's in the Room of the Saints that you find the work of Pinturicchio, whose real name was Bernardino Betti. He personally did most of the frescoes. The Martyrdom of Saint Sebastian shows the Colosseum in the background and also the Palatine Hill and the churches of Saint John and Saint Paul. Another painting depicts Events From The Life of Saint Barbara, showing her escape from the tower and the search by her irate father. In the background of the painting you see Barbara meeting Saint Juliana and the shepherd who will be turning her in to her father who shows determination to put her to death because she had taken up the Christian religion.

The fresco called Saint Catherine Disputing has her standing in the presence of Emperor Maximinus. (Constantine's Arch is in the background.) Catherine, with her long waves of blond hair, is arguing with the philosophers. Many of the portraits in this fresco are those of well-known persons of the era, and this is what makes the painting one of the most ironic in art history. As witness: the Turk with the white turban is Catherine's brother, Cesare (with whom she was known to be having a love affair). The man with the drooping mustache on the left side of the throne is Andrea Palaeologus, the despot of Morea and a son of the last Byzantium Imperial Family. In back of him is Antonio da Sangallo the Elder, seen holding a square. On his left is Pinturicchio who drew himself into the scene; he stands there in his long hair with a golden chain on his red doublet. One little mystery in the picture is Prince Zi-Zim (the brother of Sultan Bajazid), who at the time was living in Rome as either a hostage or a guest of the Emperor (whichever is your preference). There is controversy as to whether the Prince is the oriental figure on horseback or the figure next to the emperor. The full scene is done in front of a triumphal arch in Rome crowned by a golden bull, the heraldic symbol of the Borgias. In spite of the fact that Cesare Borgia was mostly responsible for the campaigns of conquest—and the times were anything but peaceful—the Borgia coat-of-arms is inscribed with the words, *Pacis cultori* ("To the Peacemaker").

In *The Visitation* are scenes from the myth of Isis and Osiris. Their presence with the bull Apis is a direct allusion to the pope. Osiris is seen teaching the Egyptian how to plough the ground and how to plant vines and apple trees. Also shown is the wedding of Osiris and Isis. Another scene shows Seth killing Osiris and Isis finding the limb of Osiris. The final part has Osiris leaving the pyramid looking like Apis, and then Apis is carried in triumph by the populace.

On the large arch, one can study scenes from the myth of Io and Argus—Mercury lulling Argus to sleep with the music of a panpipe, Hera asking Zeus to hand over Io, Io being tempted by Zeus, Isis sitting between Horus and Mercury, and Mercury killing Argus. Also note that above the door leading to the Room of the Mysteries is a Pinturicchio scene of the Madonna and Child which may be a portrait of Giulia Farnese.

The Room of the Mysteries, the last of the rooms done by Pinturicchio, shows the Mysteries of the Faith depicted in the lunettes. Here you have the Ascension, the Pentecost, the Assumption of the Virgin, the Annunciation, the Nativity, the Adoration of the Magi, and the Resurrection. In the Resurrection portrait there is an outstanding depiction of Alexander VI kneeling. He is in full regalia in his position next to the redeemer who apparently ''understands'' how the pope — a majestic and imposing individual — is able to keep both the virtues and vices he practiced in ingenious equilibrium, to say nothing of his children. As for the soldier in the middle brandishing a lance, it is pretty certain to be a portrait of Cesare Borgia. The figure on the right in the Ascension is the papal manservant, Francesco Borgia.

Actually the official wing of the Apartment, the Room of the Pontiffs is so named because of a series of inscriptions above lunettes in honor of 10 popes who served before 1500. Built in the fourteenth century, this room was used for papal audiences, dinners, consistories, and other official functions. The original beam ceiling collapsed in 1500, nearly killing Pope Alexander VI, and was replaced by a false vault.

Under Leo X the ceiling was done with stucco ornaments and grotesques, depicting the 12 signs of the Zodiac, the constellations, the seven planets then known, and a set of dancing angels.

Six other rooms follow, the first of which is Alexander's private Audience Room, whose vault frescoes were painted in 1576–1577 by Lorenzo Sabbatini and his students. These depict Saint Peter and Saint Paul and eight stories from the Acts of the Apostles. Another room is called Second of The Vestments (Room IX, once known as the Room of the Pappagallo, then the Dressing Room, then the Consistory). It was in this room that the pope would put on his vestments and also meet with state officials, cardinals, and other clergymen. In this same room the pope would conduct special ceremonies like the Benediction of the Golden Rose and the Christmas Benediction of the Sword. The rich ceiling was made under Pius IV in 1563 and restored under Gregory XIII. Known as the Room of the Vestments, the adjoining room is the one used by cardinals to dress.

Collection of
Modern Religious Art

SET UP BY Pope Paul VI as a record of the capacity of contemporary art for religious expression in 1973, the Collection of Modern Religious Art opens with the works of Matisse, Rodin, and Goya. Represented from the so-called Novecento Movement of Italian artists are painters like Rosai, Soffici, Casorati, Sironi, and Guidi. From Italy's so-called Corrente Movement are Cassinari, Guttuso, and Sassu, and from the so-called Roman School there are Cagli, Purificato, Gentilini, and Pirandello.

A more firm resolution to revive religious art is depicted in the paintings of Denis, Desvallieres, and Couturier (who were the founders of the Ateliers d'Art Sacre in France) and in the works of Previati, Carpi, Saetti, Consadori, Filocamo, Ferrazzi, Brindisi, and Avenali. A series of sketches for sculptures are on hand, as executed by Biagini, Nagni, and Monteleone for the doors of Saint Peter's; Minguzzi and Fontana for the doors of the Cathedral of Milan; and Greco for the doors of the Cathedral of Orvieto. There are also sketches for bronzes by Barlach, Messina, Berti, Fazzini, and Manfrini.

Giacomo Manzù, who did the doors of Saint Peter's Basilica, prepared the Chapel of Peace in Room XIV on the upper floor —this is a homogeneous collection of vestments and vessels for church ceremonies from the birthplace of Pope John XXIII (Bergamo). Room XV is given over entirely to Roualt, and Rooms XVI–XVIII contain works by the late nineteenth century artists who rebelled against impressionism—Gauguin, Bernard, Redon, Denis, and Valloton. This group also includes the so-called Ecole de Paris artists like Chagall, Zadkine, Dali, Foujita, and Utrillo. Rooms XIX–XXII house the graphic arts collection with drawings and engravings by Morandi, Casorati, Bucci, Marini, Modigliani, Sutherland, Nicholson, Klee, Kandinsky, Le Corbusier, Braque, Munch, and Henry Moore.

The impressive lineup of painters continues in Rooms XXIII–XXVIII where on exhibit are the works of Balla, Sironi, Carra, Rosai, Martini, Semenghini, Tosi, Guidi, de Pisis, Spazzapan, Levi, Morlotti, Omiccioli, Longaretti, and Tomea. There is an extraordinary display of high-fired ceramics by Biancini. In Rooms XXIX–XXXII are mosaics by Cantatore Ferrazzi; stained glass windows by Leger, Bissiere, Villon, Thorn-Prikker, and Campendonk; bronzes by Selva, Mestrovic, Scorzelli, Mirko, Bodini, Ciminaghi, Baskin, and Hillebrand; marble and stone sculpture by Fontana, Mastroianni, Marini, and Mazzullo; and paintings by Buffet and Hajnal.

The works on display in Rooms XXXIII–LV are arranged by nationality and artistic movement. To start things off, the United States has works by Shahn, Evergood, Levine, Feininger, Weber, Lipchitz, Rattner, Watkins. Room XXXVIII houses a big group of works by Severini from the fifties and sixties and give a good account of the artist's activity as decorator of the Cathedral of Cortona, the Church of Saint Pierre in Fribourg, and the University of Fribourg. Rooms XL–XLIII house an excellent series of Expressionist paintings, most of which are by German artists. A wide range, however, is collected here: Modersohn-Becker, Ensor, Kirchner, Heckel, Schmidt-Rottluff, Nolde, Rohlfs, Dix, Beckmann and Kokoschka. Included nearby are several ceramics by Picasso, paintings by Bacon and Sutherland, Rivera, Orozco, Siqueiros, and Tamayo. Spain is represented by the works of Chillida, Serrano, Aguilar, and Palenciu; Yugoslavia is represented by the works of Mestrovic, Dulcic, and the naifs of the so-called School of Hlebine; France is represented by the works of Bazaine, Manessier, and Villon. Also included in this collection are paintings by Mastroianni, Capogrossi, Aaltona, Botero, Djanira, Crooke, Zack, Azuma, Hantai, and Hansing.

The Sistine Chapel

AS ONE OF THE glories of the world, the Sistine Chapel stands by itself by standards and measurements. Next to Saint Peter's Cathedral itself, it is by far the biggest drawing card in Italy. No matter what religion a tourist in Rome may profess, sooner or later a magnet pulls him to the Vatican, and once there, he is "programmed" to pay a call on both Saint Peter's and the Sistine Chapel. Not to visit the Sistine Chapel is not to have visited Rome.

Standing in the southwest corner of the old medieval section of the Apostolic Palace, the Sistine Chapel takes its name from Pope Sixtus IV della Rovere who ordered it built, a job that lasted from 1475 to 1480. From a plan laid out by Baccio Pontelli, a Florentine architect, the Sistine edifice was designed with two purposes in mind: to house the new palatine chapel and to defend the Apostolic Palace—hence the defensive nature of the building as evidenced by the stern, massive appearance of its exterior and by the battlements on top. The chapel is still used for some papal functions and for the Conclave of Cardinals when a new pope is to be elected. Built on a simple rectangular plan, the Sistine has no apse and is covered with a barrel vault with weight-bearing vaulting cells that come down between each of the 12 arched windows. Measuring 132 feet in length, 44 feet in width, and 68 feet in height, the edifice has a floor of inlaid marble of different colors.

Using events from the lives of Moses and Christ (not to mention the portraits of popes), the painters who worked on the walls worked as a team. These included some of the biggest names in art—Perugino, Botticelli, Ghirlandaio, and Rosselli—who were helped by members of their workshops that included such men as Pinturicchio, Piero di Cosimo, and Bartolomeo della Gatta, later joined by Luca Signorelli (he, by the way, painted the last two frescoes of the Mosaic series). It was Perugino who coordinated the work of the various artists, since he was the first to be engaged and had painted the altarpiece with the Virgin Mary and the first two panels of both the Mosaic and Christian cycles. Dedicating the Sistine Chapel to the Virgin Mary, Sixtus IV consecrated it on August 15, 1483.

There followed after Sixtus' death, three popes; all of them left the chapel as Sixtus had left it. Then in 1506 Julius II della Rovere (nephew of Sixtus IV) wanted to make changes in the vault decorations, and in 1508 he called in Michelangelo who, basically, did not want to do any work on the chapel, nor even touch any of the decorations which he admired. Though he tried everything to get himself out of the commission, Michelangelo eventually succumbed to the pope's pressure, and on May 10, 1508, he began to work on the ceiling with two of his assistants (Jacopo d'Indaco and Francesco Granacci). Once Michelangelo had learned the fresco technique, which was new to him, he decided to let his painting partners go because he would do the work himself. By September 1510, Michelangelo had actually done half of the vault. Almost a year later, on August 14, 1511, Pope Julius—who could not wait to see the unfinished product —ordered the scaffolding be taken down. It is generally believed that when Raffaello got a glimpse of the paintings on the vault, he changed his own style from that day forward. In October 1512 the ceiling was done, and on November 1 (All Saint's Day) Julius II inaugurated the ceiling with a solemn high mass.

With Pope Clement VII de' Medici sitting on Saint Peter's Throne in 1533, Michelangelo accepted another commission to paint *The Last Judgment* on the altar wall (with that commission, by the way, Michelangelo was also supposed to do another painting on the opposite wall, *The Fall of the Rebel Angels,* but he never undertook the actual job). Michelangelo did not begin to work on the painting until 1535, and then only under heavy pressure from Pope Paul III. Since the wall to be used was already covered with other fifteenth century paintings, Michelangelo had these erased and the wall covered with a sloping layer of bricks. It

Not to visit the Sistine Chapel is not to have visited Rome. *(Photo by Carlo Piccolo)*

was on this surface that Michelangelo started his painting in the summer of 1536 and completed it in the autumn of 1541. Having followed the artist's progress with considerable impatience, Paul III celebrated vespers on October 31, 1541, in front of the colossal painting which takes up 2,152 square feet and contains over 390 figures. At the time, *The Last Judgment* astonished all Italy; today it is still a wonderment for anybody who comes to Rome, for it is the masterpiece of Michelangelo's maturity—he was then in his 60s.

The work takes as its sources the Bible and Ezekiel in particular, the Dies Irae, Dante, and the motives of pre-Tridentine religious polemic. Although the figures are placed on different levels, the whole composition is absorbed into the dynamic vortex and Christ's gesture of condemnation. Note the symbols of the Passion borne by angels in the two lunettes. Down a bit further in the central part is Christ the Judge, which is an anti-traditional image; he has the features of the Apollo Belvedere and the limbs of Hercules. Next to him is Mary who has turned away her head out of pity; the patron saints of Rome (Saint Lawrence and Saint Bartholomew) are at Christ's and Mary's feet. Pay particular notice to the face of Saint Bartholomew since it is a self-portrait of Michelangelo.

Pictured on the right are Peter with the keys, Adam and Eve, the reconciling embrace of Esau and Jacob, Simon of Cyrene (with the cross on his shoulders), Saint Sebastian holding an arrow, Saint Catherine of Alexandria, Saint Blaise, Saint Philip with the cross, Simon Zelotes with the saw. Depicted on the left are John the Baptist with an animal-skin cloak, the group with the personification of the mother, the nude Eve, and Virgil. On the level underneath are the trumpeting angels in the center, and on the right, you see the damned being hurled down by demons. On the left, the selected ascend—special note must be taken of the two redeemed suspended by a rosary. On the earth (below, left) are the resurrected whose bodies are being formed again and (right) hell with two Dante-esque figures—Charon who, unlike his counterpart in the Divine Comedy, is shoving the damned ones out of the boat, and Minos who is watching it all. In the figure of Minos, Michelangelo left behind a marvelous practical joke. As he was about to finish the big painting, the pope's master of ceremonies (one Biagio da Cesena) got a glimpse of it and objected to the majority of figures being unclothed. So Michelangelo added another figure down in the corner (the 391st) which depicted Biagio da Cesena in the nude with the ears of a donkey. Though da Cesena complained loudly to Pope Paul III, the painting was not changed—and today da Cesena is still in *The Last Judgment*—still with donkey ears and still naked!

In the minds of some tourists superstar Michelangelo and the Sistine Chapel are virtually synonymous. Understandable as this may be, the Sistine Chapel nevertheless houses a proliferation of art done by other famous painters that warrants radar attention. This is especially true of the side walls and the entrance wall. Depicting the lives of Moses and Christ, the wall frescoes are very closely intertwined, and the Latin description above each picture makes this relationship quite clear. Bear in mind that the writing sometimes makes references to a main episode in the frescoes and sometimes to a secondary episode, for which a counterpart shows up on the opposite wall (illustrated by the same words). Hence, it is important to keep in mind that a thorough understanding of the cycle makes it necessary for the two lives to be looked at simultaneously. This rather complex iconographic setup was dictated by Pope Sixtus IV on the recommendation of one of his court theologians, and there is a specific political rationale: the choice of the episodes stresses the role of Christ and that of his "precursor," Moses, as leaders of the people.

When Christ is seen handing over the keys, this is intended as a symbolic gesture wherein these roles are being transmitted to Peter, founder of the papacy. The Payment of the Tribute—as shown in the painting's background—makes a strong reference to the independence of spiritual from temporal power. This independence is also recognized by Emperor Constantine, whose arch of triumph you see two times; the scene deals with his legendary donation to Pope Silvester. In the Punishment of Korah, the fresco tells of the divine punishment that awaits all persons, including those clergy allied to the Church, who take exception to any authority of the pope. (There is a similar message to be found in the gallery of portraits of the first 30 popes which serves as a record of the historical origins of papal power. [Since the first 4 portraits on the altar wall were wiped off, only 26 of the popes remain.])

On the south wall is the Journey of Moses. Moses is shown taking leave of his father-in-law before going back to Egypt. Now the prophet meets the angel dispatched to punish him for not having circumcised his son. On the right is shown the Circumcision. This fresco was done by Perugino, and the two popes next to the window are Clement I (on the right) and Evaristus (on the left), done respectively by Ghirlandaio and Botticelli. The north wall carries the Baptism of Christ, and in the background on the left is a sermon by the Redeemer and a sermon by John the Baptist on the right. This fresco is by Perugino, and you see his signature on the marble frame above God. Pictured are Pope Anaclete by Ghirlandaio and Pope Alexander I on the right by Fra Diamante.

Back to the south wall again. Here are various events from the life of Moses: Moses kills the Egyptian who maltreated an Israelite, Moses escapes from Egypt, Moses defends Jethro's daughters from the shepherds and helps the girls to water the flock, Moses takes off his shoes and prostrates himself before the burning bush, Moses leads the Jews out of Egypt. This fresco is by Botticelli. Ghirlandaio did the portrait of Pope Hyginos, but the picture of Sixtus I is by an undetermined artist. On the north wall once more, the Temptations of Christ (as interpreted by Botticelli) appear in the background. In the foreground is the Purification of the Leper. A number of onlookers are present, and the figure on the far right (holding a baton) is Girolamo Riario, the pope's condottiere. The two popes in portrait are Pius I by Botticelli and Telesphorus by Fra Diamante.

Again the south wall: here you have the Crossing of the Red Sea. At the left are depicted the jubilant populace that gathers around Moses, and at the right the Egyptians are seen being swept away by the sea. Moses and Aaron are before the Pharoah in the background. The old man holding a case at Moses' right is Cardinal Bessarione. Piero di Cosimo is also present—he's the youth in black. Roberto Malatesta is the warrior with his back turned to the viewer. Cosimo Rosselli was the painter of this fresco, and Fra Diamante was the painter of the two popes pictured here—Anicetus and Eleutherius. The Calling of the First Apostles (on the north wall), as depicted by Ghirlandaio who also did the two papal portraits, deals with Peter and Andrew kneeling before Christ. In the background are John and James. Among the various portaits are the humanist Argiropolos in the foreground and on his right, the pope's treasurer, Giovanni Tornabuoni and his son Lorenzo. The popes are Soter and Victor.

Cosimo Rosselli undertook the responsibility of both the south and north wall for the next episodes that were painted. On the south is Moses receiving The Ten Commandments. Below are depicted the people worshipping the golden calf. In the background you see the Punishment of the Idolaters, and on the left Moses as he returns with the tablets. Pope Zephyrinus and Pope Urban I are the work of Fra Diamante. The north wall has the Sermon on the Mount, which is squarely in the center. On the right is the Healing of the Leper. The two figures standing in the foreground are Jaime (in oriental dress) and Fernando de Almeida. Over to the far left is the Queen of Cyprus standing, and behind her (in black) the painter Rosselli has put himself into the fresco. Rosselli also did Pope Calixtus I, but the Pope Pontianus portrait was executed by an anonymous artist.

The south wall this time has the Punishment of Korah, Datan, and Abiron. The Attempted Stoning of Moses is on the right, and in the background is the Arch of Constantine. The portraits include Alessandro Farnese and Pomponio Leto standing behind the bearded figure of Moses. Note that Botticelli, who painted this fresco, has inserted his own likeness, and he can be detected behind Moses dressed in black. Botticelli did one of the popes, Cornelius, and Fra Diamante did Pope Anteros. The theme of the Handing Over of The Keys occupies the north wall as we see the Payment of the Tribute, the Attempted Stoning of Christ, and the two scenes of the Arch of Constantine. Among the portraits are the painters Pinturicchio and Perugino (the latter having done the fresco). An unkown painter did the portrait of Pope Fabian, but Botticelli did Pope Lucius I.

Occupying the south wall this time is the Testament of Moses, and we see him giving his staff to Joshua. Now you view in the background the angel showing Moses the Promised Land, Moses descending from Mount Horeb, and the Death of Moses. Luca Signorelli, who did this fresco, took the occasion to portray himself in the picture—he's the third figure from the left in the background. Botticelli painted Pope Stephen I, and Rosselli painted Pope Dionysus. As for the north wall, we come at last to The Last Supper as done by Rosselli. We also see the Prayer in the Garden, Christ taken Prisoner, and the Crucifixion. The popes are Sixtus II (by Botticelli) and Felix I (by Ghirlandaio).

The entrance wall on the south side concerns itself with the Disputation Over the Body of Moses, as done by Matteo da Lecce. This work replaces the lost masterpiece by Signorelli. An unknown artist did the portrait of Pope Marcellus I, while that of Pope Eutychianus was done by Ghirlandaio. The north side of the entrance wall has Arrigo Paludano's Resurrection, replacing the masterpiece by Ghirlandaio. Pope Marcellinus is a Botticelli work, and Pope Caius is a work by Ghirlandaio.

An interesting aspect about the ceiling of the Sistine Chapel is that Michelangelo originally wanted to paint the 12 apostles, but then he came up with the idea of doing the history of mankind as recorded before the birth of Christ, thereby tying in the ceiling decorations with those on the walls. Although he did not seek to create special fourth dimensional effects, he parceled out the vault by painting monumental architecture into panels so that each would enclose a separate scene. The nine panels describe the events from Genesis.

Represented in the spaces between the vaulting cells are the five Sibyls and seven prophets, pagan and Hebrew harbingers of the future Grace. Also shown are the miraculous Salvations of Israel, prefigurations of the redemption (which form a convincing the matic link with the fifteenth century cycle found on the walls). In the lunettes below you see the Ancestors of Christ. Observe the nude young men to the sides, for they have both an ornamental and symbolic function; various interpretations hold them to be genii of the golden age of Pope Julius II, personifications of various kinds, expressions of Michelangelo's Neoplatonic ideas. Their function is similar to that of the plaque-bearers you see between the lunettes and to the nudes above the vaulting cells. Each pair of young men holds a monochrome medallion with stories from Genesis, II Samuel, and II Kings.

Going against usual procedures, Michelangelo started the ceiling from the entrance and worked towards the altar. It is believed he did it this way because the crowd scenes presented fewer technical problems to a painter not yet familiar enough with the fresco technique. Facing *The Last Judgment,* you look up at the ceiling and observe in the right corner Judith and Holofernes. Judith is covering the head of the dead man — this visage is said to be a self-portrait of Michelangelo. In the left corner there is a scene of David and Goliath — David is in the act of slicing off the head of the giant. In the middle of the fresco, thoughtfully leafing through a book, is the prophet Zachariah.

The central panel shows the Drunkenness of Noah. With his head turned away from the viewer, Cam is mocking his sleeping father, while Japheth covers his dad and Shem reproaches Cam. Noah is also seen on the left, planting a vine. Over on the right is the Delphic Sibyl, absorbed in a prophecy as she reads. On the left, studying a parchment, is Joel, whose face is that of the painter Donato Bramante. The Flood occupies the central panel — this was the first of the historical events to be painted. This portion was finished by Michelangelo in January 1509, but in 1797 an explosion in Castel Sant' Angelo caused a fracture and a triangular portion of the right-hand side of the fresco fell off (it has now been restored with a work phase completed in 1986). In the center background we find the Ark represented as a house, and in front of the ark a boat is sinking because of excessive freight. There is a small island at the right in which you observe a populace of selfish people preventing others from reaching dry land. Providing contrast to this is an old man who is striving desperately to save an unconscious person he has clasped. Included in the scene are embracing lovers who bravely await death together, while a mother with her terrified children awaits the same fate. There is a nude man with fierce eyes transporting his wife on his shoulders as he seeks to save himself. The central panel shows Noah's sacrifice after the flood.

In the central panel we also see the Fall of Adam and Eve. This is one of the loveliest nudes ever painted by Michelangelo. They are seen tempted by the demon in the guise of a human-like snake. On the right is the Expulsion from Eden. Art experts point that this panel marks the beginning of the stylistic maturity of Michelangelo who from this point on started to draw forms of increasing grandeur, as witness his work in the Temptation scene.

In the Creation of Eve we are shown Adam who is sound asleep near the stump of a tree, which is a symbolic allusion to the Cross. The wrinkled female figure is that of the Cumaean Sibyl who is seen searching for a passage in a book. Nearby is the prophet Ezekiel. Seized by inspiration, he wears a Syriac turban and holds a scroll of prophecies. The Creation of Adam is seen and he is shown in the moment the Creator instills life into him with a gesture of His hand.

The center panel also includes the Division of the Land from The Waters. At the base is a nude young man, the likeness of which was inspired by the Belvedere Torso which is in the Room of the Muses in the Pio-Clementine Museum. With his hair and clothing mussed by a gentle wind, Daniel the prophet is intent on making notes from a text. Bent with age, the elderly female figure is the Persian Sibyl. The Creation of the Heavens: God is creating the sun and moon on the right, and on the left you see Him, with His back to the viewer, eating the plant life on Earth. Now we come to the Division of Day from Night, and the female figure that is immediately prominent is the Libyan Sibyl who, having stopped her reading, is now getting ready to get up from her chair. Of extra special interest is the face of Jeremiah the prophet; Michelangelo gave vent to his innermost self and used his own face for that of the prophet. Particular attention should be paid to this version of Jeremiah for its special aspects.

The Bronze Serpent, with which Moses saved the Israelites from divine punishment, is in the right corner, as you look towards the altar. Two other scenes are included—The Punishment of Haman and the recumbent Ahasuerus as he calls Mordecai. Over on the left Haman is being condemned by the king's council and then he is seen as a crucified figure (which Michelangelo drew from the famous Laocoön). In the center is the monumental figure of Jonah, supposed to be a prefiguration of Christ and symbol of the Faith.

Now here's a nifty tip to save you neck pains that develop from looking up too long at the Sistine ceiling: bring along a small hand mirror or a larger sized one, and instead of craning your neck constantly to view the masterpiece art (this applies also to other ceilings and vaults in other parts of the Vatican Museums!), place your mirror in a horizontal position near your chin and look "down" at the artwork without straining or tiring the muscles in your neck. Moreover, if you place the mirror on the floor, you can get a better picture of some of the details—albeit all of the figures will be left-handed instead of right-handed, or vice versa.

And here's another nifty tip: the official entrance of the Sistine Chapel is the Sala Regia—which has to be the most magnificent anteroom in Europe. At one time the popes used to give audiences in the Sala Regia. If time permits, and you can work out a deal for yourself to get permission to visit this glorious room, do so by all means. The walls of this chamber are filled with a series of historic frescoes by Giorgio Vasari as, for example, *The Naval Battle of Lepanto 1571* and *The Death of King Henry IV of France,* which were done with the collaboration of many of Vasari's pupils. The permission you obtain will also be good for the Cappella Paolina (also not to be overlooked), in which Michelangelo did some frescoes between 1514 and 1549—such as the *Conversion of Saint Paul* and the *Crucifixion of Saint Peter.* The latter composition is magnificently done; it shows Peter suffering upside down on a cross that is about to be put into a hole from which a worker is digging out clumps of dirt by hand. In spite of the pain the nails and position are giving him, Peter manages to give a stern look of disapproval as bound Christians are being led to their execution. Both the Michelangelos and the Vasaris are excellent works that rarely get a fair viewing by visitors who are usually too rushed going somewhere else—alas!

The Vatican Library

OWING ITS INSTITUTIONALIZATION to some 1,500 manuscripts that had been collected by Nicholas V, the Vatican Library was founded in June 1475 by Sixtus IV. Upon visiting the Vatican Library today many tourists are often confused; in fact many tourists actually walk through the Vatican Library without being aware of it. This happens very often because the part of the Vatican Library open to the public looks more like a series of exhibition rooms in a museum and not like a place where books are on the shelves and people are seated at tables reading or doing research. In actual fact, the book and manuscript part and the reading rooms of the Vatican Library are not open to tourists, but anyone who wants to consult a book or use the reading room for research will get special permission if he can show he is doing scholarly research. (For more details on this part of the Vatican Library, see the Addendum Chapter devoted to it.) Herewith will be presented the Vatican Library that tourists can go through at any time the Vatican Museums are open.

Since the Vatican Library is divided into various segments, let's start out according to a "new" one-way tour that is the easiest way to see-and-conquer it—by directly entering into the Room of the Addresses of Pope Pius IX:

This Room XIII was originally set up to preserve all the messages of homage sent to the papal office by Catholics all over the world. The collection also includes all the addresses that have been "saved" by popes. In the showcases you will find vestments of various periods from the fourteenth to the eighteenth century. Two antique pieces that stand out are a pair of mitres of the fourteenth century—the first, in yellow damask silk (with pictures of

150

parrots and four-legged animals), was found in the tomb of Pope John XXII in Avignon (France), and the second is decorated with a series of circles. Also included is a stole given by the Grand Duke of Tuscany Ferdinand I to Pope Clement VIII, woven in 1587 in the Medici workshop. In this collection are the altar aprons of the Dead Christ and Christ Among the Apostles and Christ and Magdalen.

Built between 1566 and 1572, the Chapel of Saint Pius VI is decorated from designs by Giorgio Vasari with stories from the life of Saint Peter the Martyr. In the showcase are objects from the Sancta Sanctorum treasury that include the following: an ivory lid showing the healing of a blind man; part of a case that once belonged to a sixth century oculist; two figures, Saint Peter and Saint Paul, forming a diptych; a silver shrine representing Christ seated between Saint Peter and Saint Paul (on the sides are scenes showing Christ's childhood), a shrine made in Rome in the ninth century which contained an enamelled cross with stories of Christ; a reliquary of the head of Saint Praxedes, and a ring with the seal of Pope Nicholas III, found inside the reliquary.

In still a second room called the Room of the Addresses (this one bearing the number XI) are a display of Byzantine icons and primitive paintings. Here you will find Roman and early Christian glassware and church ornaments, vestments and cult objects in enamel, ivory, and precious metals dating from the Middle Ages on. Among the many things in this room worth noting are the *Rambona Diptych* with the enthroned Madonna and Crucifixion, made by a North Italy workshop. Also: a Cover of the Codex Aureus of Lorsch in which Christ is seen trampling a lion and a dragon; Christ and five apostles in a series of enamels from the antependium of the ''Confession'' in the Constantine Basilica in Limoges (thirteenth century); and an encrusted drinking glass with marine creatures in the design, made in Cologne around 300 A.D. and found in the Catacombs of Saint Calixtus.

Stories of Samson are to be found in the Room of the Aldobrandini Wedding, which was built in 1611 and decorated by Guido Reni. This is an Augustan Age fresco and got its name because the first owner was named Aldobrandini. On the side walls is a fresco cycle with landscapes and scenes from the Odyssey. This is from the first century B.C. In Room IX (called the Room of the Papyri because it was intended to house the sixth–ninth century papyri of Ravenna) has showcases of gilded, early Christian glass objects with pagan and sacred scenes, among which are the portrait of Dedale the ship builder—this one has six scenes of carpenters busily at work and was found in the Catacomb of Saint Saturninus on the old Via Salaria. Two other scenes here include the Resurrection of Lazarus and the Wedding at Cana, both from the fourth century. The ceiling fresco commemorates the 1973 inauguration of the Clemetine Museum.

Set up in 1756, the Christian Museum (Room VIII) houses early Christian antiquities displayed in showcases. An unusual mosaic in this room, which Pope Benedict XIV provided for, is a traveling icon showing Saint Theodore. This twelfth/thirteenth century piece of art is very similar to those preserved in the monasteries of Mount Athos. The Gallery of Urban VIII (Room numbered VII) contains the manuscripts of the Palatine Library. In the lunettes are views of buildings constructed or renovated during Pope Benedict XIV's term in office from 1740 to 1758.

Perhaps the two most important rooms in the Vatican Library's public part are the Sistine Rooms numbered V and VI. The latter room was laid out by Sixtus V to house documents from the papal archives. On the walls of this room are episodes from the papacy of Sixtus V. In the lunettes facing each other are two frescoes done by Cesare Nebbia and Giovanni Guerra in 1590, which show a view of Saint Peter's according to the project of Michelangelo and the Transportation of the Obelisk to Saint Peter's Square during May to September in 1586.

The more elaborate of the two rooms is the one numbered V, which is usually called the Sistine Salon and which once served as the Library reading room. At the entrance and exit are two frescoes with views of the Pope's Lateran Palace before and after its reconstruction in 1598. In the vestibule are representations of the papal chapels in the basilicas of Saint Lawrence's Outside the Walls, Saint Paul's Outside the Walls, Santa Maria Maggiore, Santa Maria del Popolo, and also of the Council of Trent and the

Lateran Council. One of the pilasters is devoted to the inventors of the alphabet.

The showcases contain important autographs, illustrations by known artists, coins of the State of Vatican City, ancient manuscripts, and miniatures. This chamber quite often puts on exhibitions of books and manuscripts from the stacks of the Vatican Library reading room.

In the Pauline Rooms (IV) are paintings done by Giovanni Battista Ricci in 1610 and 1611 showing episodes from the reign of Pope Paul V. This is followed by the Alexandrine Room (III), set up in 1609 by Pope Alexander VIII to depict episodes from the papacy of Pius VI. The artist was Domenico De Angelis who executed the work in 1818. In one of the showcases is a skillfully embroidered linen altar cloth from the Sancta Sanctorum (eleventh century).

The Clementine Gallery (II) is divided into five rooms, and on its walls are episodes from the papacy of Pius VII. In the showcase are Gian Lorenzo Bernini's models of Charity, the prophet Habakkuk and Daniel in the lion's den, and studies for the Chigi Chapel in Santa Maria del Popolo and for the monument to Pope Urban VIII in Saint Peter's. The so-called Profane Museum (I), set up by Pope Clement XIII in 1767, houses various objects from the Etruscan, Roman, and medieval periods. Most of these are what is left over from the rich collection taken to Paris in 1797. The ornate furniture in this room, by the way, is from the skilled hand of Luigi Valadier.

The Pinacoteca

WITH PAINTINGS dating from the eleventh to the nineteenth century, the Pinacoteca has rooms devoted to one or more schools of painting, to individual artists, or to a period. The Pinacoteca owes its founding to Pope Pius XI in 1932 when the masterpieces taken away from Italy by Napoleon (under the 1797 Treaty of Tolentino) and returned after the 1815 Congress of Vienna were finally exhibited to the public. This brought about the opening of the Pinacoteca, one of the best-stocked masterpiece museums in the world, though taking a back seat to the Louvre in Paris, the Prado in Madrid, and Kunsthistorisches Museum in Vienna, and the Uffizi Palace in Florence.

Stocked with Primitives, Room I of the Pinacoteca gives every visitor a hint of great things to come, starting with the School of Giunta Pisano. Saint Francis and stories of his life done in tempera on wood is a panel attributed to the Pisan master in the Church of San Francesco in Assisi. The central part of the painting has the saint, and at the sides are four of his miracles (the Healing of the benumbed child, the Healing of the cripple, the Possessed woman freed of the demon, and an Old Man praying at the altar of the saint).

The Last Judgment by Giovanni and Niccolò (tempera on wood) is from the Roman school, datable to the second half of the twelfth century. Two Benedictine nuns, who are depicted on the left at the bottom, commissioned Giovanni and Niccolo to create this piece of art. Unusual is the fact that the panel is round in shape and has a rectangular piece attached at the base. Various scenes are on different levels: on top is Christ with seraphim and angels; below is Christ with symbols of the Passion, standing before an altar surrounded by apostles; and farther down is Saint

Paul leading the resurrected. Also represented are Dismas the good thief, the Virgin, the saintly innocents, Saint Stephen, and the Works of Mercy shown in three episodes. At the next level are the Resurrection of the dead, those condemned devoured by wild animals and fish, those who were buried, two allegories of classical derivation—and on the lowest level Paradise and the torments of Hell.

The School of Rimini from the fourteenth century has the guardian angel with the child John the Baptist (tempera on wood), attributed to Giovanni Baronzio. There is the Madonna and Child by Allegretto Nuzi depicting donors at the Virgin's feet in the center panel. Next is a Madonna and Child with Saints by Giovanni del Biondo (tempera on wood) which shows four saints on either side of Mary, and below a skeleton eaten by worms. Giovanni Bonsi's Madonna and Child with Saints (tempera on wood) has the Virgin and the Christ Baby in the middle; on the left are Saint Honophrius and Saint Nicholas, and on the right Saint Bartholomew and Saint John the Evangelist. Bonsi signed this painting in 1372, and it is said to be the only work certain to come from his brush. This painting, therefore, is of special interest to art connoisseurs and art historians.

Room II (the School of Giotto and Late Gothic) comes at you strong. Giotto is represented with his Stefaneschi triptych (tempera on wood), painted for Cardinal Jacopo Gaetani Stefaneschi. Originally made for the high altar of Constantine's Basilica, the work was done in about 1315, since Pope Celestine V is haloed, and he was canonized in 1313. Painted on both sides, the work is a delight to all viewers: the front side shows Christ enthroned with angels and Cardinal Stefaneschi; the side panels show the beheading of Saint Paul and the Crucifixion of Saint Peter; the back central panel shows Saint Peter on the throne surrounded by angels and Cardinal Stefaneschi. The side panels show Saint Mark and Saint John the Evangelist on the right and Saint James and Saint Paul on the left. On the predella front center is the Madonna enthroned and surrounded by the angels Saint Peter and Paul; to the right and left are apostles. On the predella back are three saints; the side panels are lost.

Jacopo del Casentino, who was born in 1297 and who died in 1358, is represented with a tempera on wood called Madonna and Child, one of the few works attributed to this Florentine painter. Pietro Lorenzetti is represented with a tempera on wood with his Christ before Pilate. The Redeemer giving his blessing by Simone Martini is a tempera on wood that was at one time the crown of an altarpiece. With its upper part restored, Bernardo Daddi's Madonna of the Magnificat is a tempera on wood that came from the Vatican library collection.

Next, from the fourteenth century Florentine school comes a painting called The Coronation of the Virgin, done in the manner of Pietro Gerini. Giovanni di Paolo's Prayer in the Garden and The Deposition are both temperas on wood, as is Stefano di Giovanni's Saint Thomas Aquinas before the Crucifix. A scene showing Saint Benedict freeing a monk from the temptations of the devil is from the brush of Lorenzo Monaco (tempera on wood).

Gentile da Fabriano is represented with tempera on wood works that include Stories of Saint Nicholas, the Birth of the Saint, Saint Nicholas gives three golden balls to some poor girls, Saint Nicholas revives three children cut up in pieces in a barrel, Saint Nicholas saves a ship. The missing parts of this polyptych are in the Florence Uffizi Gallery and in London's National Gallery.

In Room III the works of Fra Angelico, Filippo Lippi, and Benozzo Gozzoli dominate the chamber. Fra Giovanni da Fiesole, who is better known as Fra Angelico, has a tempera on wood that came from the collection of Lord Dudley called Madonna and Child with Saint Dominic, Saint Catherine, and Angels. This work was done in 1435. There is a Fra Angelico tempera on wood called Stories of Saint Nicholas of Bari, made in 1437 for the Church of San Domenico in Perugia. The work shows the Birth of Saint Nicholas, his summons from God, the alms to three poor girls, the meeting with the emperor's messenger, and the miraculous rescue of a sailboat. Pope Urban VIII made Fra Angelico a saint, and when asked what the miracles actually were that supported canonization, he replied ''His works!'' Fra

Angelico, therefore, holds the distinction of being the only painter ever to be elevated to sainthood because of his masterpieces.

The triptych painted by Filippo Lippi for the Chapel of Saint Bernard in the Monastery of Monteoliveto in Arezzo is called Coronation of the Virgin. Commissioned by Carlo Marsuppini, secretary of the Republic of Florence, the works show him kneeling in the left panel. After the order was suppressed, the triptych first went to the Lippi Family in Arenzo and then in 1841 to Ugo Baldi. It was bought by Pope Gregory XVI and later transferred to the Vatican.

Painted in 1450 by Benozzo Gozzoli, the Madonna of the Girdle, a tempera on wood, demonstrates the Birth of the Virgin, the Wedding, the Annunciation, the Nativity, the Circumcision, and the Death of the Virgin.

Melozzo da Forli and Marco Palmezzano are the two painters whose works take up Room IV. Da Forli's Sixtus IV and Platina is a fresco transferred to canvas and originally decorated one of the rooms of Pope Sixtus IV's personal library. Painted in 1477, it represents the nomination of Bartolomeo Platina as prefect of the Vatican Library in 1475. A curiosity about this work is that the figure of a person bedecked as a cardinal is Giuliano della Rovere, nephew of Pope Sixtus and the future Pope Julius II. The Madonna and Child with Saints (tempera on wood) by Marco Palmezzano shows the Saints Francis, Lawrence, John the Baptist, Anthony, Dominic, and Peter at the foot of the throne. It was made in 1537.

Various fifteenth century painters are exhibited in Room V, and they include Ercole de Roberti's Miracles of Saint Vincent Ferreri (tempera on wood), a part of an altarpiece done by Francesco del Cossa for the Griffoni Chapel in Bologna (the central panel of the altar piece is to be found in London's National Gallery and the side panels are in the Brera Gallery in Milan), which depicts a number of miracles. These include the Revival of a Child Killed by His Mad, Pregnant Mother, the Extinguishing of a Fire, the Rescue of a Youth in Danger, the Resurrection of the Jewess, and the Healing of the Crippled Woman. The Pieta of

Lucas Cranach the Elder (tempera on wood) has a quite visible Cranach monogram (a small winged snake) at the base of the tomb.

Polyptychs is the main category in Room VI. You'll find two works by Carlo Crivelli—Madonna and Child and Pieta (both tempera on wood). Then there is a tempera on wood, the Camerino triptych, by Niccolo di Liberatore (also called Alunno). The central panel shows Christ crucified, the two Marys, and Saint John. Other panels contain likenesses of Saint Peter, Saint Venantius, Saint Porphyry, and Saint John the Evangelist. David, the Resurrection, and Isaiah are in the pinnacles. The missing pinnacles, by the way, are on display in the Louvre. Antonio Vivarini did a wood painting in tempera in 1469 of Saint Anthony Abbot and other saints. This is a rather complex polyptych comprising a wooden statue of Saint Anthony and a series of panels painted with figures of Christ in the tomb and Saints Peter, Paul, Jerome, Benedict, Christopher, Venantius, Sebastian, and Vitus.

The fifteenth century Umbrian School is given good representation in Room VII what with such painters as Bernardino di Betto (better known as Pinturicchio), Pietro Vannucci (better known as Perugino), and Giovanni Santi (better known as Raphael's father). Pinturicchio's Coronation of the Virgin (tempera on canvas) shows the apostles and Saints Francis, Bernardino, Anthony of Padua, Louis of Toulouse, and Bonaventura at the Virgin's feet. Pinturicchio did this in 1502 for a minor order of Umbertide's Monastery near Perugia.

The Perugino tempera on wood is called Madonna and Child with Saints, and though commissioned in 1483, it was completed in 1495 for the Chapel of the Palazzo dei Priori Perugia. Shown in the masterpiece are the patron saints of Perugia (Lawrence, Louis, Herculanus, and Constant) who are at the Virgin's feet. The original frame and the Crown of this work are presently in Perugia and will very likely remain there forever. Giovanni Santi produced a tempera on canvas called Saint Jerome Enthroned. Though Raphael may have learned some of his art under his father, the painting on exhibit is a decidedly mediocre work that was done for the Church of Saint Bartholomew in Pesaro. Raphael's father's signature in Latin—Johannes Santis De Urbino P.—can be seen on the step of the throne.

It's easy to compare Raphael's works with that of his less-talented dad by stepping into the next chamber, Room VIII which is wholly devoted to Raphael (whose name in Italian is Raffaello Santi). This room could easily take up a whole hour of your time —and should! The Coronation of the Virgin (tempera on canvas) has the apostles and Saints Thomas, Peter, Paul, and John witnessing the event. Raphael did this painting for the Oddi Family in 1502–1503, and at one time adorned the Church of San Francesco in Perugia and even made a trip to Paris in 1797. The Madonna of Foligno (another tempera on canvas) was commissioned in 1512 by Sigismondo de' Conti who is shown kneeling before Saint Jerome, praying for the protection of his house from lightning.

Raphael's Transfiguration (an oil on wood commissioned in 1517 and finished in 1520) has Christ between Moses and Elijah with Saints Peter, John, James, and at the side Saints Julian and Lawrence. Below shows the apostles and the episode of the possessed child whose relatives are seen begging for God's mercy. This masterpiece was finished a very short while before Raphael's death, and, since it was done entirely by his own hand (with a few minor contributions by his workshop), is considered by cognoscenti to be the ''manifesto'' of the artist's style in his last years. The painting was commissioned by Cardinal Giulio de' Medici who intended to donate it to the Cathedral of Narbonne, but after Raphael died in 1520, the Cardinal decided against that and presented it to the Church of San Pietro in Montorio, Rome, and in 1523 it was unveiled there.

Another special treat in this room are the tapestries of Raphael with 10 scenes from the Acts of the Apostles—these being the Blinding of Elima, the Conversion of Saul, the Stoning of Saint Stephen, Saint Peter healing a cripple, the Death of Ananias, the Handing over of the Keys, the Miraculous Draught of Fishes, Saint Paul's Sermon in Athens, the Sacrifice of Lystra, and Saint Paul in Prison. These tapestries were commissioned by Pope Leo

X in 1515 to decorate the side walls of the presbytery of the Sistine Chapel. For these Raphael, assisted by his students, did the cartoons; the execution was by Pieter van Aelst in Brussels.

In Room IX you will find Leonardo da Vinci's Saint Jerome (tempera on wood), a work with a most unusual history. It was once owned by one of the greatest women artists in history, Angelika Kauffmann, who apparently lost it while living in Rome. Years later Cardinal Joseph Fesch's agents found the work in two different places: the part with the Saint Jerome's torso was being used as the lid to a trunk in an antique dealer's shop, and the part with the head was being used by a shoemaker as the seat of his stool. This lost Leonardo was expertly restored. The other major painting in Room IX is part of Giovanni Bellini's Pieta (tempera on wood) which shows the dead Christ, Mary Magdalen, Nicodemus, and Joseph of Arimathea. Bellini painted this in 1470 for the Church of San Francesco in Pesaro. The French removed this work to Paris, but some years later it was returned to Italy and placed in the Vatican Pinacoteca.

The sixteenth century Venetian painters that occupy Room X include Titian as the ''star'' and his Madonna of the Frari (oil on canvas), an altarpiece that was done in 1525 for the Church of San Niccolo dei Frari on Lido Island in Venice, is marred by the fact that the upper part, alas, has been lost. The painting shows the Madonna, at whose feet are Saints Sebastian, Francis, Anthony of Padua, Nicholas, Peter, and Catherine of Alexandria. Though only partial, this painting is an exquisite work that has been given a value of well over $1 million.

Better known by his pen name (brush name?) of Veronese, the artist Paolo Caliari did an oil of Saint Helen that at one time belonged to the Pio di Carpi Family. Pope Benedict XIV purchased this work for the Pinacoteca. An oil on wood called Saint George and the Dragon is the work of one Paris Bordone and once belonged to the parish church of Noale, near Treviso. Giulio Pippi (also known as Giulio Romano) and Francesco Penni collaborated in 1525 on an oil called the Coronation of the Virgin which they did for the nuns of the Convent of Monteluce in Perugia. The upper part is the work of Giulio Romano and the lower part that of

Penni. Originally, the commission was given to Raphael, but after his death, his two students carried out the work according to his designs.

Late sixteenth century works are featured in Room XI. There's an oil on wood by Giorgio Vasari (The Stoning of Saint Stephen), an oil on canvas by Giuseppe Cesari, also known as Cavaliere d'Arpino (Annunciation), an oil on canvas by Girolamo Muziano (the Resurrection of Lazarus) that received high praise from Michelangelo (a fact that zoomed Muziano to fame), a tempera on wood by Niccolo Filotesio (Assumption), an oil on canvas by Federico Barocci (Rest on the Flight into Egypt) and another oil on canvas by Barocci (Blessed Michelina). Barocci's oil on the Flight into Egypt also goes under another name, Madonna of the Cherries. It has been donated to the Church of the Jesuits in Perugia, and after the Society was suppressed the painting was taken to Rome and in 1802 was given to the Vatican.

Baroque works occupy all of Room XII. Painted by Jean de Boulogne (known as Valentin), an oil on canvas called Martyrdom of Saint Processus and Saint Martinian was originally for an altar in Saint Peter's. It was removed (and replaced by a mosaic copy) and taken to the Quirinal Palace, then to Paris in 1797, and eventually was brought to the Vatican. Domenico Zampieri (also known as Domenichino) did an oil on canvas in 1614 called Communion of Saint Jerome which he painted in 1614 for the Church of San Gerolamo della Carita. Caravaggio (whose real name was Michelangelo Amerighi) is represented with an oil on canvas that is entitled Deposition. This painting, which was done in 1604, has the distinction of having versions of it painted by Rubens and Cézanne.

Commissioned by Cardinal Scipione Borghese for the Abbey of Saint Paul of the Tre Fontane in Rome, the Crucifixion of Saint Peter is an oil on canvas by Guido Reni. Giovan Francesco Barbieri (known also as Guercino) did an oil on canvas in 1623 called Saint Mary Magdalen. The painting was executed for the Church of Saint Magdalen of the Convertite of Rome, but this church is now destroyed and the painting hangs in the Pinacoteca. The largest painting ever made by Nicholas Poussin (an oil on canvas that measures 10.5 feet by 9.3 feet) is the Martyrdom of Saint Erasmus that had been commissioned by Cardinal Francesco Barberini in 1630. It was for the left tribune of Saint Peter's where it was eventually replaced by a mosaic copy.

Room XIII occupies itself with the seventeenth and eighteenth century. While living in Rome, Anton van Dyck did an oil on canvas, Saint Francis Xavier, over a period that embraced the years 1622–1623 for the Church Il Gesu. Nearby is a work of Pietro Berrettini da Cortona, The Virgin Appears to Saint Francis, an oil on canvas. In Leningrad there is a copy of this mature work. The Martyrdom of Saint Lawrence by Jose de Ribera (known often as Spagnoletto) is an oil on canvas, done by the artist while still a young man.

Room XIV has various subjects that include Daniele Segher's Garland of Flowers with Madonna and Child, Nicolas Poussin's The Battle of Gideon, and Donato Creti's Astronomical Observations. This last work, executed for the observatory of Bologna devoted to astronomy, shows the sun, moon, Mercury, Venus, Mars, Jupiter, Saturn, and a comet. The Poussin work, by the way, is one of his early attempts and was made in 1624 soon after he went to Rome.

Room XV is devoted to portraits that show Titian at his best in this particular type of painting. His The Doge Niccolo Marcello is a posthumous portrait of the man and was painted on canvas around 1542. Of special interest in this masterwork is Titian's use of Niccolo Marcello's innovation of painting dogal garments interwoven with gold, a fact that brought the custom later on. Thomas Lawrence's George IV of England is an oil on canvas that is signed in capital letters: SIR THO. LAWRENCE on the lower part of the curtain. The painting shows an opened letter, dated 1816, sent by the pope to the King, on whose left leg is the Badge of the Garter. King George IV donated the painting to Pope Pius VII. Painted in 1669, Carlo Maratta's Clement IX is an oil on canvas that Louis Mendelssohn of Detroit donated to the Vatican. One of the most curious paintings in the Pinacoteca is to be found in this room: it is Giuseppe Maria Cresci's Benedict XIV, an oil on canvas. It was painted for Prospero Lambertini while he was still a Cardinal and Archbishop of Bologna. After he was elected pope, the robes of cardinal that Cresci had painted were repainted as papal vestments.

Room XVI is usually used for exhibits of short duration. Room XVII houses an array of original clay models fashioned by Bernini, built for the Chapel of the Holy Sacrament in Saint Peter's. Room XVIII contains the Vatican's Byzantine Icon collection, 115 paintings in all of tempera on wood, dating from the fifteenth to the nineteenth century, most of which are Greek and Slavic in origin. The works represent biblical and evangelical calendars with saints.

The Pinacoteca is one of the best-stocked masterpiece museums in the world. *(Photo by Irene Rooney)*

The Gregorian
Profane Museum

MOST OF THE MATERIAL from the sites in the former Papal States—which existed from 754 to 1870—are contained in the so-called Gregorian Profane Museum, which Pope John XXIII opened to the public in 1970. Actually this museum is the collection of antiquities that were previously on exhibit in the Lateran Museum, a collection set up by Pope Gregory XVI which opened in May 1844. The main sections of the Profane Museum are the sections devoted to the Roman Imperial Age (first to third centuries A.D.), copies and versions of Greek originals of the classical age (fifth to fourth centuries B.C.), and an array of Roman sculpture set up in chronological order. These include such things as historical portraits and reliefs, urns, funeral monuments, sarcophagi, cult sculpture, and decorative reliefs.

Section I of the Profane Museum is devoted to Roman Imperial Age copies and versions of Greek originals from the first to the third centuries A.D. In the first room you will find copies of Myron's famous bronze group of Athena and Marsyas and a cast of the Lancellotti Athena. There are a Statue of Marsyas from the Esquiline, u Torso of Marsyas from Castel Gandolfo, and a Fragment of the Head of Athene, completed in plaster. The group of bronzes by Myron of Eleutherae were put in as a votive offering in the Athenian Acropolis in about the middle of the fifth century B.C. Described by Pausanias and Pliny, it was also depicted on coins. Through Roman copies in marble, only parts of it have been preserved. The scene shows the imperious gesture of the goddess as she prevents the satyr Marsyas from taking away the double flute which she has just devised.

Among a group of heads on the left is a 440 B.C. basalt head, a copy of a Greek honorary statue known as *Idolino,* representing a
164

young athlete who is the victor at the Delphic (Olympian) games. He is offering a drink with a sacrificial patera in the style of Polyclitus.

Nearby are a number of portraits of famous Greeks. The statue of Sophocles, the Athenian tragic dramatist, is in the center of the room. On stylistic grounds this is thought to be the copy of the statue on display in the Theatre of Dionysus in Athens that had been commissioned by Sophocles' son Iophon. The dramatist is shown in his prime—self-confident, his cloak thrown casually around his shoulders, his gaze fixed on something in the distance. The headband shows his status as priest of the cult of Aesculapius. When this cult initially appeared in Athens, Sophocles brought it directly into his own home. Although Sophocles was always criticized by his peers as being ''a favorite of the gods,'' namely ''blessed'' and ''protected'' from man's problems, Sophocles' plays (7 out of 123 he wrote) survived, proving he definitely could relate to human feelings.

A portrait of Homer (broken) and a portrait of the Greek lyric poet, Anacreon, are next in view. The latter is a marble copy of a portrait statue which Pericles commissioned from Phidias in 440 B.C. for the Acropolis. The adjoining small chamber contains a Hellenistic relief from the first century B.C., with figures of a woman and a comedian poet holding a theatrical mask. The male figure is thought to be that of Menander, the most prominent author of Greek New Comedy (the so-called Attic comedy of the fourth century B.C.). The female figure is probably a Muse or a personification of comedy.

The large floor mosaic has been reconstructed from fragments that were dug out of an old building on the Aventine. Lost are the central part and other parts of the framing strips. The inner part is decorated with figures of animals from the Nile region. The outer strip shows the floor of a dining room covered with the leftover food of a lush banquet; there is even a mouse gnawing away at a nut. Along one side of the white stripe are six theatrical masks and some other objects.

On the right-hand side is a gallery of hermae (the word now used for any kind of statue that is in the form of a pillar). Also note nearby a triangular base with reliefs depicting Dionysian festivals. Attributed to Praxiteles are copies of the Resting Satyr—this is a fourth century B.C. famous Attic work that has often been copied. A statue of Neptune (or the Colossus of Poseidon) shows the god of the sea resting his right foot on the bow of a ship, alongside which is a large dolphin that is holding up the statue. Since the eyes are looking down, it is apparent that the statue once stood in an elevated position. Emphasizing the greatness of the statue is the crown of flowing hair and the expression of controlled passion. It is believed that the model of this work was a fourth century A.D. bronze that was famous in its day as it was depicted on silver coins of the Hellenistic period.

Behind the statue just outside the room there is a relief with Medea and the daughters of Pelias. The theme of this work is based on a story about the witch Medea who has convinced Pelias' daughters that they can rejuvenate their father by segmenting him into pieces and boiling the parts with magic herbs in a pot which is being watched by one of the daughters while the other is holding a sword pensively. This scene comes across with a strong sense of dramatic tension. This work is a first century B.C. copy of a late fifth century B.C. original.

On the right is a room with robed male torsos, Roman copies of Greek statues of heroes and gods. The copyists have apparently added portrait heads of Roman personages. Nearby are copies of female statues of the classical age, and on the right is the upper part of a statue of Artemis. The remaining fragments of a goat are visible on the left arm. Next is a headless statue (probably of Diana) and then a torso of a statue of Athene (of the Rospigliosi type, the original of which is linked with Timotheos' work of 360 B.C.). Also included are two draped female statues of Aurae, copies from Palestrina.

Of particular interest is the Chiaramonti Niobid. Niobe was the wife of the King of Thebes, with whom she had seven sons and seven daughters and often bragged about her many children to Leto who only had two children, Apollo and Artemis. Both of them were enraged by the insult to their mother and killed all 14 of Niobe's children with arrows. Nearby is the torso of a statue of Diana the Huntress; the swift forward movement of the figure is emphasized by her flowing drapery. This is a Roman copy of a Greek original from the fourth century B.C.

Section II of the Profane Museum keeps Roman sculpture of the first and early second century. Almost upon entering you are struck immediately with an art curio—two portraits of the same man side by side. The man's identity is controversial (and some observers say it's not the same man), but the general consensus is that it is Virgil. Less impressive are the three funeral reliefs with portraits of families of Roman freedmen.

There is a round altar dedicated to Mercy, which is decorated with garlands of fruit and 10-stringed citherns. Under each garland are such things as hammer, tongs, anvil, and a cap worn by artisans. Reminiscent of the magnificent festoons of the Ara Pacis of Augustus found at Veii are the finely carved, gracefully arranged ornaments on a copy of the altar dedicated by Scribonius Libo in the Roman Forum. There is also an idealized statue of Drusus the Elder, brother of Tiberius (or Drusus the Younger) who is seen with a mantle around his hips. Since it has always been difficult to identify with any degree of certainty the members of the Julian-Claudian Family, because they all, remarkably, look alike, it is hard to decide which of the Drusi it is.

From the round tomb near Vicovaro, 21 marble fragments have been assembled in an effort to give a general idea of what the original structure looked like. The pieces include four fragments, with palmette frieze, from the upper edge of the drum, eight fragments of the cornice at the top of the drum, and nine roof blocks arranged in alternating vertical and horizontal ways. On the outer surfaces are the decorations of reliefs of ox skulls and festoons. The ornaments and the shape of the tomb make it quite clear that it was constructed in 20–40 A.D. during the time of Tiberius or Claudius. In front of the Vicovaro Tomb are sculptures of the first century A.D. found in the Roman theater at Cerveteri during archeological diggings that lasted from 1840 to 1846.

Next in line is a pair of sleeping sileni, their heads resting on a wineskin. This work was very likely a fountain. The togated statue nearby has a restored neck, and art experts are not yet convinced that the head and body belong together. The draped female figure, which is a copy of a Greek original from the fourth century B.C., was made in the nineteenth century.

Three Etruscan cities — Vetulonia, Vulci, and Tarquinia — are inscribed on a relief with personifications: a man standing under a pine tree with an oar over his left shoulder, a veiled woman sitting on a throne holding a flower in her right hand, a man wearing a toga (he is believed to be Tarchon, the mythical founder of Tarquinia). The relief was found together with the seated statue of Claudius and may have formed part of the throne of the same statue; this work is thought to comprise an expression of gratitude for the emperor who had taken a special interest in the region. Close to this work is a so-called Colossal, a seated statue of Emperor Claudius (41–54 A.D.). He is wearing a civic crown of oak leaves. There is another Colossal, this one of Emperor Tiberius (14–37 A.D.) seated with a civic crown of oak leaves. On the metal trellis are inscriptions from the area of the Theater of Caere in honor of Augustus, Germanicus Caesar, Drusilia, Agrippina the Younger, Claudius, and the senate of Caere.

In front of the hemicycle is an altar dedicated to Manlius, censor of Caere. The scene shows the sacrifice of a bull. On the back is a female deity who sits on a rock and is surrounded by worshippers; the deity may be Fortune, a local goddess. On each side a protective local god of houses or fields dances between two olive trees. This work is from the first century B.C. Three statues — one a draped female statue and the other two wearing loricas — have special interest for historians, for she is Agrippina the Younger (15–59 A.D.), who was the wife of Emperor Claudius and the mother of Nero. The hairstyle she has is typical of the early Empire. This copy of a fifth century B.C. original idealizes the body of the empress to the point that it has the appearance of a goddess.

Standing opposite the Caere group, towards the back, is a relief from the altar of the Vicomagistri, found sometime in 1939 on the site of the present Palace of the Apostolic Chancery. This relief very likely decorated the base of a large altar of the Imperial Age. Expertly shown is a sacrificial procession in which two consuls are accompanied by Roman soldiers acting as bodyguards; the three victims are accompanied by their executioners, while flutists and cithern-players march along, together with five veiled youths and figures wearing togas and laurel wreaths (the Vico-magistri). The youths who walk in front of the Vicomagistri are holding statuettes in their left hands, one of which represents two dancing lares with drinking horn and the other a togated figure (the Genius Augusti).

Once you move away from the Vicomagistri Altar, you come upon the Altar of Augustus Pontifex Maximus, a twelfth century A.D. work. Relief art is to be found on all four sides: on the front is a winged Victory with a round shield bearing the words, ''The senate and people of Rome have dedicated this altar to the emperor Augustus, son of the divine Caesar in his capacity as Pontifex Maximus.'' On the back is a deification of Caesar and on the two sides are seen a sacrifice to the lares and the prophecy made to Aeneas regarding Laurentus' son.

On the next trellis are portraits of the Julian-Claudian age. There is a portrait of Livia, the second wife of Augustus who died at the age of 86 and was defied under Claudius in 41 A.D. There is a Colossal head of Augustus from Veii who became emperor in 31 B.C., which is the date of the naval victory at Actium. Augustus died in August 14 A.D. at the age of 76, and the portrait was made after his death. Other works included in this group are the Princes of the Julian Claudian Family, Tiberius (stepson and successor of the Emperor Augustus), and, behind the wall, funeral urns and altars of the first century A.D. Most of the funeral altars on exhibit here were found in 1825 in the Volussi Columbarium on the Appian Way. The urns here are varied in shape, with their lids in the form of a sloping roof. Into these urns — square, rectangular, or round — the remains of the cremated were placed.

The ashes urn in the form of a richly decorated altar also belongs to this group — it is located in the area below the stairs at the left. At the corners are two candelabra, and on the face are the inscription, the head of Medusa, and a large festoon. An amusing scene below gives light to a cockfight organized by two cupids, the winner of the two being embraced by its owner as it holds a wreath in its claws. Meanwhile the weeping master of the loser carries away his defeated bird. The other side shows festoons and nests of baby birds that are being fed by their mothers. This first century A.D. work is an example of rare workmanship.

Another cinerary urn shows two men pressing grapes in a vat. Nearby, below the stairs, is a funeral altar of Claudius Dionysius who is shown standing as he holds his wife's hand. A second relief depicts the same Claudius resting in bed with his wife sitting next to him; her hairstyle is typical of the Claudian age.

With the Altar of Gaius Julius Postumus, the first century A.D. decorations suggest that the deceased was a child. On the front side a boy is feeding grapes to a hare, and next to him a taller boy is wearing a toga. On the right a boy plays with a dog, and on the left a boy wheels a carriage with a child in it. Up until the Year 1025 this funeral altar was used as a Holy Water basin in the Church of the Navicella. On the left is the base of a column from the Julian Basilica in the Roman Forum, an example of advanced skill achieved in the carving of marble architectural ornaments in the early Flavian age. As for the two large reliefs that follow, these are known as the Chancery Reliefs because they were found under the Palace of the Apostolic Chancery.

Frieze B is the Arrival of the Emperor Vespasian (69–70 A.D.) in Rome. Easily recognizable, he is the noble-looking, togated figure on the right side of the frieze. His son (Domitian), also wearing a toga, is welcoming his father. The scene is set in the outskirts of Rome. Included in the emperor's retinue are a winged Victory, holding a wreath of oak leaves over the emperor's head. Domitian is flanked by the Genius of the senate and the Genius of the people—the latter resting one foot on the boundary stone. Vespasian greets the Roman population, and as he sits on the throne on the left, he is surrounded by Vestal Virgins. The artwork of this historic event was commissioned by Domitian who later himself became emperor and ruled from 81 to 96 A.D.

Frieze A is the departure of Emperor Domitian. Dressed in a tunic and a traveling cloak, Domitian is surrounded by deities, genii, lictors, and soldiers. Preceding him are Minerva, Mars, lictors, and Victory, whose left wing is still visible, though about a

yard of the left slab is missing. The emperor is led by the arm by
Virtue, and the Genius of the senate and the Genius of the people
are both behind him, bidding him farewell. They are followed by
freelance professional soldiers and the regular army. In one hand
Domitian is holding a scroll, and he raises the other in a command gesture. Curiously, Domitian's face was later scratched out
and replaced with that of Nerva, his successor who ruled from 96
to 98 A.D.

To the right on the wall is a fragment of a portrait of Titus who
was emperor from 79 to 81 A.D. Most of the skullcap, the nape of
his neck, and part of his forehead are missing. That which remains, especially of the face, shows a beautifully modeled portrait
that is untouched by the hands of restorers. Beyond Frieze A are
39 fragments from the Haterii Tomb, excavated in 1848 and discovered outside Porta Maggiore, near Centocelle. Additional
excavations undertaken in early 1970 resulted in the discovery of
new epigraphical and sculptural material, which is now owned by
the Italian State. On the other side of the trellis where Frieze A is
on display are shrines with the busts of a man and woman of the
Haterii Family, which are in perfect condition. Under his short
curly hair, the man has a most expressive face dominated by bristly
eyebrows. He wears a garment thrown over his left shoulder. The
bust is supported by a writhing serpent, an allusion to the man's
heroic past.

Not far away is a relief representing five buildings from ancient
Rome. From left to right, they are (1) Arch with three barrel
vaults and the inscription, Arcus ad Isis. This served as the
monumental entrance to the Temple of Isis and Serapis in the
Campus Martius. During the eleventh century it was known as
the Arch of Camillo, probably erected to commemorate the victory over Judea. (2) The Flavian amphitheatre, known to everybody as the Colosseum. (3) Triumphal Arch, generally identified
as the one erected in 81 A.D. in Titus' honor. Through the
passage of the Circus Maximus, you can distinguish the Magna
Mater enthroned between lions. (4) This is the Triumphal Arch
with the inscription, *Arcus in Sacra Via Summa.* This arch was
erected in honor of Titus on the highest point of the Velia. (5)

Temple of the Thunderer at the approach to the Capitoline Hill; behind the altar there is a cult statue of Jove with thunderbolts and sceptre. Destroyed by fire in 80 A.D., the temple was reconstructed during the time of Domitian. It is understood that the tomb was built for Domitian and his family by a building contractor who had been involved in the reconstruction of all the edifices shown here, all of which are of the Flavian age.

The exhibit continues with a relief in two parts—with scenes of corpse and mourners. The lamps and torches are arranged around the large funeral bed, which is in the atrium of a house. Behind the bed are wailing women and below are mourning servants and a flutist. The Fragment of a portal with busts of four gods of the Underworld show Mercury, Proserpine, Pluto, and Ceres. The missing section underneath was also decorated.

A relief representing a funeral edifice and crane stands on a high podium, lined with columns and pilasters. Richly decorated, it has the busts of three children, and on the pediment is the bust of a woman, probably the one who has died. The scene above the building shows the inside of the tomb, with the dead woman lying on a bed. Down beneath is depicted a woman performing a sacrifice at a burning altar, in front of which three children are seen playing. To the right is a small shrine with a statue of Venus. Below the stairs on the podium are a canopied altar and what is probably the place of cremation. The crane on the left was operated by the force of the weight of the workmen inside the wheel.

One of the finest examples of Roman decorative art is the Pillar of the Roses, two sides ornamented with the same motif: a candelabrum with roses and olive branches and two long-tailed birds. In the first window compartment on the right is a bust of L. Julius Ursus (he was a confidant of Emperors Trajan and Domitian). Ursus was the man who prevented the execution of Empress Domitia Longina. This work was once the property of the Duke of Wellington. On a trellis is a relief with the procession of Roman magistrates before a temple. On the temple pediment is depicted the myth of Rhea Silvia, the twins and the wolf. The second figure is the head of Trajan, a restoration by Bertel Thorvaldsen, a Danish sculptor.

Behind the columns on the wall is a fragment of a tomb relief, which has an inscription missing on its central slab. On the left is a togated figure offering a drink, and below is a man asleep in a grotto. Above, while cupids are carrying garlands, a cockfight is taking place. Another tomb relief shows circus races in honor of a dead man. A Roman chariot with four horses abreast is racing along the wall separating two tracks; several signposts are prominent, including an obelisk, two columns with statues, and a shrine with four dolphins on the roof. A winner is seen holding a palm leaf. The large figure on the left is the deceased, dressed in a toga and holding a scroll in his left hand, while his right hand is extended towards his wife.

On the left, above, is a fragment of a pediment of a funeral monument which is on the Appian Way. Supporting the bust (meant to represent the soul of the dead woman — Claudia Semne) are cupids. Below is a tomb relief of Ulpia Epigone who is shown supine on a couch. At her feet is a sewing box, and under her arm is a lapdog. Her hairstyle is typical of the Flavian-Trajan period. An unfinished statue to the Dacian campaign (the Dacians were a Balkan people conquered by Trajan) is the Colossus of a barbarian prisoner. This statue was from another monument and used again here.

On the trellis in front of the hemicycle is a fragment of relief with standard bearer. The insignia is that of the Praetorian Guards, and it makes frequent appearances on columns erected by Trajan and Marcus Aurelius. Evidently part of a military scene, this fragment is from the second century A.D. As you move to the right, you see two fragments of the same architectural frieze that are probably from Trajan's Forum. On the amphora are relief decorations depicting a satyr and two maenads. Two cupids at the sides of the amphora are watering griffins. The legs of both cupids are transformed into acanthus leaves and spirals that harmonize with the abundant floral decorations.

Section III is devoted to sarcophagi and begins with those having mythological themes. The first one on the left deals with the labors of Hercules, the capture of the Cretan bull, the capture of the mares of King Diomedes, and the victory over Geryon. Above on the sarcophagus front is a scene of Meleager killing the Caledonian boar. And on the right in front of the trellis is a sarcophagus with scenes of the myth of Adonis. The young hunter Adonis takes leave of Aphrodite who is seated on a throne surrounded by cupids. You see on the right a boar who is about to attack and another scene in which Adonis falls mortally wounded. Now you see Aphrodite who is grieving after the loss of Adonis and is begging the god of the underworld to let him spend six months of the year on earth. This is quite indicative of the theme of life after death. Both the faces of Adonis and Aphrodite are portraits. The lid on the Adonis sarcophagus has scenes from the saga of Oedipus (note: the lid does not belong to this). From left to right are Laius' sacrifice before the Delphic Apollo, Laius and the exposure of Oedipus, and Oedipus fleeing from Corinth. Also there is a second series in which Oedipus kills Laius in the chariot and in which you are given the riddle of the Sphinx and its interpretations by a Theban shepherd.

Moving to the other side of the pillar you come across a sarcophagus slab with the myth of Adonis. There is the scene of Adonis taking leave of Aphrodite, and also a picture of the struggle with the boar. Note that the style and treatment of the same subject preceding are different. At the right is a sarcophagus with scenes from the myth of Phaedra and Hippolytus. The wife of Theseus, Phaedra (who is the stepmother of Hippolytus), reveals her love for the youth. Leaving for the hunt Hippolytus turns down his stepmother's offers. Another scene shows Hippolytus hunting boar, accompanied by a female figure wearing a helmet. On the fragments of the lid are hunting scenes, the sacrifice to Artemis, and hunters on horseback.

Bearing seals from the years 132 and 134 A.D., the tiles are from the tomb in which the next three sarcophagi were found in 1839 near the Porta Viminalis. The sarcophagus with scenes from the myth of Orestes shows him and Pylades at the tomb of Agamemnon who can be distinguished as the shadowy figure below the vault. Other pictures include the death of Aegisthus from whom Orestes is taking the royal cloak, the murder of Clytemnestra, and Orestes' purification at Delphi, to which the tripod, laurel and omphalos allude. On the left side are the shadowy figures of Aegisthus and Clytemnestra on Charon's boat. The lid contains a picture of Orestes and Iphigenia in Tauris.

Nearby on the right is a sarcophagus with two Gorgonian masks and festoons of fruit supported by a small satyr and two cupids. On the lid are some cupids racing various animals. The third sarcophagus represents the slaughter of the Niobids. On the lid are Apollo and Artemis in small size. To avenge their mother, Artemis is shooting arrows at Niobe's helpless children, as the powerless parents are forced to watch. Niobe and Amphion are then shown at their children's tomb, but there is also a scene with a shepherd and his oxen in a rocky landscape.

As you enter the next compartment, you see on the outer wall a sarcophagus slab with the myths of Mars and Rhea Silvia on the left side and Selene and Endymion on the right. The two myths are symbolic of the participation of mortals in the lives of the gods. The heads of Mars and Rhea Silvia are portraits, while those of Selene and Endymion are restorations.

On the opposite side is a sarcophagus with a Bacchic scene. Dionysis (Bacchus) is seen in a chariot drawn by two centaurs. On the right is Ariadne in a similar chariot. Both are flanked by followers. Both the lid and the sarcophagus are in excellent condition. This is a good example of a Roman sarcophagus in its original state and is from the second century A.D.

Sarcophagus with the Seasons follows. This piece has two cupids holding a medallion that has on it a portrait of a woman. Down beneath, a cupid disguises himself with a big mask of Silenus to scare his small friend. Both on the left and the right sides are four more cupids who represent the Seasons. This is from the third century A.D. Next, on the outer wall is the front of a large sarcophagus with philosophers. Enthroned in the center, the sage is reading from a scroll to a man and two veiled women, one of whom holds a closed scroll. Bearded figures appear on both sides, and on the right is a sundial that is barely visible. As for the imposing figure in the middle, he is believed to be Plotinus who reached Rome from Alexandria in 244 A.D., lived in The Eternal City and died in Minturnum in 270.

On the opposite side is a fragment of an oval sarcophagus

which bears a bearded philosopher and the hands of a cloaked figure holding a scroll. There is a fragment of a lid on which a cockfight is going on. Near the end of the Gallery of the Sarcophagi, to the left of the glass door, is a sarcophagus of a child with representations of athletes who are boxing, wrestling, and engaging in a contest consisting of the combination of boxing and wrestling (known as pancratium at the time). The judges, all bearded, are holding palms. At the left the victor is getting his award, while a herald blows his trumpet to let everybody know of the victory.

The exhibit of sarcophagi terminates with a third century A.D. sarcophagus with representations of the growing and processing of wheat. This one is at the left in front of the stairs. In the upper part a peasant is seen working a plough drawn by two oxen and another turning the soil over. The right side shows a cart taking the wheat to the mill, followed by two workmen turning the millstone, and a scene of bread being baked. The central part offers a portrait of the deceased man, a baker, dressed in a toga and holding a scroll. On the lid is his name and a bit of Latin verse based on a Greek epigram in which the deceased dismisses Hope and Fortune, leaving them to make fools of everybody who will survive him.

Section IV deals with Roman sculpture of the second and third century A.D. Behind the statue of the Dacian are three fragments from a large historical frieze from the time of Hadrian. In patrician boots, the figure in a toga is the Emperor Hadrian, although some art experts are still not in agreement about this. On the left is a portrait of a member of his retinue, and it may be that of one of the Caesernii brothers who accompanied Hadrian. Nearby is the Statue of Antinous, and since the original head has never been found, the present one is a restoration. The following portrait of a bearded man in a Greek helmet has the type of face and the treatment of eyes that show it is a late work from the time of Hadrian, depicting Mars.

Skillfully carved, the relief fragments with two wrestlers is believed to have decorated a large monument that inspired Raphael to make a drawing of it, mostly to fill in the missing parts. A heavily restored funeral relief stands on the opposite side of the trellis. It shows a young warrior astride a horse as he greets a woman sitting on a throne, while a slave holds his master's spear in the background. Serving as an allusion to the heroization of the deceased are a laurel and a serpent. On the left are fragments of togated statues in porphyry, reserved for representations of Roman emperors, and on the right there is a torso wearing a lorica—a masterly work in porphyry (very likely a representation of Trajan or Hadrian).

On the left in the initial window compartment there is a relief from the Fountain of Amalthea. You see a nymph offering water to a young satyr from a large vase. Young Pan is playing his syrinx in a grotto nearby; water spouts from the hole in the drinking horn. In front of the partition that separates the two windows are eight Roman portraits of the first half of the third century A.D., among which is to be found the young Caracalla (211–217 A.D.), son and successor of Septimius Severus. In the second window compartment are two fragments of ornate pillar facings and a statue of Omphale. Although the statuary style is reminiscent of Aphrodite, it is now certain that the club and lion-skin identify the subject as Omphale—she was the Lydian queen whom Hercules was ordered to serve but who took on his attributes in a reversal of roles.

Now follow Roman portraits of the third century. At the entrance to the next room is a togated statue of Dogmatius (Gaius Caelius Saturninus). Underneath him is an inscription that lists the offices held by Dogmatius, who was a consul and intimate of the Emperor Constantine. By turning right you come to a room of Roman statues associated with mystery cults, and this is the Room of the Statue of Mithras. First you see Omphalos wrapped in bands, and this is attributed to the Delphic Apollo who took the sacred navel-stones from the goddess of the earth, the original mistress of Delphi. Next, the triangular base of a candelabrum has all three sides decorated: (1) Poseidon with a cloak and trident, one foot resting on a mound of earth. (2) Pluto with a cornucopia. (3) A goddess with peplos and sceptre. This is a neo-Attic work of classical inspiration made during the Roman Imperial Age.

In the Mithraic group, Mithras is seen killing the primigenial bull. The god in Persian dress is seen plunging his sword into the bull's neck. This scene is an important one in Mithraism because followers of the Mithras cult firmly believed that life on earth originated from the death of the primigenial bull. Notice the five ears of corn on the tail; they are symbols of vegetative energy. The dog seizes the soul by drinking the blood, while the serpent and scorpion force Darkness and Evil to try to impede the act of creation by drinking down the life-giving blood and seed of the bull.

An altar with the 12 labors of Hercules: according to the inscription, Publius Decimus Lucrio has fulfilled a vow to Hercules. The labors of Hercules are now depicted from left to right: the Nemean lion, the Hydra of Lerna, the Boar of Mount Erymanthus, the Hind of Ceryneia, the Stymphalian birds, the cleaning of the Augean stables, the victory over the Amazons, the horses of Diomedes, the Cretal bull, the struggle against Geryon, the capture of the dog Cerberus from the underworld, and the apples of the Hesperides.

The acts of the Apostles indicate the extent and power of the cult of Diana of Ephesus, who was an Asian deity similar to the Great Mother of the Gods. To respond to Paul's attempt to convert them, the Ephesians shouted their praise for Diana, but the town scribe reassured the populace with the words: ''Men of Ephesus, who knoweth not that the city of the Ephesians is temple-keeper of the great Diana and of the image that fell down from the skies?''

Identified by a staff with a snake coiled around it is Aesculapius who is depicted with a long cloak thrown over his left shoulder (his chest bare). Outside this room in a semicircular court is one of two floor mosaics discovered in 1824 at the Baths of Caracalla. To get a good view of the first mosaic, go up the stairs and you see the winding band dividing the mosaic into series of squares and rectangles that show Roman referees and athletes. The latter hold such things as a boxer's basket, a disc, sword, and victory palms. Some of the squares also contain objects that allude to the training sessions that used to go on at the Baths, such as an ointment jar, weights, discs, a crown, and a strigil.

Along the corridor are heads of satyrs and Dionysiac reliefs on display. To the right at the end of the corridor, in front of the window, are two matching hermae of a faun carrying the young Dionysus on his shoulders. A highly refined work, this was probably used to decorate a court or a garden. Down at the end of the corridor there is a semi-circular balcony, and from here you'll get a superb view of the second mosaic from the Baths of Caracalla, which is equally decorated with the figures of athletes and referees.

The Statue of Saint Peter overlooks the serenity of the Vatican Gardens. *(Photo by Irene Rooney)*

The Pio Christian Museum

AFTER HE SET UP a Commission for Christian Archeology to deal with excavations and maintenance of the catacombs, Pope Pius IX founded in 1854 the Pio Christian Museum which has a collection of Christian antiquities that has been on exhibit in the Lateran Palace up till 1963. The museum is divided into two sections—one dealing with sculpture, mosaics, and architectural fragments. The other concerns epigraphical material. Only the first section is open to visitors. It will be detailed here, for it comprises the best collection of sarcophagi to be found anywhere in the world; many clerics feel that the Museum should be renamed The Sarcophagi Museum. (In the second section, by the way, are historical inscriptions that have to do with public monuments bearing consular dates or with Christian dogmas and symbolic inscriptions. Correctly, the Vatican keeps this part closed because it holds little interest to the average tourist. Catholic clergy or scholars from abroad can visit, however, upon petition.)

Truly one of the most fascinating pieces of the fine collection of Christian epigraphs is the fragment (originally two fragments that have now been fused) discovered in Hieropolis in 1883. The inscriptions on the two fragments were identified as part of a metrical epigraph dictated by the Bishop Albercius of Hieropolis in the Acta Sanctorum. Proclaiming himself the ''disciple of the pure shepherd who leads his sheep to grace on the hills and plains,'' Bishop Albercius tells about his trip to Rome on the fragments. There, he reports, he saw a ''queen in golden robes and golden shoes. And I also saw there a people which possess a golden seal.'' Then the Bishop adds: ''Faith led me everywhere and set before me to eat in every place fish from the springs, big

180

and clean, caught by a pure virgin. And this she (Faith) offered always her friends to eat, and together with it a fine wine and to mix with the wine she offered bread.'' The Vatican believes that if the Christian interpretation of the text is accurate, then the two assembled fragments constitute one of the most important Christian epigraphs of Eucharistical content extant. If nothing else, it is the earliest one known (161–180 A.D.).

In a narrow passage that follows, you will see on a wall opposite a large window a sarcophagus panel from Saint Lawrence Outside the Walls, showing a young, beardless Christ who is wearing a short tunic and mantle. Christ is escorted by 12 bearded apostles —in the forefront are Peter and Paul. In the foreground are 15 sheep to symbolize the Christian flock.

After leaving the narrow passage, you come upon the Statue of the Good Shepherd. Expertly restored, the statue once belonged to the Mariotti Collection in the eighteenth century before it was donated to the Vatican. The figure represents a young shepherd with long curly hair. Dressed in a tunic, he is carrying a bag across his shoulders. This is a rare statue, and it represents The Good Shepherd himself.

Next to the statue there is a fourth century sarcophagus that has decorations on all the sides. The front side shows three shepherds standing on ornate pedestals—the bearded shepherd is standing in the center carrying a ram on his shoulders. The other two shepherds are each holding a sheep. The background is replete with a crowded wine scene with winged genii climbing the vine shoots, picking clusters of grapes, and putting them into a vat to be pressed. At the right side a small Psyche is offering grapes to a genie at repose. Below, on the left, another genie is milking a goat. The decorations on the end of the sarcophagus show scenes of country life during the four seasons of the year.

Nearby is another sarcophagus from the middle of the third century in the form of a bathtub. This was found in 1881 on the Via Salaria and purchased by Pope Leo XIII in 1891. This one has a shepherd with a ram on his shoulders and two other rams at his feet. On the left is a bearded man dressed as a philosopher who is seated between two persons who are listening. There are three women in the scene, one of them sitting down. A unique aspect to this frieze is that it is faithful to the art customs of the time, to place all the heads at the same level, irrespective of the different heights of the various figures. Thus, the two seated figures are somewhat larger in conception.

The next important sarcophagus—this one with a lid—is placed in front of a small niche on the outer wall. It was found in 1818 on the Via Prenestina on an estate of Massimi Family. Displaying its good condition, the sarcophagus is the only one in the Vatican that still retains traces of its original blue, red, and gold colors, although these have faded a lot.

In the center of the lid are three inscribed Bs and some hunting scenes. There is a bust of a man against the background of drapery supported by small genii. To the right a woman is depicted against a background of drapery as she prays. The central part has some lively agricultural and pastoral scenes.

Halfway through the next gallery, after you go down a few steps, is another sarcophagus (early fourth century) from the Cemetery of Saint Calixtus. The scenes on this one are the Resurrection of Lazarus, the Multiplication of the loaves and fishes, the Miracle of Cana, praying woman between Peter and Paul, healing of an injured woman, Peter taken prisoner, Miracle of the spring, the manger scene, and scenes of Jonah. There is a long metrical inscription on the upper edge which says that Crescens was buried here after four months of marriage and that his widow had him placed here against the wishes of her father-in-law but with the help of her mother-in-law.

In the dimly lit room at the end of the gallery, a visitor will see the so-called "dogmatic" sarcophagus, which was unearthed in the foundations of Saint Paul's Outside the Walls. Only the front part of this is decorated—the busts of the deceased couple are in the center. Another scene at the top shows God creating man and woman, Christ giving Adam an ear of corn and Eve a sheep. This is intended as a symbolic condemnation for Adam and Eve to work for their sustenance. Behind Eve is the tree of knowledge of Good and Evil. Other scenes include the Miracle of the Loaves, the Wedding at Cana, the Resurrection of Lazarus, the Adoration of the Magi, Daniel in the lion's den, Prophecy of Peter's denial, Peter taken prisoner, and Miracle of the spring.

In the same room is a cast of the sarcophagus in the Basilica of Sant'Ambrogio of Milan. This one has decorations on each of the four sides. Set against a background of the city walls of Jerusalem, the various scenes show Christ and the apostles, Elijah ascending to Heaven, Noah leaving the ark, the smaller figures of Adam and Eve under the tree of knowledge of Good and Evil, the sacrifice of Isaac and four apostles, the three young Judeans (Shadrach, Meshack, and Abednego) who are refusing to worship a statue erected by Nebuchadnezzar, the Magi before Herod, the manger scene, the tympanum monogram of Christ within a laurel wreath, and Alpha and Omega (the two apocalyptic letters).

Now come two fourth century sarcophagus fronts, both with two rows of reliefs, depicting scenes from the Old and New Testament. There now follows a sarcophagus taken from the area near the Basilica of San Sebastiano. The scenes on this sarcophagus, besides a portrait of the dead couple, have Christ entering Jerusalem, Christ between Adam and Eve, Moses receiving the tablet of the Law. One striking scene depicts the hand of the Angel of the Lord stopping the sacrifice of Isaac. Other scenes on this sarcophagus show Daniel in the lions' den, the healing of a man with palsy and of a man born blind, Peter taken prisoner, and the Prophecy of Peter's denial.

When you go down the stairs on the left side you see a sarcophagus with decorated ends, bearing an inscription from the Vatican Necropolis that reads: ''To my dearest wife Agapene who lived with her husband 55 years, one month, and five days and who was laid to rest 23 December. Crescentianus made this when he was alive.'' In letters that are a bit sloppy, the following was added after he died: ''Buried 30 August at the age of 101.'' The front part of this sarcophagus is divided into seven niches by spiral fluted columns with scenes of the Sacrifice of Isaac, Moses receiving the Law on Sinai, Christ healing the man born blind, Christ prophesying Peter's denial, healing of the bleeding woman, multiplication of the loaves, miracle of the spring, three youths in the furnace.

Past the stairs, in the center of a raised podium, there is a cast of the sarcophagus of Junius Bassus, the original of which (found in 1595) is now kept in the Room of Junius Bassus in the Treasury of Saint Peter's because of its iconographical importance. At the left end of the podium will be found a fourth century sarcophagus with five niches from Saint Paul's Outside the Walls. This shows the monogram of Christ within a laurel wreath. At the sides are two sentinels, one who is sleeping and the other contemplating the symbol of Christ. In the other niches formed by olive trees, are shown God with Abel and Cain, Peter taken prisoner, Martyrdom of Paul, Job (scolded by his wife for patience) being comforted by his friends.

In the center of the niche is an unusual sarcophagus dealing with the Crossing of the Red Sea. Viewable is a scene of a pharaoh and the Egyptian army pursuing the people of Israel who are passing "into the midst of the sea upon the dry ground while the waters were a wall unto them on their right hand and on their left." To the right you are shown Moses as he stretches out his hand towards the sea to make the waters close over the Egyptian army. Also included is a portrayal of the Prophetess Miriam singing a hymn of victory and thanksgiving.

Not much further on, by the outer, yellow wall is a series of sarcophagal fragments that do artistic justice to the Nativity and the Epiphany. In one of his sermons Saint Augustine explains that from the second century on, the Epiphany was a most common theme in early Christian art. "The Magi," he wrote, "were the first pagans to know Christ our Lord, and these early Gentiles deserve to symbolize all peoples." Depicted in short tunics and Phrygian caps, the Magi are accompanied by their camels. In another tract, Saint Matthew states that the Magi came from the East, led by a star, to the Temple of Herod in Jerusalem. Herod directed them to Bethlehem, where they found the Messiah, worshipped Him, and offered Him gifts of gold, frankincense, and myrrh.

Among these remarkable fragments, you should take special note of the enthroned Madonna as she holds the Christ Child, to whom the Magi are offering gifts. Then there's a manger scene between two palms, the wrapped Child in a wicker cradle, a mule, and an ox. The central part shows Daniel in the lion's den and also Crispina reading a codex bearing the engraved monogram of Christ—the Lex Christi which was given to her at her baptism and which guided her through her life. Another fragment from the fourth century, the front part of a sarcophagus lid, has the theme of the Epiphany occupying the whole right side—the first king offers the Baby a golden crown with his left hand and points to the star with his right hand.

There is an unusual story behind the 64-ton marble base of a column you will come upon in the courtyard that joins the new building of Pio Christian Museum and the Pinacoteca with that of the Vatican Library. Around 161 A.D. the base was erected in Rome's Montecitorio Square by Emperor Marcus Aurelius and his brother, Lucius Verus, in honor of Antoninus Pius, their adoptive father. The base is carved with many flourishes, scenes and inscriptions to give glory to the man and his wife, Faustina. During the seventeenth century it underwent considerable damage from a fire, and over the centuries neglect brought on additional corrosion. Then it was brought over to the Vatican City where it remained unattended until 1980 when Vatican workers laboriously moved it several hundred yards to its present location —an incredible accomplishment involving hydraulic lifts and engineering skills. The base forthwith underwent a miraculous restoration by Ulderico Grispigni, the Vatican's chief sculpture restoration expert.

The Missionary-
Ethnological Museum

INAUGURATED ON December 21, 1926, in the Lateran Palace
by Pope Pius XI, the Missionary-Ethnological Museum was
transferred by Pope John XXIII during his administration to the
Vatican Museums and set up in its new building. Altogether this
museum houses a vast collection of artifacts collected by missionaries to most of the countries of the world and also includes
donations made privately by other persons and groups and many
items from the Borgia Museum. Basically, the theme of the Missionary Ethnological Museum is to display objects that illustrate
various forms of religion from countries that are not located on
the European Continent. Although the museum is sectioned off
into two segments, the main part is open to the public at all times,
while the ''secondary itinerary'' is available only to scholars and
other specialists on written application and presentation of credentials. Since the part open to tourists is a maze of complex ''ins
and outs,'' you are advised to follow the itinerary guided by
arrows. This means starting with the extensive display on China.

Upon entering you are confronted with two Takuchai lions in
enamel, both of them from Peking—the male facing the entrance
and the female the internal part. These lions represent two essential principles in Chinese philosophy and religion—Yang is male,
sky, round, perfect; Ying is female, earth, square, imperfect
—which, together, combine to form Tao (supreme law, order,
universe). To the right is a model of the Temple of the Sky. Built
in 1420 in Peking in wood, the Temple was then rebuilt in 1755
in marble. It was then used during the winter solstice by the
emperor who would stand on the top platform of the altar to make
a sacrifice to his ancestors (the Sky and all the former emperors of
his dynasty). At the same time from a lower platform an official
186

would make a sacrifice to the sun, moon, stars, wind, and rain. The last time this was done was in the year 1916.

In a showcase marked A1, to the left, are objects associated with the cult of the dead, tomb gifts from the time of the Ch'ing (221–206 B.C.), Han (206 B.C.–220 A.D.), and Tang (618–906 A.D.) dynasties. Also included is a reproduction of a typical funeral procession from the last Ch'ing dynasty (1644–1912). The A2 showcase houses objects dealing with the cult of the ancestors (statues of deified ancestors, tablets, household altars, and the like). Each of the articles, except the household altar on the right, are from Aberdeen near Hong Kong.

In the nearby niche is a model of a pagoda from Fukien, and on the right you see a Taoist painting with a finely carved frame. From the last dynasty there is a Taoist altar with emblems and sacrificial vases. By following the arrow, you now reach a reproduction of the red altar of Confucius (from Küfu, where he was born and buried). With permission granted from the descendents of Confucius, this reproduction was made in 1934 by noted Chinese artists. Wearing the imperial insignia of the Chou dynasty (1129–258 B.C.), Confucius—who lived from 551 to 479 B.C.—is seen holding a tablet of honor, which is the imperial sceptre of dominion in the reign of thought. In front of the philosopher's statue is a table for sacrifices and three sacred vases from the eleventh century, above which is a gilded tablet with the inscription, "Spiritual Throne of Confucius, master of holy doctrines."

Now you reach a section devoted to Chinese Buddhism. In Showcase A3 you see Buddha and two of his satellites. In the front are three sacred vases from a Buddhist temple in Peking. A wooden statue of Kwanyin (the ancient fertility goddess and the most popular Bodhisattva in China) stands outside the showcase; a Bodhisattva is a compassionate being bent on saving others and a future Buddha. There are various representations of Buddha and Kwanyin in Showcase A4, plus various stone sculptures of them both on the outside. Especially interesting are the head of a monk from Lohan and a statue of a Buddhist monk from the Ming dynasty (1368–1644).

Across the way to the right in Showcase A5 is some Chinese

pottery which has Arabic inscriptions (serving as a record of the presence of Islam in China). Next to that is a large stone stele from 781, China's first Christian document. Unearthed in the year 1615 in the Province of Shensi, it was copied carefully, said copy presented to Pope Benedict XV by Fritz Holm in 1916. Now follow a small block of showcases in which you can see a Christian altar in the Chinese style, near which is the bronze statue of Father Marcellus Sterkendries; to make this statue, ancient bronze vases were melted down. He is credited, while serving as a missionary in King Chow, with saving the city from extermination in 1912. So to show their gratitude, the converts to Christianity in King Chow sacrificed their most valuable vases to make the statue. Against a red screen next to it is a Chinese bronze Madonna and Child that the diocese of Taiwan donated to Pope Paul VI.

The part devoted to Japan begins with two lions in gilded wood —these are guardians against evil spirits. In Showcase B2 is a model of a Shintoist temple in the ancient capital of Nara, and in Showcase B3 there are three small Shintoist garden temples and sacrificial vases for wine, water, and perfume. Also included are a mirror, which is the symbol of the sun goddess Amaterasu, and foxes, which serve as symbols of the god of rice and riches. Against the wall in showcase B4 are several Shintoist-Buddhist masks. Pay special attention to the ones marked with Number 10068 and 10069, since they are carved in sacred Sughi-di-Dohi wood in the ancient manner.

Outside the showcase is a large, metal perfume burner with scenes and statuettes depicting figures from Shintoist mythology. In the central medallion is a scene of the sun goddess struggling against the moon and the earth. In showcase B5 are many objects that pertain to Japanese Buddhism. Noteworthy is the monk in ceremonial dress. On exhibit are eight prayer scrolls that are a copy of the Book of Hokekyo, written in Kansho in 1289 and pre served in the Temple of Nyohoji.

Showcases B6 and B7 contain two Putsudan (household altars) with sacrificial vases, statues of Buddhist and Shintoist deities, and ancestral tablets. Showcase B8 has paintings by Okayama Shunkyo of Kyoto of the Japanese martyrs killed in Nagasaki in 1597. The wooden tablets bear the persecution edicts.

In the collection of Korea, the museum keeps domestic objects in the first three sections. One part consists of a model of the main building of the Imperial Palace in Seoul, a model of a house of a rich man and a model of a house belonging to a poor man. Included in this part are lacquered wooden boxes with mother-of-pearl decorations, a wardrobe in the ancient Korean style, and five vases of a special porcelain from China. Ordinary everyday crockery, typical Korean games, and ornaments are on exhibit in Section C3. Section 4 has a variety of samples of Korean dress, traditional costumes, a number of ceremonial hats, and ordinary hats for everyday use. Nearby is a model of a loom. Religious life in Korea occupies much of Section C5—this would include a household altar, sacrificial vases, and a statue of a departed relative. On view is a shield once used for traditional festivals. Of special interest are the dies used to print the first Korean catechism and two tablets with The Ten Commandments.

The four sections devoted to Tibet and Mongolia, where Lamaism is the main religion, have objects that pertain to the religion and to the original Tibetan Bon-pö religion. These include representations of spirits, drums made from human skulls, flutes made from human bones, which show the Shamanistic influence. Section D2 features two figures of monks who are dressed in yellow (to represent the more orthodox aspect of Lamaism) and in red. In the third section are Lamaistic reliquaries, cult implements, and vases. This section has a tent used by a Mongolian lama on his trips. The middle part of the room is a model of the lamasery founded in 1700 by the lama Tchuo-eul-tsi, who was sent to Mongolia by the Dalai-Lama of Lhasa. The first temple is the so-called Pagoda of The Four Guardians of The Four Main Parts of the World. In the second one, the Pagoda of Prayer, religious assemblies were staged on important feast days, and in the third, the Pagoda of Beneficence, there were daily rites celebrated at dawn and at dusk. A large collection of Tibetan standards and religious books are on hand.

The Indochina exhibits include things from Cambodia, Burma, Laos, Siam, and Vietnam. Showcase 1 deals with the cult of the dead in Vietnam and displays rice baskets for tomb offerings, a wooden fence with ancestral figures, and two vases for minor burials. Also from Vietnam is a model of a Buddhist monastery. From Siam in the seventeenth century one finds a religious book in a case and statuettes of Buddha made from the ashes of Buddhist monks, which display the Tibetan influence on Siam. Siam is also the theme of the third showcase which demonstrates chairs that have been dedicated to ancestors.

Another showcase contains statuettes of Buddhas and Bodhisattvas from various Indochinese countries. Make particular note of the Sleeping Buddha, a white marble statuette found in the ruins of the Temple of Ara in Burma during the sixteenth and seventeenth centuries. There follows the large Christian sedan chair in gilded wood which was made in 1846 and was used in the procession of the Madonna of the Rosary. Ten men were required to carry this Vietnam artifact. Showcase 5 is filled with Christian statues in the Annamite Style (Vietnam).

The Indian subcontinent is well represented with exhibits on Bangladesh, Sri Lanka, India, and Pakistan. From central India are three rural deities and five funerary stelae carved out of wood. Since Hinduism is the principal religion of India, the two main currents of the religion are illustrated—Sivaism and Vishnuism. At the entrance to the large Indian room one can see a votive ox (Nandi), Siva's legendary means of transport. There is a small votive temple honoring Siva and a wooden door with carved stone.

There follows a large block of showcases on the right with paintings of Siva and his wife Kali, as well as statues of both. Going on further there begins a series of objects that deal with Vishnuism, starting with a painting of Vishnu and a collection of statuettes. Close by, in Showcase F4 are two lovely household altars with representations of Vishnu. Ceremonial masks used in ritual dances in various magic rites are on display in the next case. These combine both the elements of Hinduism and the primitive religions of Sri Lanka and southern India. Of unique interest is the triptych mask of Maha Kola who is known as the demon of the 18 diseases. Below is the large statue of Bhima, protector against serpents. Showcase F6 against the wall has various Hindu cult objects that include rattles, knives, vases, and altars.

In another showcase is a model from northern India showing the Golden Temple at Amritsar, the spiritual center of the Sikhs. Showcase F8 deals with Buddhism and tells how it was widespread in the Indian sub-continent in the last centuries before Christ and how it is not limited to Sri Lanka. On the other hand, Islam, which was widely practiced in India from the Middle Ages up to the British conquest, still is very much in operation in Pakistan and Bangladesh, and Showcase F9 deals with this subject rather well. Pay particular notice to the Koran from the nineteenth century, the jewels with inscription from the Koran, and the alabaster model of the Taj Mahal. Christianity gets treatment in Showcase F10 with Indian, Sri Lankan, and Portuguese influences on the statues of the Madonna and the Saints from the seventeenth and eighteenth centuries. Going over to another showcase, one can see a large wooden urn with carved scenes of Hindu mythology on the base. A rather impressive collection of more than a hundred small statues of Hindu gods is on view.

In the section devoted to Indonesia and the Philippines, on the left wall, is one of 24 bas-reliefs that depict the life of Buddha from the time he was born to his first sermon (the originals are in Java). A good collection on the primitive cults of Indonesia is available in the showcase at the wall where you can inspect a basket for offering rice to the dead, sacred birds, a model of a tomb, and many wooden statuettes of ancestors and heroes. The next showcase contains iron and bronze statuettes of Hindu-Buddhist deities from Java, and in an adjoining showcase is a display of particular interest: a shadow theater (called Wayang) from Indonesia. You get a good picture from this of the influence of the Hindu religion, a religion that is still professed on the Island of Bali. The chief Hindu deities (Siva, Vishnu, and Kali) are well represented here with many painted wooden statues.

Currently the main religion of Indonesia, Islam is the subject of Showcase G4, where examples of vases used in everyday life from Borneo, Java, and the Philippines are on display. The next showcase shows many illustrations of Christianity in this particular zone, not excluding a large altar by the Javanese sculptors Iho and Adi.

In the section on Polynesia, many of the exhibits deal with the cult of the dead, such as the showcase on the right which shows two boats used for taking souls to the hereafter. Various mourning wreaths on display as is an ancestral casket. In the following showcase, marked H2, are to be found wooden and stone statues of Polynesian gods (from the Marquesas and Tahiti). There are two remarkable wooden statues to the God Tu of the Mangarewa Islands, cited as masterpieces of Polynesian sculpture. The four-legged one, by the way, is the only one of its kind. The last showcase is of prime importance, for it bears witness to the presence of Christianity in Indonesia. There are many objects that once belonged to both Father Damien and Father Nicouleau, both of whom spent their lives caring for lepers and both of whom contracted leprosy and died of it.

Divided into two parts, the next collection has to do with the Melanesian Islands and New Guinea. The large sculptures in talevis wood on the left are intended to display the protective spirits of the home (New Caledonia). The cult of the dead is represented on the right with several objects. The small hut on the wooden pillar is for the cremation of a tribal chief in the Solomon Islands. The statues are in honor of deified ancestors, and on the wall are several New Hebrides funeral mats. Showcase I2 contains ceremonial masks representing departed relatives and protective spirits. From New Ireland there is an excellent triptych mask with carved figures of an ancestor and mythological birds.

On the right you can look at various cult implements, with ancient stone hatchets that were used for human sacrifices on the

Loyalty Islands. Note the oar shields with the spirit of death and the drums and other shields from the Solomon Islands. Christianity in Melanesa gets representation with three crucifixes from New Ireland, New Guinea, and the Solomon Islands. Also on view is the earliest Christian sculpture from the Solomons, a painted wooden statue of the Madonna.

As you reach the section devoted to New Guinea, you come upon two big masks of the secret society called Tubuan in New Britain. In the center of this exhibit is the so-called Hut of the Spirits which anthropologists have shown to be the social and religious center of New Guinean villages. There are also huts allied with the cult of the spirits which have been carefully built by men of the village. The pillars and supports are richly carved. According to tribal customs, some of the huts were built on the ground and others on piles—the huts here were all reconstructed from original pieces of materials that came from central New Guinea. Over the entrance are five painted skulls of dead villagers and a shield-shaped mask.

In the back of the hut, inside, is a big wooden statue of the god of war and a mythological heron whose feathers are decorated. Also included are hand drums, skull masks, wooden horns, torture instruments (for initiations), and stone shields, not excluding head-rests, plumed lances, painted human skulls, masks, and sacrificial vessels. Outside the hut are weapons, flutes, oars, and figures of the spirits, and in the front of the hut are drums that were used for communicating with people far away. Initiation rites were performed in these huts, to which women were never allowed. Over at the left are two showcases that display religious sculptures from New Guinea—these being figures of Buna, Nor, Kanengara, Worawari, and Tuo. Also on exhibit are various ritual masks and a master dancer with a spectacular headdress of colored feathers, a very rare object.

Australia's exhibit runs too skimpy, and the Vatican has hopes of enlarging it. There are ten carved and painted tomb poles from the Northern Territory and the Melville Islands. Showcase J1 has 13 paintings on stone which are representative of mythological motifs like sun, rain, ancestors, and totemic animals of the Australian aborigines. From Western Australia and the Northern Territory are included various cult implements like funerary wreaths and shields.

Showcases K1, K2, and K3 deal with North Africa, more particularly Algeria, Morocco, Tunisia, Libya, and Egypt. The first showcase has religious statuettes that demonstrate various religious influences of the ancient Middle East on North Africa. Showcase K2 has many Christian objects that include Coptic bracelets from the second to third century. There are terra-cotta molds and two stamps from the Catholic mission of the Minor Friars. In the back is a throne given as a gift to Pope Pius XI by the King of Egypt. The large showcase on the right illustrates the chief religion of North Africa, Islam. Fragments of colored terra-cotta vases made by Arab workers in Egypt from the ninth to the sixteenth century are shown, together with typical Arab ornaments from Algeria and vases for everyday use with inscriptions in Arabic from Algeria and Morocco. In the back is a curiosity: a Turkish inscription in Arabic characters invoking the protection of Allah. This was taken from a fortress in Algeria in 1830.

Now you reach a cubical showcase in the section on Ethiopia. This houses ornaments and other objects of the nomadic peoples from southern Sudan and northern Uganda. At the right is a plaster statue of Cardinal Guglielmo Massaia (1809–1889), apostle of Ethiopia. The next case displays Coptic cult objects from Ethiopia, a processional cross, an iron lectern, censers and a cross-shaped altar stone. In the tiny, adjoining room are four Ethiopian icons, copies that were made in ancient Ethiopia.

The Madagascar exhibit shows how the color white is the symbol of death. Six tomb stelae carved out of wood make this clear. Three showcases against the wall are set aside for the cult of the dead and ancestors: there are two ancestral statuettes of soldiers who were killed in action during the First World War in Europe. Also on exhibit is an ancestral head of wood put into use during magic rites and several Betsileo models of tombs. Revealing the influence of the Orient on the beliefs of Madagascar are four lamps in stone, wood, and iron.

When you enter the West Africa collection room, you are confronted with a large array of showcases, in the first of which is a group of small statues in painted terra-cotta. These represent priests, gods, and ancestors of the Ashanti tribe in Benin. Now comes a collection of wrought iron objects and some abstract sculptures of ancestors and totemic animals used for tomb ceremonies in Togo. The third showcase houses a series of vases, wooden objects, and sculptures relative to the cult of ancestors in Benin and Nigeria. This is followed by wooden and stone statuettes and representations of gods of the various tribes of West Africa. The last showcase holds ceremonial masks for spirits of the dead, gods, and sacred animals from secret societies.

Three showcases constitute the entire collection on Central Africa, and there are items from Gabon, Cameroon, Zaire, Congo, Angola, and Zambia. In the first exhibit on the right you find a series of wooden statuettes, which, known as ''fetishes,'' are used by magic cults. Ranging in quality from the roughly carved to those well stylized, these statuettes are representations of ancestors or protective spirits. If these spirits do not receive their due respect, according to anthropologists, they become vindictive —which is why they must be venerated through sacrifices and prayers. Several of the figures have mirrors on the abdominal part; these were imported by the Portuguese in the seventeenth century.

In the next showcase against the wall are three crucifixes. The two small ones are of European origin and were brought to Africa by the first missionaries who arrived during the seventeenth century. Found in a cave in the Lower Congo, the large crucifix has a decoration with the figures of four baby monkeys. The natives who owned these items looked upon them as representations of protective spirits. Representing ancestors are three metal-plated wooden sculptures which are from Gabon. The last exhibit is devoted to ceremonial masks.

As for the small display given to Ruanda, Burundi, Uganda,

Kenya, Tanzania, and Malawi, this comprises small straw huts, which are found in the forest and which are used as a place to worship the departed. Whenever there are calamities, sacrifices would be offered in these huts to appease the spirits of ancestors. In the back are to be found a series of horn amulets, which are filled with herbs and other ingredients believed to have magical powers that provide a lifetime of protection against evils. These evils include diseases, tribal enemies, and lightning. Also implied are those problems that come from the return of the dead.

Southern Africa's Zambia, Southern Rhodesia, Bechuanaland, Lesotho, Mozambique, and South Africa are dealt with in a small exhibit of two showcases, the second of which contains items from the trousseau of a Zulu bride. The first one has various wooden statuettes of ancestors and deities. Observe carefully the clay statuettes that are covered with beads. These represent ancestors venerated by the women of Basutoland as spirits associated with fertility. The wall is covered with a variety of ceremonial masks from Mozambique and a good collection of protective amulets from all over the area.

A special exhibit on Christianity in Africa has been set up in a section two steps below the main floor. Showcase R1 contains several statuettes carved out of ebony and forming a nativity scene with the Christ Child carved out of ivory. All the figures in the scene suggest strong European influences. As components of another crib scene, two other groups of statuettes are in painted metal. The second exhibit is replete with statuettes of the Madonna. Although the ones in ivory are simple imitations of representations from Europe, all of the others manifest a complete Africanization of Christian sculptural stylism.

In the last showcase are housed four groups of brass figures (the Martyrdom, story of the prophet Jonah, the Good Shepherd, and the Prayer). The style here is indigenous to Benin, but the interpretations are definitely from ancient Roman examples. A favorite motif of African sculpture is to show Christ as the Good Shepherd, and many examples of this are in this same showcase.

Not all of the countries of South America are represented in the section devoted to that part of the Western Hemisphere; the countries that receive treatment here are Argentina, Brazil, Chile, Peru, Surinam, Guyana, Colombia, Ecuador, and Venezuela. An unusual item from a now almost extinct tribe from Tierra del Fuego is a hat used for initiation rites. As you go up the stairs, you are bombarded with six showcases that house feather ornaments from countries like Argentina, Brazil, Peru, and Colombia, used during religious ceremonies and dances. In the room itself are two showcases dealing with primitive cults. A collection of five wooden sculptures is of immediate interest. Originally from Santa Marta, Colombia, these were shipped to Rome in 1692 and are the oldest Colombian wooden sculptures to be found on the Continent. The last showcase has a layout on cult objects which include flutes, maracas, ceremonial staffs, and masks.

The semicircular room that follows houses materials that go back to the higher pre-Columbian religions. Four plaster-copy sculptures that represent the goddess Bachue from Chibcha, Colombia, and two Inca gods from Huaraz, Peru, are on view. In another showcase are many articles from Colombia done in gold in honor of Colombian gods. In the central showcase are housed vases and fragments of sculptures that illustrate the religions of Peru from Nasca, Tiahuanaco, and the Trujillo Plateau. There is a large funerary urn with decorations of painted geometrical designs and a human figure in relief presumed to be the image of the deceased one.

Central America is well represented through materials from Guatemala, Honduras, Nicaragua, Costa Rica, Panama, and Mexico (though the last named is actually part of North America). Upon entering the section you note two plaster reliefs, one representing the destructive god of fire (a man dancing with a skeleton), and the other on the right representing a Mayan tribal chieftan from Guatemala. Above, on the wall, is a relief portraying the god of the wind (Quetzalcoatl) from the Yucatan, and below you see the ruins of the Temple of Copan in Honduras. Nearby is a sculpture in stone as a symbol of the sun (from Mexico). A Honduran cast is nearby from a carved column found in the ruins of Copan.

Over at the right two plastic models are on hand. One is of the Temple of the Cross, at the top of which is a skull. The arms of the figure are decorated with serpents and Mayan mythological figures and hieroglyphics. There are also figures of mythological birds and priests offering sacrifices. The other deals with the Pyramid of Papantla from the Gulf of Mexico: the style of the steps is reminiscent of Indochinese temples. The showcase on the left is full of minor pieces of sculpture from Mexico.

The central part of the room displays an attractive sculpture in a reddish stone from the Mexican plateau in classical Aztec style. Then there are five fragments of stone statues of gods. Against the wall are four statues of the main Aztec gods—there are Tlaloc, the god of rain; Chicomecoatl, the goddess of grain; Quetzalcoatl, the god of wind, and Chalchiuthlicue, the goddess of water. Nearby is a model of the Temple of the Shields and Jaguars, dedicated to the Yucatan goddess Kukulkan. Now come two casts of the cornerstone of the pyramid of Monte Alban in Mexico. Note also the model of the Temple of Xochicalco, dedicated to the goddess of rain and fertility. This is an Aztec work found on the Mexican plateau. And as you go out, on the right side, are two casts—one of a drum and the other serving as symbols of the four prehistoric suns. Nearby is a large cylindrical basin in the form of an ape carrying a vase on its back. This was used in Guatemala by the Mayans for sacrificial fires.

The section dealing with North America (both the United States and Canada) houses a wealth of material dealing with Christianity in the Americas—such as lecterns, sculptures, and cult implements. An outstanding relic is the wooden lectern that once belonged to Christopher Columbus' chaplain (Fra Bartolomeo de Las Heras) during the voyage to America. This object, made by the Caribs of Cuba, is decorated with shell-shaped appliques in mother-of-pearl.

A massive collection of sculptures by Ferdinand Pettrich, who went to the United States in 1835 and made sketches for his works, is on display. After making life-size sculptures during his long stay in Brazil, he presented them as a gift to Pope Pius IX.

Upon entering you are confronted by a Pettrich work, a bas-relief depicting a war dance of the Sauks-Foxes and Mississippi Sioux tribes, together with a statue of a young hunter. The showcase also keeps Eskimo masks and sculptures from Alaska and Canada. Next there is a bas-relief of a battle between two hostile tribes — the Winnebagos and the Creeks. This work was inspired by stories told to Pettrich by Indians, but all the figures are based on real people he met. An outstanding example of Pettrich's art is his statue of the dying Tecumseh, who — wounded during the Battle of Thames in 1813 — propped himself up on one elbow to become an inspiration for his warriors.

Another showcase has masks and sculptures made by the Indians of British Columbia, which is followed by a bas-relief demonstrating a buffalo hunt. The large Pettrich statue on the left is of Tahtapesaah, chief of the Sioux of the Mississippi Area. On the wall are many busts of various chiefs and priests of the Sioux, the Sauks-Fox, the Creeks, and the Winnebagos. A bas-relief in the middle reports on the council staged in Washington in 1837 between the United States and the chiefs of the Mississippi Sioux and the Sauks-Fox regarding the sale of the lands that belonged to the two tribes.

The stairway on the right leads you to a doorway to the Persian section which has a good array of Persian and Oriental majolicas. Especially interesting are the two star-shaped majolicas with verses from the Koran that are printed along the edges. Although some of the writing is meaningless arabesques, one can distinguish the words, ". . . in the name of the clement and merciful god." All these pieces are from Imam Zadeh Veramin (thirteenth century). A particularly lovely square tile on exhibit carries the image of the mythological bird Simurgh of thirteenth and fourteenth century Persia. Just before you take leave of this section, take a good look at a picture on the right that is composed of small piece of vitreous enamel. On these are various travel scenes of Persia in the seventeenth and eighteenth century and a large arch of 14 human figures on colored majolicas involved in hunting activities. These are from Teheran.

Comprising religious art from Turkey, Lebanon, Syria, Jordan, Israel, Iraq, and Saudi Arabia, the next section has artifacts that were all found in the Middle East and pertain to the ancient cultures of that widespread area. In the collection are a necklace made of seals that represent Oriental gods, a clay tablet with cuneiform writing that goes back to 2000 B.C., fragments of stone bearing Hittite hieroglyphics from 1400 B.C., reliefs, statuettes, vases, lamps, crystal bottles, and the like—all of which do reveal Hellenistic-Roman influences.

In the next room are items dedicated to the various Middle East religions of today. For instance, the first showcase houses items regarding the Jewish religion—a scroll from 1400 of the Torah, a Hanukija candlestick from a synagogue, and two Meghillat Esthers. One of them is in a silver gilded case which was a wedding gift to a bride. The next showcase has items of a Christian religion nature—small icons, silver crucifixes, a representation in mother-of-pearl, the Last Supper, and the Resurrection. There is a remarkable reproduction on the wall of a mosaic of a map of the Holy Land. Finally, there are many objects used in daily life that have to do with Islam, which is the Middle East's predominant religion.

The final segment of the Missionary Ethnological Museum keeps on display an excellent set of works of Christian art from mission countries. From Japan there is on hand a richly gilded altar carved out of wood, and from China there are sacred handiworks that included enamelled metal decorations for altars, wooden and enamelled candlesticks, and crosiers. Lacquered and on gilded wood is a tabernacle that was made in Vietnam, based on models from Europe. A particularly interesting Christian painting from Vietnam done by an anonymous artist is the Last Judgment in which the painter made use of both European and Buddhist elements. The artist has created a lifelike vision of the end of the world, a hell-purgatory and a paradise. The hell, by the way, is a typically Buddhist kind of hell, consisting of eight hot hells and eight cold hells and tortures from hunger and thirst.

Not to be overlooked is the painting of the Last Supper on white silk in Chinese ink done by Wang-Su-Ta. By the same artist are two panels of the Madonna. The last painting in this display shows the arrival of Christianity in Japan, the arrival of Saint Francis Xavier, the sermon, the martyrs of Nagasaki, and the Madonna as the Queen of Japan. Luca Hasegawa was the artist. Models of tabernacles from China and churches from Vietnam are on display in the atrium; these are quite illustrative of Christian architecture. Included is a model of a pagoda that was erected in the seventeenth century in honor of Father Faber, a Jesuit priest who was received into the Chinese pantheon as the protective deity Fang.

The Historical Museum

SET UP BY Pope Paul VI in 1973, the Historical Museum is housed in a large room below what is known as the Square Garden. As you enter the vestibule you come upon a bronze bust of Paul VI by Guarino Roscioli, and on the table is a small model of the first locomotive that entered the State of Vatican City on its own railroad. The railway, by the way, was built in keeping with the terms of the 1929 Lateran Pacts between Italy and the Vatican.

Divided into two sections, the museum keeps in Section I a collection of carriages used by popes and cardinals before the advent of the automobile. The sides of the walls are rife with harnesses for ordinary events (called by the Vatican *mezza gala*) and harnesses for *gran gala* that are made of red velvet and studded with shiny ornaments. Included are saddles, trappings, cushions, luggage, reins, and other equine items.

The walls also have representations of the 1912 Eucharistic Congress, which took place in Vienna and papal processions before 1870. Clement XIV is seen astride a horse, a rare photograph of a pope on horseback. There is a wealth of photographs of popes aboard their vehicles, and nearby are a collection of whips and bronze carriage lamps. For nonceremonial occasions popes used to travel in black landaus, but these were used until the early days of Pope Pius XI's reign. The sturdier carriages, built for long journeys where bad roads were expected, are also on display. One of the carriages used in November 1849 gave Pope Pius IX a most difficult time because his trip from Rome to Gaeta and back followed some of Italy's worst roads.

One of the high points of this collection is the so-called *gala Berlin* red-and-gold carriage of Cardinal Lucien Louis Bonaparte

(1829–1895), who was a cousin of Napoleon III. This carriage carries a brass coat-of-arms with the Napoleonic eagle. There are also two other Cardinal Bonaparte Berlin carriages — one was a *terza gala Berlin* in red, black, and gold, with a throne that was used for lesser occasions, and the other was a *mezza gala Berlin* in red, black, and gold with a throne that had plumes that were used for occasions above the *terza gala.*

Perhaps the most interesting piece in the collection is the *gran gala Berlin* that Pope Leo XII commissioned from Gaetano Peroni, the then-famous coach-maker of Rome. This carriage was so impressive that after Leo's death, subsequent popes used it up till the time of Pope Pius IX.

Another means of papal transport was the sedan-chair. Several of these used by Pope Leo XIII are on exhibit, and the one upholstered in red damask was also used by his successors. One wooden sedan-chair was presented to Leo XIII by the faithful of Naples in 1887 on the 50th anniversary of his priesthood, but the pope never got around to using it. Another curiosity is the flag of the papal military steamer, "San Pietro," which was taken in a battle on September 26, 1860, off the coast at Ancona. There are also a model and the flag of the papal corvette, *Immacolata Concezione,* the last ship of the pope's navy.

Section II begins with a collaboration of uniforms of the papal armed forces, which were disbanded in 1871 when the pope's temporal powers were abrogated (restored in 1929). There are many other materials relative to the army of the Pontifical State, not exluding arms and armor. Pay particular note to the well-preserved and beautiful suit of armor of the papal guards called "The Broken Lances," a type used up to the time of Pius VII in 1801. Directly nearby are two showcases against the wall that display mannequins wearing uniforms of the Noble Pontifical Guard Corps, founded by Pius VI in May 1801; these military men were part of the popes' guard corps until they were disbanded during this century. Another showcase has mannequins wearing the uniforms of the Swiss Guards. Other mannequins display uniforms of the Pontifical Gendarme Corps, which Pius VII set up in July 1816 as a police service, and this group was stopped by

Paul VI on September 15, 1970. His Holiness' Palatine Guards of Honor, a volunteer corps founded in December 1850, have their uniforms on view—these are the men who attended the pope on ceremonial occasions in Saint Peter's.

As for armaments and ammunition, there are several showcases full on hand. The Chassepot gun was used for the first time by French troops at Mentana in 1867. There are various types of muskets of French, Swiss, Austrian, English, Piedmontese, and Neapolitan make, not to mention a Remington carbine and an array of revolvers, swords, daggers, axes, and picks (many of these belonged to the French Imperial Engineers). On exhibit is also a collection of 78 Remington muskets, made in 1868, which not only have considerable historical and technical interest but also have an artistic value.

In a showcase against the wall is a collection of flags belonging to the Palatine Guard. Every time there was a change of pope, there would be a change in flag for the new pontiff. Two other showcases have uniforms of the Pontifical State army, including those of the papal zouaves who were the Algerian infantrymen in baggy trousers in the employ of the pope. The uniform of a captain of the reserve volunteers known as the Caccialepri and the uniform of a papal artillery officer are of special interest, too.

On the columns in this large room, in the center part, is a series of helmets, basinets, morions, and so-called "Burgundy helmets" of the sixteenth and seventeenth centuries and various sidearms and a 120.3 mm. cannon, made in Turin in 1820. This is all that remains of the expansive Vatican armory which was still in existence during the latter half of the nineteenth century. A special showcase keeps the standards of the various pontifical soldiers and especially of the regiment of Pontifical Dragoons and of Pontifical Artillery.

The wall is replete with the portraits of all the commanders of the Noble Pontifical Guards, together with the papal coats-of-arms. One of the most valuable of all relics here is the gala harness of the standard-bearer of the Holy Roman Church—he had the rank of Lieutenant-General.

The Vatican Radio

THERE'S A FAVORITE STORY that gets told in Rome every now and then about the time that one of Leonid Brezhnev's aides went into his Kremlin office with needle and thread. When the aide said he had come to sew the top button on Brezhnev's pants, the Soviet chief asked how he knew that the button was missing. The aid replied, ''I just heard it on Vatican Radio.''

All levity aside, the anecdote does point up the worldwide reputation Vatican Radio has earned for itself in the well over 50 years that it has been in operation, broadcasting 225 hours a week in 33 languages (including Esperanto) to a hundred countries by FM, shortwave, and medium-wave. Without Vatican Radio, the pope's spy system would probably not function well.

An estimated 80 million people listen to Vatican Radio, but it is virtually impossible to gauge the actual size of its worldwide audience. Not the least of these are the polyglot monitors and Vaticanologists inside the Kremlin and in other parts of the Soviet Union, as far away as Siberia, Sverdlovsk, Novosibirsk, Samarkanda, and Karaganda where listening posts have been set up. From time to time Moscow has seen fit to jam Radio Vatican whenever news bulletins are being broadcast that the Kremlin has already held back for internal consumption. One clever deception Vatican Radio uses, which the Communists are wise to now, is to insert a particularly sensitive news item into just one foreign language broadcast that goes into Russia, while leaving the same item out of all the other newscasts of the same day, in order to get the message past the monitors and avoid being jammed. This to-day still works some of the time—but in the past it worked all of the time.

The Soviet Union also keeps daily close tabs on Radio Vatican broadcasts that go into Bloc countries that are heavily populated with Roman Catholics—especially Poland, which the Vatican knows listens to Radio Vatican with a much greater statistical intensity than do any other Red nations, with the possible exception of Czechoslovakia. Neither the Czech regime nor the Polish regime has jamming equipment and both depend on Moscow to provide this "service." That Radio Vatican is listened to more comprehensively by subjected peoples is borne out by the report given Pope Paul VI by a Lithuanian priest who had spent ten years in a Siberian slave camp. He said that Lithuanian transmissions from Rome were listened to by the prisoner-workers over their hidden radios while on their knees "as if it were a prayer" coming from Vatican City.

Run by Jesuit priests with modern equipment that includes the world's largest rotating antenna and a 500-kilowatt transmitter, Vatican Radio made its first broadcast in 1931 on equipment supplied by Guglielmo Marconi, inventor of wireless radio. In fact, it was Marconi's voice that emitted the first words ever broadcast over Radio Vatican when he introduced Pope Pius XI on February 12, 1931, who then said to his few hundred listeners: "Using this admirable invention of Marconi, we can talk to all creatures and all men using the words of the Scriptures. Distant peoples, lend your ears . . . ." For several years after that Marconi lent his know-how and made improvements on Vatican Radio's setup which at the time was located inside the walls of Vatican City. Today the main transmitting center is situated 11 miles north of Rome in a compound ten times the size of Vatican City, though one antenna is still on Vatican grounds. Only once since Marconi inaugurated the station has it gone off the air, and that came about on December 19, 1979, when lightning silenced it for 18 hours.

Unknown to most people, even regular listeners, is the fact that during the early morning hours of each weekday the office of the Vatican's Secretary of State broadcasts messages—many of them in code—to priests, nuncios, apostolic delegates, and cardinals in all parts of the world. Each Church dignitary knows about what time to expect special announcements pertaining to his region or for him. He also receives coded signals from the Vatican to remind him of the "date" he has with his receiver. In contrast with other stations, Vatican Radio often communicates private messages that will not be understood by anyone but the papal representative for whom they are intended. One might, for example, hear something like this: ''Father Tizio, with reference to the information in your letter of the eighth of September, re the peasant woman who sees visions of the Virgin Mary, we have considered your suggestion, but suggest that *ad captandum vulgus* . . . .''

With a staff of more than 300 men and women, many of whom are multi-lingual non-Italians, Radio Vatican sends out nearly 500 programs a week. These range from papal speeches and blessings to international newscasts and from jazz music to Masses. The Vatican hymn—written by French composer Charles Gounod—is played at least once a week. Technical religious discussions are kept to a minimum because Vatican Radio officers feel these are not easily understood and would bore most of its listeners. From the some 50,000 letters it gets from all parts of the world every year, Vatican Radio is able to guide itself as to what its audiences want.

One special feature Vatican Radio put on in September 1979 brought its biggest avalanche of mailbags in history. This was a show that involved an imaginary interview with the Virgin Mary during which she was questioned on what she thought of today's women libbers, the suicide deaths of Marilyn Monroe and Jean Seberg, world pollution, nuclear war, the holocaust in which six million Jews were massacred, and the Palestinians' drive for a homeland of their own. Each of Mary's answers was taken from quotes in the Gospels. Here is a sample from the script which was broadcast in Italian, Spanish, Polish, English, German, French, Portuguese, and Esperanto:

QUESTION: What do you think of the tragic death of film actress Jean Seberg who committed suicide like Marilyn Monroe?
ANSWER: *Daughter, why have you treated us so? Behold, your Father and I have been looking for you anxiously. (from the Gospel according to Saint Luke)*
QUESTION: We are scared. The threat of nuclear war, pollution of the environment, the exhaustion of energy sources, terrorism,

delinquency, corruption, torture . . . . Do you think the Lord will still have patience with this poor world gone astray?

ANSWER: *His mercy is on those who fear him from generation to generation. (from the Gospel according to Saint Luke)*

QUESTION: Would you have ever thought of the holocaust of the people which gave birth to you?

ANSWER: *He has scattered the proud in the imagination of their hearts, He has put down the mighty from their thrones, and exalted those of low degree. (from the Gospel according to Saint John)*

QUESTION: But where were you in those tragic moments of world history, which unfortunately continue to be repeated, as we see today in the sufferings of the Palestinians, Indochinese refugees, and others?

ANSWER: *Standing by the cross of Jesus was his mother. (from the Gospel according to Saint John)*

Although the answers in the simulated interview were necessarily vague and rather cryptic, the program grabbed listeners everywhere.

Successes of that type, as with every medium of communication, are tempered by moments of great stress and near-catastrophe. Such was the case for Vatican Radio one year when the world awaited a special Easter message from Pius XII. Five minutes before he was to begin his discourse in front of a live mike in the Vatican Radio studio, Pius XII (who suffered all his life from a hiccup affliction — a fact that for a long time was kept away from public knowledge) suddenly developed a case of hiccups. With an international radio hook-up to millions of people tuned in from everywhere, the pope could not seem to shake of this most tricky of ailments. As the second-hand of the studio clock raced towards the On-The-Air deadline, staff members tried all kinds of devices to get the pope to stop hiccupping; they spun him to the right nine times, covered his head with a paper bag, made him hold his breath, got him to drink some water from the far side of the glass, and even tried to ''scare'' him with a sudden movement. Someone even tried pounding his back, and someone else suggested pulling his tongue with a thumb and forefinger. But nothing worked. Yet a few seconds before the pope was due to go on the air, the hiccups disappeared as mysteriously as they had come, and the pope delivered his words with nary a fluff.

Like every major news organization, Radio Vatican has ready-prepared programs and tapes for the eventual death of Pope John Paul II. These are coded by the staff as ''Day X'' and would have been used in May 1981 when a moslem Turkish gunman put two bullets into the pontiff in Saint Peter's Square in an assassination attempt that failed. The ''Day X'' programs consist of a series of broadcasts that can run for several days (in each of 33 languages) and include speeches and statements made in public by the Polish pontiff. There are also a large number of prepared scripts that Vatican Radio announcers can read from, after minor alterations have been made to fit the events surrounding the pope's demise.

One of the geographical areas in which Vatican Radio is relatively weak is North America. It is not easy, if you live in the United States and Canada, to get any of the English-language programs because Vatican strategy is to penetrate officially atheist countries like the Communist states of Europe. People in mainland China, for instance, get better reception and more programs beamed to them, not only in English but in Mandarin Chinese and Esperanto. The Vatican believes that its Esperanto broadcasts, by the way, are more valuable than most of the other languages, with the exception of English which papal authorities are convinced has become the world's most important international tongue and the most widespread ''second language'' in nearly all countries, having replaced French as the most diffused diplomatic language. French broadcasts are still very strong into North Africa and the Middle East, as are Spanish, which has the distinction of being the one language that is officially spoken in more countries (19 in all) than any other. Curiously enough, though Latin is officially the Holy's See's language, hardly any broadcasts are beamed out in that tongue.

General director of Vatican Radio is Reverend Roberto Tucci who keeps in constant communication with the Vatican Secretary of State. The latter supervises Vatican Radio quite closely but gives Father Tucci considerable leeway nevertheless. Though Reverend Tucci does confer with John Paul II from time to time, he depends on Cardinal Casaroli to alert him on highly sensitive matters to make sure that a broadcast does not bring on problems for some Church officer under political or social pressures somewhere.

Father Tucci has admitted that his annual budget of nearly $4.5 million is really too small to do the thoroughly professional job he would like. Therefore, Vatican Radio, despite its shoestring operation, is a successful mixture of professionalism and amateurism. So, many of the staff announcers—quite a few of whom are priests and nuns—learn while on the job, but because they are dedicated in a like mission to spread the faith all over the world, and especially to the Communist and atheist world, they are truly a motivated group of people which learns fast and functions effectively. Though earning considerably less than what they could make in private radio broadcasting (in some cases the priests and nuns receive no pay whatever), the staff and its officials are most proud of the fact that on the occasion of Vatican Radio's 50th anniversary when John Paul II visited the radio's studios, he revealed to the assemblage that while he was a cleric in Cracow, Poland, both as a lowly priest and later as archbishop and cardinal, he rarely missed any of Vatican Radio's Polish broadcasts.

The Vatican
Daily Newspaper

NOT LONG AGO John Paul II discovered that the Vatican's semi-official daily newspaper, *L'Osservatore Romano,* had censored some of his own stylistic pearls from his papal speeches. The pope was not amused. In fact, he was quite miffed and let the paper's editors know that from that day forward he would personally supervise the editing and proofreading of his addresses before they appeared in the paper. He even went a bit further during 1981 and began to interfere with certain headlines that were to appear on the first page by rewriting them after they had been set in type. John Paul had particularly ruled out of the paper such statements that preface his speeches with: ''We present the following discourse from our illustrious and enlightened supreme pontiff, the Holy Father, as we have gathered it from his august lips.'' The pope also told intimates that he considered *L'Osservatore Romano* a dull newspaper and that its grayness should undergo changes, reaching towards heaven, so to speak, where there would be more light and less grayness.

The pope is not alone in his opinion, for down virtually to the last journalist and editor in Italy, the professional feeling is that ''the pope's newspaper'' is without doubt one of the dullest newspapers anywhere and of all time. It carries no sports reports, no crime stories, never prints any financial news, uses few ads, uses no book reviews, has no comic strips, does not print a letters-to-the-editor column or ''people'' notices, carries no regular columnists, uses no scandals, almost never runs photographs (unless it is of the pope), and often places an earth-shattering news item on an inside page while every other newspaper in the world has given it justifiable headline treatment on the first page (a case in

point is the end of the Vietnam War, which appeared on Page 4).
As a matter of fact, *L'Osservatore* has even been known to
publish a hot headline story several days after it has happened
(such as President Nixon's resignation which was reported two
days later). In addition, the Vatican newspaper thinks nothing of
running an article entirely in Latin—or in any one of 33 different
languages, including Sanskrit, with no translation.

Yet it is one of the world's most carefully read newspapers, cir-
culating in over a hundred countries and wielding an influence
well beyond its relatively small circulation of 60,000. Though
banned in the U.S.S.R., seven copies are sent to the Kremlin each
day (Josef Stalin took out the subscriptions), and several copies
are put on permanent file at the Lenin Library in Moscow. Copies
of the paper go every day to heads of state in Peking, Washington,
Senegal, London, Bonn, Paris, and just about every capital in the
world, not to mention such places as the Island of Hvar, the
Republic of San Marino, Tibet, Alaska, Northern Ireland,
Andorra, and to the office of the *Daily Worker* in New York City.
It is also one of the world's most quoted newspapers, for besides
being carefully scanned by foreign correspondents stationed in
Rome looking for quotes or nuggets, its views and opinions are
frequently reprinted by other newspapers.

As witness the time *L'Osservatore* printed a guest essay on
boxing, in which the writer expressed his disparaging view that
the sport was "mayhem." Despite the fact that the essayist was
reflecting only a personal opinion, many publications and the
wire services picked up the story and reported that the Vatican
was against boxing. Later an editor threw up his hands in disgust
and shook his head: "We don't know if there is even any Vatican
view about boxing. Nobody has ever told us about it."

Founded in 1861 "to denounce and refute all calumnies
against Rome and its pontificate," *L'Osservatore Romano* must
go into the books as one of the world's most unusual newspapers
—noted more for what it omits than for what it publishes. Its
staple diet is a mixture of papal speeches, Vatican documents,
cultural articles, religious news from all over (mostly Catholic),
feature stories with a strong Catholic thrust, obituaries, and

"news" articles that point up the failure of totalitarian regimes to treat Catholic clergy humanely. As an example this report:

The news agency, ANSA, quoting the Czech agency, CTK, reports that it has publicly admitted for the first time that some Catholic priests were unjustly condemned during the Stalinist era. The daily newspaper, *Lidova Demokracie,* the organ of the Czech popular party, today quoted statements to that effect by representatives of the Secretariat for religious affairs.

The officials stated that it is impossible to know how many priests had been tried and condemned during the years of Stalinism; but, they added, some of them had been granted an amnesty. Priests who had been freed under amnesty were required to engage in "productive work."

L'Osservatore, open in its use of invective when it tackles Communism (which it describes as "the unfeeling omnipotence of a materialistic state, without any ideal beyond this world, without religion and without God"), does not hesitate to take on totalitarian giants of other stripes. For instance, its feud with Benito Mussolini provided *L'Osservatore* not only with perhaps its finest moment but also increased its daily circulation to over 440,000 during World War II because it was the only paper in Italy that printed news reports from the Allied camp which were not available under the Mussolini dictatorship. Mostly what raised the hackles on Mussolini's head was that the editor, Count Giuseppe dalla Torre (who ran the paper for more than 40 years, until he retired in 1961) steadfastly refused to call Mussolini by his pet title, "Duce."

A blunt outspoken man who wrote nearly all the hard-hitting editorials himself, dalla Torre showed his contempt for Hitler when he went to Rome in May 1938 to meet Mussolini, a big news event to which the world press gave flair coverage. Instead of running a news item on the Hitler-Mussolini summit conference in Rome, dalla Torre used the editorial column of *L'Osservatore* to insult the two Fascist leaders: he pointed out that Pope Pius XI had left Rome for his summer villa at Castel Gandolfo in the hills outside Rome because "His Holiness finds the air in the hills preferable to that in Rome."

For Mussolini—already enraged that he was never referred to as Il Duce—this was the insult supreme. He ordered dalla Torre's arrest. While the pugnacious Count one day was walking across Saint Peter's Square, he crossed the white marble line on the pavement that marked the border of the sovereign State of Vatican City and Italy. Immediately the two Fascist plainclothesmen accosted him and "invited him to go with them to the *Questura,* Rome's police headquarters, because he was under arrest. Nodding an agreement, dalla Torre began walking with the two men making casual conversation and joking about the invitation—which threw both the cops off their guard. Then, suddenly and swiftly the editor broke into a run, managed to cross back over the white border of the Vatican State before the policemen could stop him, turned around with only inches separating him from Italian soil, and snarled at the two agents: "Tell your Boss he knows where my office is and if he has anything to ask me, let him make an appointment with my secretary—and perhaps I will find time to see him!''

This kind of defiant behavior was not what Mussolini was used to in a country he was ruling with an iron thumb. The Big Jaw ordered dalla Torre assassinated and assigned two of his Black Shirt hit men to go after the cantankerous editor. But word from a Vatican spy in Mussolini's office swiftly got to the pope who ordered his bad-guy editor not to leave Vatican grounds until the war was over. Accordingly, dalla Torre walked from his office to his one-room apartment inside the Vatican using a different route each day, just to make sure the cop men did not violate international boundaries on their own volition. Dalla Torre not only out lived Mussolini but he outlived Fascism in Italy. And Hitler.

Strangely enough, when the Allies liberated Rome in April 1944 and the Nazi troops that had been occupying The Eternal City fled to the north, dalla Torre chose not to give this major event any kind of play. Instead he ran an eight-column headline on Page 1 that had nothing to do with the liberation but was an important Church ruling that had been ratified by Pope Pius XII. The Rome liberation story got a few lines on the back page, and that issue has become a collector's item today.

Another issue that has become a collector's item, worth a good price on the open market, is the one with the front-page announcement in Latin on the election of Cardinal Albino Luciani of Venice on August 26, 1978, as Pope John Paul I, an issue that was hurriedly put out in just 24 minutes. Overlooked by the *Osservatore* staff and the Vatican's Latinologists was the fact that the streamer headline:

HABEMUS PAPAM ALBINUM LUCIANI QUI SIBI NOMINEM IMPOSUIT IOANNEM PAULUM I

contained a nonexistent Latin word. The error, amusingly enough, was found by the editor's high-school son, who had just finished first-year Latin. Apologizing for not being an expert in Latin, he pointed out to his father that the word *nominem* did not exist at all in Latin and that the word *nomen* (which means "name") should have been used.

With an editorial staff of 30 writers and editors, only two of whom are priests, and a mechanical staff of 60 employees, the eccentric *L'Osservatore Romano* has its offices in a two-story building just inside the Vatican walls near the Saint Anne Gate. Since most of the writing is done with a pen, the sound of typewriters is rarely heard in the cloistered calm newsroom. Silence reigns in its many private offices (there is no large, open newsroom per se, as is found in American newspapers) which have old-fashioned furniture, high ceilings, and religious paintings and crucifixes on the walls. The same is true of the dark corridors that connect the offices, many of which do not even have telephones. The *Osservatore* is a standard size, eight-page evening paper that comes out five days a week but carries the date of the next day (it publishes no issue on Mondays). Since April 4, 1968, the Vatican has been publishing a tabloid weekly edition full of feature stories and papal speeches; these are issued in Italian, English French, Spanish, Portuguese, and German. Although the Vatican is secretive about its circulation figures, a printer inside the Vatican has revealed that the Sunday number sells about 100,000 copies. Most of these are subscriptions through the mails, since very few copies are purchased from newsstands in Rome, even though each newsstand gets two or three copies delivered each day by about 6 P.M. when the last editions of Italy's dailies go out. The paper operates at a loss of $2 million a year.

The editor of L'Osservatore today is Valerio Volpini, who succeeded Raimondo Manzini, who in turn had succeeded Giuseppe dalla Torre. Volpini had the distinction of being the only one of L'Osservatore's nine chief editors to be sued for libel. He was found guilty in 1979 in an Italian court of accusing an editor of a Catholic biweekly publication of ''encouraging division with the Church'' in an editorial entitled, ''Sower of Discontent.'' Volpini was fined $299, but the court suspended the penalty because he had never been convicted of anything before. The pope did not stand behind Volpini during the trial because he had not seen the editorial before it was printed and because he personally found it unpalatable when he read his copy that day.

This raises the question: how ''official'' is anything printed in L'Osservatore and to what extent do its editorials reflect what the Vatican or the pope officially think on a given issue? Reporters who scour the newspaper looking for clues or hints sometimes make the mistake of misleading readers by not calling L'Osservatore, ''the Vatican's semiofficial daily,'' or by warning a reader that the opinion expressed, if not directly attributed to the pope or an official Vatican spokesman, may or may not be what the Vatican is actually thinking. In spite of this, the government officials in over a hundred countries who get the paper look at it with a most careful eye in an attempt to read between the lines and understand its pronouncements on morality, religion, politics, international events, and future Vatican policy on one issue or another.

Almost as if it serves a special mysterious purpose, the Vatican will not allow its daily newspaper to be called an official newspaper, though it is generally considered to be the voice of the Vatican. It is. And it isn't. The Vatican's only official newspaper is the Acta Apostolicae Sedis which comes out four times a year and publishes Church documents, Vatican legislation, and official information in Latin—this would make it the Vatican equivalent of *The Congressional Record.* The quarterly newspaper, with its world circulation (mostly distributed by air mail), is a rather authoritative mirror of the pope's views, serves as the most visible sword against the foes of the Roman Catholic Church, and wields an influence well beyond its relatively small circulation.[1]

Sometimes what's left out of *L'Osservatore Romano* speaks in more miraculous voice than what is put in, as many a Vatican-ologist has found out. On the occasion of Pope Paul's *Humane Vitae,* which forbade under pain of mortal sin the use of artificial birth control methods, *L'Osservatore* never reported or commented on the storm of protest his pronouncement had created among Catholics all over the world, especially in the United States.

The pope's interference with the daily came to the fore in June 1983 after he came back from his trip to Poland where he had had secret talks with that country's leader, General Wojciech Jaruzelski, on a possible future dialogue in Poland. The managing editor of the *Osservatore,* the Reverend Virgilio Levi, had written a first-page editorial about the pontiff's talk with Lech Walesa, the champion of the outlawed Polish Solidarity movement, in which he expressed his own journalistic opinion that Walesa was soon going to remove himself from the labor movement and become a private person. From Levi's editorial, readers inferred that John Paul II had asked Walesa to withdraw from the public scene for a short period in order to reduce tensions in Poland. The article, which was run under the headline, ''Honor to the Sacrifice,'' proved embarrassing to Church watchdogs, and especially to the Polish Pope who was trying to pave the way for the abolition of martial law in his home country and bring about an amnesty for political prisoners.

---

[1] Before the Acta was first published, the Vatican did indeed have an official newspaper called *Diario di Roma,* first printed in February 1829. Only one column wide, it had the distinction of being the smallest newspaper ever printed, measuring 2.7 inches by 4.3 inches. In its masthead it made mention of the fact that it was published ''con privilegio pontificio'' (with the pope's permission), and today the only extant copy of this minitabloid is in Germany, on display in Aachen's Newspaper Museum.

The roof fell in on Father Levi, and when on orders from a peeved John Paul II he was asked to submit his resignation, the priest editor did so. He followed up with the explanation that he had indeed asked, in writing, for editorial guidance on how to deal with the pope's trip and the meetings but never received an answer. Father Levi, who had been expected eventually to take over the chief editorship of the paper, had been to Poland several times and was quite knowledgeable on that country's politics, though he had not accompanied the pope on his last trip there. Nor had he seen John Paul on his return from Poland. Privately, he admitted he may have torpedoed the papacy's negotiating position by printing his own opinion rather than the Vatican's official view. No sooner had Levi quit than the pontiff himself selected a new managing editor, an Italian layman of Polish family background—one Gianfranco Svidercoschi, who had been a respected writer on Vatican affairs for the Rome conservative daily, *Il Tempo.* Among his first acts was to have the *Osservatore* printing plant bring in type faces with all the diacritical signs of the Polish alphabet.

Aware of how closely *L'Osservatore* is fine-toothcombed by its readership, the ''publisher'' (i.e., the Vatican) has, since the Virgilio Levi fiasco, been even more paranoid as to what gets printed. Even the meager advertisements come under scrutiny by uptight Vatican biggies. Most of the advertisements come through an ad agency, and they invariably include banks, insurance companies, funeral parlors, books, and other ''quiet'' advertisements. Most other categories are considered unsuitable; from time to time ads that have appeared in the paper suddenly are ''invited'' to advertise elsewhere. There is the case a few years ago when Johnson's Wax placed full-page ads on two different days: the ad on the back page showed a large blow-up of the front of Saint Peter's Basilica with the caption—''Truly Splendid'' —the Basilica of Saint Peter's Recently Cleaned With Johnson's Wax Products.''

Though indeed Saint Peter's had actually been waxed with Johnson's Wax, the Vatican decided the ad was in bad taste because it showed the basilica and because the Vatican had paid for the wax and had not gotten it gratis. The Vatican made it clear to the wax company that it could not prevent people from thinking it had accepted free wax in return for the use of the basilica's photo.

The Vatican Radio Station. *(Photo by Nino Lo Bello)*

More on the
Vatican Library

ALTHOUGH THE Vatican Library is not one of the biggest libraries, it is unrivaled in importance because its shelves and stack rooms contain works on the Church that are not available anywhere. With over a million books, more than 100,000 maps and engravings, and nearly 100,000 manuscripts, the Vatican Library is only open to scholars with credentials who fill out special forms explaining the nature of their research and which books or manuscripts will be needed. Most of the scholars admitted are priests or seminary students, and lay persons who try to get in are likely to find it exceedingly difficult, if not impossible.

Two nonclerics who once managed to infiltrate the Vatican Library, however, did it their own way. They were burglars. And on an unusually dark night (for Rome, at least) in late November 1965 the pair sneaked their way into the Library. As reported by detectives attached to the Swiss Guard, the two thieves, taking advantage of no moon, monkeyed their way up a drainpipe, quietly cut open a Vatican Library window quite near the papal bedroom where Paul VI was sound asleep, crept elbow-and-knee along the floor to a glass display case, and gently removed two hefty books from their resting place.

One was a parchment manuscript by the sixteenth century writer, Torquato Tasso, and the other was a velvet-bound volume of love poems by Francesco Petrarca, a Florentine poet known outside his country as Petrarch (1304–1374), and considered the father of the Renaissance. This latter volume was written in Petrarch's own hand, and the value of the fourteenth century book, entitled *Il Canzoniere,* was conservatively put at over a million dollars by the Italian police and Interpol whom the

220

Vatican called in for help. Although the two volumes could never have been sold for anything near their worth to a museum or an antique dealer anywhere in the world, the law enforcement officers set out to track down the priceless books. They didn't have long to look, because within 48 hours a gardener in Rome's northern outskirts spotted two men in a white Fiat-600 getting out of their car and placing a large box in a thicket. After they left, the curious gardener went over to see what the men had hidden and discovered that the dark-painted tin box contained the two missing Renaissance manuscripts. He took them to the authorities, but the incredible burglary still remains unsolved. The books, however, are not only back in their glass case, but they are now wired to an alarm.

Although the real founder of the Vatican Library was Pope Nicholas V (1447–1455), who ordered that the Vatican's scattered collection of manuscripts be assembled in one place (now the Vatican Library), the actual probable date of the Library goes back to Pope Martin V (1417–1431) at the time of the return of the popes from Avignon to Rome. When he brought the papal Curia back to Rome, he also took along the old library and new purchases the popes had made in France. Many of the manuscripts carried to Rome were really handwritten copies of books by priests; these were called ''scriptores,'' a word which the Vatican's priest-librarians still use to this day.

The main entrance to the Vatican Library is from the Belvedere Courtyard, the largest of Vatican City's many courtyards. Just inside the door is a white marble statue of Saint Hippolytus, one of the first Christian scholars to catalogue the canon of the Sacred Scriptures. This statue, by the way, beats anything yet. Installed in 1959 by John XXIII, the seated figure is unique because the head is by one sculptor, the trunk by another, and the lower body by yet another, but what makes it really extraordinary is that from the belt down it is a female. The lower section was excavated nearly 440 years ago on the outskirts of eastern Rome, and for some unknown reason, one of the Renaissance popes had the headless trunk of an ancient male statue put on top of that. Then years later an artist was commissioned to sculpt a bearded head, making the Saint Hippolytus statue one of the few artworks that is the product of assembling three nonhomogeneous parts. Another curiosity is that it is known which statue the female portion once belonged to, namely a figure portraying the first female philosopher in history, the Epicurean Temistas. But the biggest wonder is: was it perhaps a private joke on the part of whoever was responsible for naming this half-man, half-woman statue as Saint Hippolytus, a noted theologian (165–235 A.D.) and an anti-pope? What is incongruous is that Hippolytus thought of the Church as a society composed exclusively of men!

Just beyond Hippolytus, through the door, is the acquisitions department, which besides purchasing new books (many books come in from scholars gratuitously), also catalogues about 1,500 magazines — most of which are scholarly journals. Every new acquisition is stamped with the Vatican Library seal on page 1 and on page 41.

Since Pope Pius XI was himself a librarian, major innovations were made during his reign, all of which helped to modernize the Vatican Library along American lines and standards. A catalogue system with duplicate cards from the Library of Congress in Washington, D.C., a new ventilating system from the United States to keep the air from becoming too damp for book bindings, a modern lighting system from New York City, and seven miles of steel shelves from Pennsylvania were introduced into the Vatican Library after Pius XI took office. These were all items Pius had wanted when he was Cardinal Acchile Ratti, prefect of the Vatican Library, but for which he found he could get no budget from Curia officials. Pius also sent four Vatican librarians to the Library of Congress, the Columbia University Library, and the University of Michigan Library to work and study methods used there.

Pius XI had a narrow escape from death in the Vatican Library on December 22, 1931. Ten minutes after he had completed a business visit to the library, the roof of the room he had been in for a half hour crashed through the floor and on down to the basement. Very few of the books and manuscripts were damaged, but one person was killed, the priest with whom the pope had been conferring.

The main library collection is contained in five floors of stacks. Whole blocks of the principal stack room are locked behind heavy wire caging which protect the library's greatest treasure—some 5,000 incunabula (books printed before 1500 A.D.). The some 100,000 manuscripts, most of which are in Latin, Greek, Syriac, and other rare languages, are also kept in this section. The most priceless manuscript in the Vatican Library is Cicero's *De Republica,* written on parchment and lost to the world until a library official found it in 1822. It is the oldest Latin manuscript known.

To consult any of the manuscripts, one has to get extra-special permission, but once admitted to the manuscript-consulting room, a scholar is left alone without supervision. This room is a long, high-ceilinged hall lined with dark oaken bookshelves and adorned with busts and paintings of former popes. Row upon row of long desks fill the center of the hall. Each place is assigned a number, and the person occupying the desk number is given a box of cards with the same number on them. Thus when he takes a book from the shelf, he places his number at that spot on the shelf so that if another scholar is by chance searching for the same volume and finds the position on the shelf empty, he will have no trouble finding the person who is using the book. Presiding over this system, which Pius XI set into motion, is an assistant librarian who sits at a desk on a dais. He not only keeps order; he is also there to answer questions or give help in tracking down a book.

Right next door is the catalogue room, a very narrow and long chamber. In addition to its own properties, the Vatican also keeps a card catalogue of ecclesiastical listings that are found in the catalogues of the United States Library of Congress, the British Museum, the French Bibliotheque Nationale, and Germany's Gesamtkatalog. The Vatican Library also maintains a number of small rooms that house the special collection of great European families who left their collections of books to the Vatican Library on condition that they be kept intact.

The Vatican Library also has a microfilming service. With the eventual goal of filming all of the library's precious manuscripts page by page, this department is constantly at work filming, developing, washing, and drying the microfilm. Another job that never seems to end is that of restoring books that are in the process of deterioration. This is work that is done with many years of experience and with methods that are of the Vatican's own invention. With each book or manuscript, the parchment pages are dismantled and trimmed of their ragged edges. Then each page is washed, dried, and pressed much like a piece of laundry. On any given day one can see manuscript pages hanging across the room from a wire, much like a Monday-morning wash. If there are any holes in a page, new pieces of parchment to match with microscopic precision are laminated in such a way that the thickness of the original page is maintained. The restored page is next covered with a sheer, almost invisible silk gauze which is then fused in such a manner that the restored page is stronger than when it was new. Paper manuscripts are patched with rice paper with such skill that it is almost impossible to detect except for a slight variation in color. The Vatican's ''manuscript hospital'' is most proud of the time it restored 56 Coptic manuscripts which had been found buried in the sands of Upper Egypt. It took ten years of solid steady work to bring the faded sheets back to life.

The Vatican Library also catalogues all of the some 4,000 books that were listed in the Vatican's Index of Forbidden Books (the *Index Librorum Prohibitorum*), which was abolished in 1966. The last such Index list came out in 508 pages in 1948 with a short supplement in 1964 that had 14 new names on the list and which included Alberto Moravia, Jean-Paul Sartre, Andre Gide, Simone de Beauvoir, and Curzio Malaparte. All the books on the condemned list made it because they were considered heretical, dangerous to morals, or offensive to pious ears. The last list contained the names of Hobbes, Hume, Locke, Kant, Montaigne, Montesquieu, Schopenhauer, Spinoza, and Voltaire —but did not include writers like Karl Marx, Boccaccio, Georg Hegel, or Friedrich Nietzsche. But it did include the name of a forgotten, seventeenth century satirist, Gregorio Letti, who held some kind of special Index record by having earned 17 condemnations in 35 years.

Quite a few of the Index listings of forbidden books forever baffled some Church executives, and these would include Maurice

Maeterlinck's *Life of the Bee,* Alexandre Dumas' *The Count of Monte Cristo,* and *The Three Musketeers* (both of which Pope John XXIII checked out of the Vatican Library and read with great pleasure), Oliver Goldsmith's *History of England,* Laurence Sterne's *Sentimental Journey Through France and Italy,* and Edward Gibbons' *Decline and Fall of the Roman Empire.* Since no reason was ever given for the anonymous bans, one can only wonder why the Index listed such things as a 1664 treatise on the use of unguents for burns, an 1844 Swiss almanac, or a pamphlet on the museums of Italy. One mysterious listing is a 1701 English treatise by a John Wilkins which had the improbable title, *'Tis Probable There May Be Another Habitable World in the Moon, With a Discourse Concerning the Possibility of Passage Thither.*

The Index had its birth in 1557 from an order given by Pope Paul IV, who of all the popes most embodied the Inquisition. He was reacting against the invention of movable type at a time when literacy was becoming widespread among the faithful.

Although the Index got frequent mentions in the popular press, little was ever printed about the so-called ''pornography'' in the Vatican Library. But every time the subject has come up, the Vatican makes a formal denial that its library maintains such a collection. When sex researcher Alfred Kinsey was putting together his two explosive reports, ''Sexual Life of the Human Male'' and ''Sexual Life of the Human Female,'' during which time his staff amassed what he believed to be the largest collection of erotica in existence, he told an interviewer once that he was pretty sure that the Vatican Library had just as good a collection.

As to whether the Vatican Library has a collection of pornography or a room devoted to erotic literature is a question that does not answer easily. The fact is that the Vatican Library does indeed have many books that could be called erotic, and some even pornographic per se. They are scattered all over the library in much the same way some of them would be in any public library. Here are three titles scribbled down during my stay as a browser with none in any special place on the shelves, other than perhaps in alphabetical order: *A Scatalogical Anthology, A Narrative of Iniquities and Barbarities Practiced in Rome in the 19th Century,* and *The Perverted Peasant.* No authors for any books were cited.

Housed in the Vatican Library is a small collection of manuscripts with illustrations of a man and woman with "their particulars nude." Whatever pornographic or erotic items the Vatican Library has, they are just not classified that way, nor are they kept in any special place or locked up. Anybody in the library has access to any book on any open shelf, including the erotic ones when he can locate them one by one.

Perhaps more interesting than any of the elusive porno books is the Library's Brobdingnagian accumulation of letters from many of history's most important people, 236 of which were put on permanent display in May 1981 in the Vatican Museum. The prime eye-grabber of these treasures is a petition from the court of King Henry VIII of England after he had fallen in love with Anne Boleyn and wanted an heir by her, which meant he had to shed his wife, Catherine of Aragon. The 75 petitioners sent off a two-foot by three-foot parchment to Pope Clement VII which they bemedaled with 75 ribbons and 75 red wax seals. This is to be found among the miscellany of letters that include messages from Copernicus, Galileo, Erasmus, Napoleon, Voltaire, Rossini, Queen Christina of Sweden, Mary Queen of Scots, Genghis Khan's grandson and heir, and a letter from Pope Paul III to Michelangelo giving him free trips on the ferry across the Po River for life. Still another set of charming correspondence is that between Queen Victoria and Pius IX, indicating what he thought of the some dozen of titles bestowed on the papacy. Queen Victoria, apparently not wanting to acknowledge any of the papal titles, began her letter with "Most Eminent Sir." Obviously offended by this lack of respect, Pius in his reply addressed Victoria as "The Most Serene and Powerful Victoria, Queen of the United Kingdom of Great Britain and Ireland and Other Regions, Illustrious Empress of India."

But what is on display is just a tiny sample of what the Vatican has, for there are millions of VIP letters in the archives. And this is the Vatican Library's biggest undone task today. To catalogue these and cross-reference them, the tiny staff would have to work several centuries more, even though over 300 years of work have already been done. The archivists tell you that one of their revered heroes, and at the same time biggest villains, is Cardinal Josephus Garampi who managed, while assigned to the library in the late eighteenth century, to catalogue an awesome 1.5 million letters which he stored into 125 large folio containers. But the bee-busy cardinal pulled a lulu of a goof: true, he arranged all the letters in alphabetical order, but that was done according to their places of origin.

"It simply means, with all due respect to the good cardinal," sighed a patient Vatican librarian assigned to the archives, who asked that his name not be used, "that in order to cross-index all his work, we just have to repeat going through every one of those 1.5 million items!"

The Swiss Guards

HELD IN UTTER fascination by the masses virtually every day of the year (and especially during big tourist months), the Swiss Guards are perhaps the world's most photographed soldiers—with nonstop cameras going clickety-split. Brandishing a seven-foot pike or halberd, the men in those colorful uniforms who look like toy soldiers have the job of guarding the State of Vatican City and the VIP who sits at its head. They comprise the world's most famous and most picturesque army—and it's no small wonder that thousands upon thousands of tourists every week seek to have their picture taken alongside one of these papal protectors standing vigil at each of the three main entrances into the Vatican.

In addition to their duties in public, the guards patrol the Apostolic Palace corridor just outside the papal apartments around the clock, and when the pope goes in or out, the uniformed sentinel on duty gives a snappy salute on bended knee. Not permitted to carry automatic weapons, the guards also do duty in the palace at Castel Gandolfo outside Rome where popes usually spend their summer months.

But what indeed is behind the pope's glamorous personal army? Are those men in the funny uniforms really trained professional soldiers or just good-looking male models hired to wear the colorful garb as part of the spectacular sideshow Saint Peter's Square is heir to?

First, let's dispel one of the biggest myths of all about the Swiss Guards. Contrary to what most tourist guides tell visitors, the weird-looking uniform—with the slashed bouffant sleeves, striped doublet and hose, all in gold, white, red, yellow, and blue—was *not* designed by Michelangelo. Nor by Raffaello. Nothing could be further from the truth.

228

Actually worn for the first time in 1914, the apparel was designed by an unknown Vatican seamstress who surpassed herself when Pope Benedict XV asked that she create ceremonial attire for his soldiers from Switzerland. The puffy sleeves, however, go back to the middle of the sixteenth century and, as nearly as can be determined, were quite possibly inspired by a Raffaello painting from a design he copied that was at that time the style in France.

And what was the inspiration for establishing the Swiss Guards? They were founded by Cardinal Giuliano della Rovere who, while Bishop of Lausanne, was so impressed by Switzerland's soldiers that he advised Pope Sixtus IV to sign an alliance with some Swiss cantons. After Cardinal della Rovere became Pope Julius II, he brought in 150 Swiss soldiers in January 1506 when the first stone of the new Saint Peter's Basilica was laid. That makes the Swiss Guards the oldest military corps in existence.

Like other volunteer armies today, the Swiss Guards have a tough time finding enough recruits to keep their complement at 100. The newcomers must be between 18 and 25 years old, about six feet tall, and must sign a contract to serve a two-year tour of duty. Most of them do not reenlist, but some make a career and stay on for as long as 30 years. The main problems are that the pay is quite low, the work is described as monotonous, the discipline is apparently the toughest of any army anywhere, private life is almost impossible, the hours are too long, and duty is, without exception, always on Sundays.

Moreover, the men are not permitted to marry while in the service. Nor are they allowed to bring any women friends into the Vatican for social visits. Most of their free time is given over to the required study of the Italian language and to special technical and commercial courses to prepare them for a future as civilians.

Sworn to protect the life of the pope at the risk of their own lives, the Swiss Guards narrowly escaped annihilation on the steps of Saint Peter's during the sack of Rome in May 1527 when a thousand German and Spanish soldiers stormed the Vatican. Three-quarters of the Swiss complement was destroyed, altogether 147 men including the commanding officer (the invaders, on the other hand, lost more than 800 soldiers). But the remaining 42 were able to give protection to Pope Clement VII and 13 of

his cardinals as they fled along Vatican ramparts into the impreg-
nable Castel Sant' Angelo fortress.

After the 1527 slaughter, the Swiss Guards never again had to
fight any battles, but on several occasions the Guards had to lay
down their arms on papal orders, rather than face extermination.
This was true in the case of Napoleon who, during his invasion of
Rome, carried the pope off to France.

In World War II Pope Pius XII made the guards store away
their firearms (all guns were later abolished by Pope Paul VI in
1970), so they patrolled the frontier between the State of Vatican
City and Italy with only their combination spear-battleaxes while
facing Nazi Germany's array of Panzer tanks that never once
dared to cross the border without an order from Hitler. It was one
of World War II's most curious sights to see the heavily armed,
efficient Nazi troops stand by rather sheepishly as a lone Swiss
Guard patrolled up and down with a hand weapon from bygone
days.

After Joe Stalin heard about the solitary Swiss Guard keeping
Hitler's army at bay—so the story goes—he shook his head in
disbelief and asked: ''So, tell me, how many divisions does the
pope have?''

Another true story that guards like to tell about their corps is
the one about the coronation of Clement XIII in 1758. On that
occasion, some Swiss Guards turned away a Franciscan friar who
did not seem to them to fit in with all the cardinals and dignitaries
on hand. Eleven years later, after that same ex-friar had been
crowned Pope Clement XIV, he said, ''I enjoyed this coronation.
This time the Swiss Guards let me in!''

Index

Note: Individual works of art are in **bold** type.